Dynamism in African Languages and Literature
Towards Conceptualisation of African Potentials

Edited by

**Keiko Takemura
and Francis B. Nyamnjoh**

In collaboration

Langaa RPCIG
Mankon Bamenda

CAAS
Kyoto University

Publisher:
Langaa RPCIG
Langaa Research & Publishing Common Initiative Group
P.O. Box 902 Mankon
Bamenda
North West Region
Cameroon
Langaagrp@gmail.com
www.langaa-rpcig.net

In Collaboration with
The Center for African Area Studies, Kyoto University, Japan

Distributed in and outside N. America by African Books Collective
orders@africanbookscollective.com
www.africanbookscollective.com

ISBN-10: 9956-551-69-4

ISBN-13: 978-9956-551-69-9

© Keiko Takemura and Francis B. Nyamnjoh 2021

All rights reserved.
No part of this book may be reproduced or transmitted in any form or by any means, mechanical or electronic, including photocopying and recording, or be stored in any information storage or retrieval system, without written permission from the publisher

Notes on Contributors

Mussa M. HANS is Senior Lecturer in the Department of Kiswahili Languages and Linguistics and Deputy Director of the Institute of Kiswahili Studies at the University of Dar es Salaam, Tanzania. He holds a PhD in Kiswahili from the University of Dar es Salaam. His areas of specialisation include development of Kiswahili language and its dialects, lexicography and translation. He is currently a Chief Editor of *Mulika*, Journal of the Institute of Kiswahili Studies, University of Dar es Salaam. Email: hansmussa@udsm.ac.tz.

Maiko KANDA is Associate Professor of the Doctoral Program for Multicultural Innovation in Human Sciences (RESPECT Program), Graduate School of Human Sciences, Osaka University, Japan. Her research in African literature concerns the influence of the colonial experience. Her recent works include: 'Approval of incomprehensibility: Explanatory notes on Namwali Serpell's short story, "Muzungu"', in S. Müller (ed.) *Embracing the Arts* (2017) and 'Thinking about multiculturalism: From the perspective of African literature', *Mirai Kyosei: Journal of Multicultural Innovation*, Vol. 6 (2017, in Japanese).

Sayaka KUTSUKAKE is a JSPS Research Fellow at the Research Institute for Languages and Cultures of Asia and Africa (ILCAA), Tokyo University of Foreign Studies, Japan. Her research concerns African sociolinguistics and her main field is Tanzania. Her recent works include: *Reconsideration of the Language Problem in Multilingual Tanzania: From the Perspective of the Gap between Globalisation and Multilingualism*, PhD thesis, Osaka University (2018, in Japanese), 'Impacts of western perspectives on "multilingualism"', *Journal of Multicultural Innovation*, Vol. 6, pp. 181–200 (2019, in Japanese) and 'Contact-induced language divergence and convergence in Tanzania: Forming new varieties as language maintenance', *Swahili Forum*, Vol. 26, pp. 181–204 (co-authored with Nobuko Yoneda, 2019).

Motoji MATSUDA is Professor of Sociology and Anthropology, Kyoto University, Japan. His research fields are Nairobi and Western

Kenya. His research topics are urbanisation, migration and conflict. His major works include: *Urbanisation from Below* (Kyoto University Press 1998), *The Manifesto of Anthropology of the Everyday Life World* (Sekai Shisosha 2008, in Japanese), *African Virtues in the Pursuit of Conviviality: Exploring Local Solutions in Light of Global Prescriptions* (co-edited with Itaru Ohta and Yntiso Gebre, Langaa RPCIG 2017) and *The Challenge of African Potentials: Conviviality, Informality and Futurity* (co-edited with Yaw Ofosu-Kusi, Langaa RPCIG 2020).

Shani Omari MCHEPANGE is Associate Professor of Kiswahili Literature at the Institute of Kiswahili Studies, University of Dar es Salaam, Tanzania. She holds a PhD in Literature from the University of Dar es Salaam. Her research interests include youth popular culture, oral and written Kiswahili literature and language and gender. Her recent works include: 'Gender representation in Simba and Yanga's joking cartoons in Tanzania', *Eastern African Literary and Cultural Studies*, 5(1): 1–15 (2019) and 'Imaging the woman through Tanzanian women's maxims', *Journal of International Women's Studies*, 19(3): 119–134 (co-authored with F. E. M. K. Senkoro, 2018). Email: shaniom@yahoo.co.uk, shaniom@udsm.ac.tz

Haruse MURATA is an independent researcher on African literature written in French. Her research field is West African countries such as Benin, Burkina Faso, Ivory Coast and Senegal. Her research concerns the expression of conflicts and genocide in literal text, and creation and publishing of children's literature. She recently translated two books of Veronique Tadjo into Japanese: *Ayanda: La Fille Qui ne Voulait pas Grandir* [*Ayanda: The Girl Who Didn't Want to Grow Up*] (Futosha 2018) and *L'Ombre d'Imana:Voyages Jusau'au Bout du Rwanda* [*The Shadow of Imana: Travels in the Heart of Rwanda*] (Edition F 2019).

Shuichiro NAKAO is Associate Professor at Osaka University where he teaches the Arabic language and cultures. He obtained a doctor's degree from Kyoto University with a thesis on 'A Grammar of Juba Arabic' (2017). He has been working on themes such as the grammatical description, lexicography, linguistic evolution and social history of East African Arabic varieties (Juba Arabic, Nubi,

Benishangul Arabic), Berta (Nilo-Saharan) and Bangala (Bantu-based pidgin), among others. Besides his interest in African linguistics, he has published articles on historical reconstruction of Old Arabic and application of linguistic methodologies in Arabic language teaching.

Francis B. NYAMNJOH is Professor of Social Anthropology at the University of Cape Town, South Africa. He is recipient of the 'ASU African Hero 2013' annual award by the African Students Union, Ohio University, USA, of the 2014 Eko Prize for African Literature and of the ASAUK 2018 Fage & Oliver Prize for the best monograph for his book *#RhodesMustFall: Nibbling at Resilient Colonialism in South Africa*. He is a B1 rated Professor and Researcher by the South African National Research Foundation (NRF), a Fellow of the Cameroon Academy of Science since August 2011, a fellow of the African Academy of Science since December 2014 and a fellow of the Academy of Science of South Africa since 2016. His scholarly books include: *Insiders and Outsiders: Citizenship and Xenophobia in Contemporary Southern Africa* (2006) and *Drinking from the Cosmic Gourd: How Amos Tutuola Can Change Our Minds* (2017).

Fuko ONODA is a JSPS Research Fellow at the Graduate School of Human and Environmental Studies, Kyoto University, Japan. Her research concerns Kiswahili literature and her main field is Tanzania. Her recent works include: 'Circular motifs and structure in Euphrase Kezilahabi's Nagona and Mzingile and an Ongoing Buddhistic study', *Swahili Forum*, 23: 76–97 (2017), '"An alienated intellectual"? Rereading E. Kezilahabi's novel Kichwamaji', *Nordic Journal of African Studies*, 26 (3): 176–190 (2017) and *Study on Euphrase Kezilahabi*, PhD thesis, Osaka University (2018, in Japanese). Recently she has been working on a translation of Kezilahabi's novel, *Nagona*, into Japanese.

Daisuke SHINAGAWA is Associate Professor at the Research Institute for Languages and Cultures of Asia and Africa (ILCAA), Tokyo University of Foreign Studies. His research field covers Swahili-speaking areas of East Africa and his research topics include linguistic description of undescribed languages, intra-genetic micro-typology of Bantu languages and linguistic dynamism in multilingual settings in Africa. He is an editor of *Swahili Forum* 26: *Variation in*

Swahili (co-edited with Nico Nassenstein, 2019, available online at https://home.uni-leipzig.de/swafo/index.html) and *Descriptive Materials of Morphosyntactic Microvariation in Bantu* (co-edited with Yuko Abe, ILCAA 2019).

Katsuhiko SHIOTA is Lecturer at the University of Hyogo and Osaka University. His research concerns West African languages, linguistics and cultures. His major publications include: *Hausago Kiso Bunpoo* [*Hausa Basic Grammar*] (Osaka University Press 2010, in Japanese), *Yorubago Nyuumon* [*Introduction to Yoruba*] (Osaka University Press 2011, in Japanese) and *Afurika Shogo Bunpoo Yooran* [*Grammatical Handbook of African Languages*] (editor, Keisuisha 2012, in Japanese).

Keiko TAKEMURA is Professor at the Graduate School of Language and Culture, Osaka University, Japan. Mainly, she teaches Kiswahili, Swahili Literature and Culture at the School of Foreign Studies, Osaka University. Her main research field is Zanzibar and Pemba Islands, Tanzania. Her research topics are language attitude, language consciousness and language use among Swahili speakers, dialectology of Kiswahili, Swahili literature and life histories of Swahili women. Her major works include: *New Express Plus Swahili* (Hakusuisha 2018, in Japanese), *How Swahili Works* (Hakusuisha 2016, in Japanese) and 'On subjunctive and imperative forms of Kichaani', *The Journal of Swahili & African Studies*, 25: 120–129 (2014, in Japanese).

Satoshi TERAO is Associate Professor of the Center for Language and Cultural Studies, University of Miyazaki, Japan. His Research fields in Africa are Angola, Equatorial Guinea and São Tomé & Príncipe. His research topics are sociolinguistics and language policy. His major works include: 'Reconsidering our linguistic diversity from Mirandese: The "latest" and the "least" among Romance languages', in D. Stern, M. Nomachi & B. Belić (eds) *Linguistic Regionalism in Eastern Europe and Beyond*, pp. 257–273 (Peter Lang 1998).

Gebriel Alazar TESFATSION is a Japanese Government (Monbukagakusho: MEXT) Scholarship graduate student at the University of Tsukuba. His research interest lies in systemic functional linguistics, specifically in the transitivity theory. Currently, he is writing his thesis on how experience is construed in a traditional conflict reconciliation of the Afar people through the transitivity theory.

Table of Contents

**Series Preface: African Potentials
for Convivial World-Making** xiii
Motoji Matsuda

**Introduction – Dynamism in African
Languages and Literature:
Towards Conceptualisation
of African Potentials** 1
Keiko Takemura and Francis B. Nyamnjoh

PART I. Language

**1. Convivial Multilingualism
as a Modern African Ethos:
Cases of East African
Non-Arab Arabophone Societies** 19
Shuichiro Nakao

**2. Socio-Linguistic Dynamism
among Languages: Sketching from
Angola as a Frame of Reflection** 47
Satoshi Terao

**3. Documentation of an Afar Traditional
Conflict Reconciliation Speech** 69
Gebriel Alazar Tesfatsion

4. Aspects of Linguistic Dynamism in
   Sheng as Kenyan Colloquial Swahili:
   Focusing on De-Standardisation and
   Re-Vernacularisation 89
   Daisuke Shinagawa

5. Flexibility and the Potential of
   'African Multilingualism':
   A Case of Language Practice in Tanzania 121
   Sayaka Kutsukake

6. Kiswahili Language and Its Potentiality
   for African Development 149
   Shani Omari Mchepange and Mussa M. Hans

Part II. Literature

7. Swahili from the Perspectives of
   'Language' and 'Literature' 169
   Keiko Takemura

8. Cultural Transformation and the
   Reconstruction of Tradition
   in Yoruba Popular Music 185
   Katsuhiko Shiota

9. Literature for African Children:
   Creation and Publication of Children's
   Books in French-Speaking
   West African Countries 209
   Haruse Murata

10. Writing from the In-between:
   Binyavanga Wainaina's Literary Practices 235
   Maiko Kanda

11. The Social Orientation of Kiswahili Poetry 259
   Fuko Onoda

12. Amos Tutuola as a Quest Hero
   for Endogenous Africa: Actively
   Anglicising the Yoruba Language and
   Yorubanising the English Language........................... 283
   Francis B. Nyamnjoh

Index.. 297

Series Preface

African Potentials for Convivial World-Making

Motoji Matsuda

1. The Idea of 'African Potentials'

The *African Potentials* series is based on the findings since 2011 of the African Potentials research project, an international collaboration involving researchers based in Japan and Africa. This project examines how to tackle the challenges of today's world using the experiences and wisdom (ingenuity and responsiveness) of African society. It has identified field sites across a variety of social domains, including areas of conflict, conciliation, environmental degradation, conservation, social development and equality, and attempts to shed light on the potential of African society to address the problems therein. Naturally, such an inquiry is deeply intertwined with the political and economic systems that control the contemporary world, and with knowledge frameworks that have long dominated the perceptions and understanding of our world. Building on unique, long-standing collaborative relationships developed between researchers in Japan and Africa, the project suggests new ways to challenge the prevailing worldview on humans, society and history, enabling those worldviews to be relativised, decentred and pluralised.

After the rose-coloured dreams of the 1960s, African society entered an era of darkness in the 1980s and 1990s. It was beleaguered by problems that included civil conflict, military dictatorship, national economic collapse, commodity shortages, environmental degradation and destruction, over-urbanisation and rampant contagious disease. In the early 21st century, the fortunes of Africa were reversed as it underwent economic growth by leveraging its abundant natural resources. However, an unequal redistribution of wealth increased social disparities and led to the emergence of new forms of conflict and discrimination. The challenges facing African society appear to be more profound than ever.

The governments of African states and the international community have attempted to resolve the many problems Africa has experienced. For example, the perpetrators of crimes during times of civil conflict have been punished by international tribunals, support for democratisation has been offered to states ruled by dictators and despots and environmental degradation has been tackled by scientific awareness campaigns conducted at huge expense.

Nonetheless, to us – the Japanese and African researchers engaging with African society in this era – the huge monetary and organisational resources expended, and scientifically grounded measures pursued, seem to have had little effect on the lives of ordinary people. The punishment of perpetrators did not consider the coexistence of perpetrators and victims, while the propagation of democratic ideals and training to raise scientific awareness was far removed from people's lived experiences. Nevertheless, while many of these 'top-down' measures prescribed to solve Africa's challenges proved ineffective, African society has found ways to heal post-conflict communities and to develop practices of political participation and environmental conservation.

Why did this happen? This question led us to examine ideas and practices African society has formulated for tackling the contemporary difficulties it has experienced. These were developed at sites where ordinary Africans live. 'African Potentials' is the name we gave to these home-grown ideas and the potential to engender them.

2. African Forum: A Unique Intellectual Collaboration between Japan and Africa

As the concept of African Potentials emerged, it required further reflection to develop ideas that could be applied in the humanities and social sciences. The context for these processes was the African Forum: a meeting held in a different part of Africa each year where African researchers from different regions and Japanese researchers studying in each of those regions came together to engage in frank discussion. The attendance of all core members of the project sympathetic to the idea of African Potentials ensured the continuity of the discussions at these African Forums. The core members who drove the project forward from the African side included Edward Kirumira (Uganda and South Africa), Kennedy Mkutu (Kenya), Yntiso Gebre (Ethiopia), the late Samson Wassara (South Sudan), the late Sam Moyo (Zimbabwe), Michael Neocosmos (South Africa), Francis B. Nyamnjoh (Cameroon and South Africa) and Yaw Ofosu-Kusi (Ghana). The researchers from Japan specialised in extremely diverse fields, including political science, sociology, anthropology, development economics, education, ecology and geography. As they built creative interdisciplinary spaces for interaction across fields over the course of a decade, project members have produced many major outcomes that serve as research models for intellectual and academic exchange between Japan and Africa, and experimental cases of educational practice in the mutual cultivation and guidance of young researchers.

African Forums have been held in Nairobi (2011), Harare (2012), Juba (2013), Yaoundé (2014), Addis Ababa (2015), Kampala (2016), Grahamstown (now Makhanda, 2017), Accra (2018) and Lusaka (2019). These meetings fostered deeper discussion of the conceptualisation and generalisation of African Potentials. This led to the development of a framework for approaching African Potentials and its distinguishing features.

3. What are African Potentials?

The first aim of African Potentials is to 'de-romanticise' the traditional values and institutions of Africa. For example, when studying conflict resolution, members of African Potentials are not interested in excessive idealisation of traditional means of conflict resolution and unconditional endorsement of a return to African traditions as an 'alternative' to modern Western conflict-resolution methods, because such ideas fix African Potentials in a static mode as they speak to a fantasy that ignores the complexities of the contemporary world; they are cognate with the mentality that depreciates African culture.

Rendering African culture static displaces it from its original context and uses it to fabricate 'African-flavoured' theatrical events, as we have seen in different conflict situations. Typical of this tendency is the 'theatre' of traditional dance by performers dressed in ethnic costume and the ceremonial slaughter of cows in an imitation of the rituals of mediation and reconciliation once observed in inter-ethnic conflicts. In our African Forums, we have criticised this tendency as the 'technologisation' and 'compartmentalisation' of traditional rituals.

Naturally, a stance that arbitrarily deems certain conflict-resolution cultures to be 'subaltern', 'backward' or 'uncivilised' needs to be critiqued and it is important to re-evaluate approaches that have been written off in this way. This does not mean that we should level unconditional praise on a fixed subject. With globalisation, African society is experiencing great changes brought about by the circulation of diverse ideas, institutions, information and physical goods. African Potentials can be found in the power to generate cultures of conflict-resolution autonomously under these fluid conditions, while re-aligning elements that were previously labelled 'traditional' and 'indigenous'. In the African Potentials project, we call this the power of 'interface function': the capacity to forge combinations and connections within assemblages of diverse values, ideas and practices that belong to disparate dimensions and different historical phases. In one sense, this is a kind of 'bricolage' created by dismantling pre-existing values and institutions and recombining them freely. It is also a convivial process in the sense that it involves enabling the coexistence of diverse, multi-dimensional elements to create new strengths that are used in contemporary society. The terms 'bricolage' and 'conviviality' are apt expressions characterising the 'interface functions' of African Potentials.

Following this outline, we can identify two features distinguishing African Potentials. First, African Potentials comprise not fixed, unchanging entities but, rather, an open process that is always dynamic and in flux. To treat African traditions and history as static is to fall into the trap of modernist thinking, in which Africa is scorned as barbaric and uncivilised, and the knowledge and practices generated there treated as subaltern and irrational – or a diametrically opposed revivalist mindset that romanticises traditions unconditionally and imbues them with exaggerated significance.

The second feature of African Potentials is its aspiration to pluralism rather than unity. For example, a basic principle of modern civil society is that conflict resolution should occur in accordance with law and judicial process. This principle is deemed to be based on common sense in our society, which means that any resolution method that runs counter to the principle is regarded as 'mistaken' from the outset. This constitutes an aspiration toward unity. It supposes that there is a single way of thinking in relation to the achievement of justice and deems all other approaches peripheral, informal and inferior. The standpoint of Africa's cultural potential, however, renders untenable the idea of a single absolute approach that represents all others as mistaken or deserving of rejection. Here, we can identify a pluralist aspiration that embraces both legal/judicial approaches and extrajudicial solutions.

An aspiration to unity, reduced to the level of dogma, can find eventual culmination in beliefs about 'purity'. In other words, thoughts, values and methods can be regarded as an absolute good, while any attempt to incorporate other (impure) elements is stridently denounced as improper behaviour that compromises purity and perfection. In direct contrast, African Potentials affirm the complexity and multiplicity of a range of elements, and attach value to that which is incomplete. This signifies a more tolerant, open attitude to ideas and values, one that differs from those of the more developed world. African Potentials are grounded in this kind of openness and tolerance.

As we have seen, African cultural potentials are distinguished by their dynamism, flexibility, pluralism, complexity, tolerance and openness. These features are completely at odds with the notion that there is a perfect, pure, uniquely correct mode of existence that competes with others in a confrontational, non-conciliatory manner – one that repels, subordinates and controls them, and occupies the position of an absolute victor. African Potentials can lead us to worldviews on humans, society and history that differ from the hegemonic worldviews that dominate contemporary realms of knowledge.

4. The African Potentials Series

In this way, the concept of African Potentials has enabled researchers from Japan and Africa to organise themselves and pursue activities in multidisciplinary research teams. The products of these activities have been classified into seven different fields for publication in this series. The authors and editors were selected by and from both Japanese and African researchers, and the resulting publications advance the research that has grown out of discussion in the African Forums. The overall structure of the series is as follows:

Volume 1
Title: *African Politics of Survival: Extraversion and Informality in the Contemporary World*
Editors: Mitsugi Endo (The University of Tokyo), Ato Kwamena Onoma (CODESRIA) and Michael Neocosmos (Rhodes University)

Volume 2
Title: *Knowledge, Education and Social Structure in Africa*
Editors: Shoko Yamada (Nagoya University), Akira Takada (Kyoto University) and Shose Kessi (University of Cape Town)

Volume 3
Title: *People, Predicaments and Potentials in Africa*
Editors: Takehiko Ochiai (Ryukoku University), Misa Hirano-Nomoto (Kyoto University) and Daniel E. Agbiboa (Harvard University)

Volume 4
Title: *Development and Subsistence in Globalising Africa: Beyond the Dichotomy*
Editors: Motoki Takahashi (Kyoto University), Shuichi Oyama (Kyoto University) and Herinjatovo Aimé Ramiarison (University of Antananarivo)

Volume 5

Title: *Dynamism in African Languages and Literature: Towards Conceptualisation of African Potentials*

Editors: Keiko Takemura (Osaka University) and Francis B. Nyamnjoh (University of Cape Town)

Volume 6

Title: *'African Potentials' for Wildlife Conservation and Natural Resource Management: Against the Images of 'Deficiency' and Tyranny of 'Fortress'*

Editors: Toshio Meguro (Hiroshima City University), Chihiro Ito (Fukuoka University) and Kariuki Kirigia (McGill University)

Volume 7

Title: *Contemporary Gender and Sexuality in Africa: African-Japanese Anthropological Approach*

Editors: Wakana Shiino (Tokyo University of Foreign Studies) and Christine Mbabazi Mpyangu (Makerere University)

Acknowledgements

This publication is based on the research project supported by the JSPS KAKENHI Grant Number JP16H06318: 'African Potential' and Overcoming the Difficulties of Modern World: Comprehensive Area Studies that will Provide a New Perspective for the Future of Humanity.

Introduction

Dynamism in African Languages and Literature: Towards Conceptualisation of African Potentials

Keiko Takemura and Francis B. Nyamnjoh

1. Background

The present volume is a research output created by the research unit that has been working on African languages and literature in the interdisciplinary joint research project titled '"African Potential" and Overcoming the Difficulties of Modern World: Comprehensive Area Studies That Will Provide a New Perspective for the Future of Humanity' (JSPS Grant-in-Aid for Scientific Research (S), JP16H06318, 2016–2021, PI. Motoji Matsuda), which is a follow-up to the project titled 'Comprehensive Area Studies on Coexistence and Conflict Resolution Realizing the African Potentials' (JSPS Grant-in-Aid for Scientific Research (S), JP23221012, 2011–2016, PI. Itaru Ohta). While the research focus of the preceding project was mainly on how people achieve coexistence and resolve conflicts with various scales in the context of contemporary Africa, the present project has expanded the scope and aimed to elucidate 'African Potentials' through investigating daily practices found in contemporary societies in Africa. It is in this context that our research unit was called for in the present project in order to discuss and define the concept of 'African Potentials' from an interdisciplinary approach consisting of sociolinguistics and literary studies. For the past five years, the group held regular study meetings to conceptualise the yet unrecognised power of the African people to solve various social problems. The group members have struggled diligently to attain the goal.

While the task was challenging, the members of the group approached it positively. During several study meetings and editorial committee meetings necessary to create this volume, the members made a wide variety of research presentations and held lively discussions. Particularly during the second meeting titled 'African People as Subjective Expressers: Language Practice in Conversations, Literature and Music', which was held in January 2017 at the University of Osaka, the participants, including many early career researchers, discussed language practices in various regions of the African continent in a cross-disciplinary manner. It was significant that not only researchers but also musicians and the general audience worked together to present and analyse the attractiveness of expression in Africa.

Through the collaboration of linguistics and literary studies as separate disciplines, our team members coordinated in order to conceptualise the notion of 'African Potentials' from various perspectives and different angles. Reflecting the number of discussions we had, the topics investigated in this volume range from multilingual practices in rural settings to dynamic processes found in urban youth languages, from cultural transformation in Yoruba pop music to the practice of children's book publication in Benin, from the history of Swahili poetry to the analysis of contemporary literature, as shown below.

2. Overview of This Volume

This volume has two parts to clarify the 'African Potentials' that each author perceives from the two main fields, i.e., 'Language' and 'Literature'. The following is the list of summaries of the various chapters.

Part I: Language

Chapter 1: Shuichiro Nakao
'Convivial Multilingualism as a Modern African Ethos: Cases of East African Non-Arab Arabophone Societies'
In his contribution, Shuichiro Nakao takes up a new approach to interpret the African multilingual realities in terms of pluralistic 'ethos', in harmony with Nyamnjoh's (2017) concepts of 'conviviality'

and 'incompleteness'. Focusing on metalinguistic conceptualisations and hybridised language uses among three ethnically non-Arab, Arabic-speaking societies in Eastern Africa, Berta/Funj the people of Ethiopia, urban spaces in South Sudan and the Nubi people of Uganda and Kenya, he demonstrates how these frontier Africans have adopted a 'racialist' language for the pursuit of vernacular cosmopolitanism (Bhabha 1996).

For example, the Sudanese Arabic term *'rutana'* 'gibberish, jargon' has lost the derogatory sense in Juba Arabic of South Sudan to mean 'ethnic language' in which people are proud. On the other hand, the Sudanese Arabic term *'lugha'* ('full-fledged language'), i.e., language with orthography and literary traditions like Arabic and English, has changed its meaning in Juba Arabic to include itself, i.e., language for conviviality, neutral language for communication in a pluralistic public sphere, regardless of whether it is a standardised variety or a 'creole' (or a 'pidgin'). Furthermore, Nakao investigates how such conceptualisations of different types of 'languages' are mitigated in real life, by describing the grammatical and lexical structures of non-Arab Arabic varieties. Nakao names these sets of (socio)linguistic phenomena – perhaps widespread in sub-Saharan Africa as suggested in this chapter, if not the only form of multilingualism in Africa – 'convivial multilingualism' and draws a line between it and Western models of envisaged multilingualism on the point that 'convivial multilingualism' is real and does not envisage assimilation as a scheduled future.

In favour of Nyamnjoh's (2017) claim for 'convivial scholarship', Nakao proposes a possibility of interpretational linguistic studies, which would draw on (socio)linguistic phenomena as expressions of people's ethos, or embodied virtue.

Chapter 2: Satoshi Terao
'Socio-Linguistic Dynamism among Languages: Sketching from Angola as a Frame of Reflection'

In African countries whose official languages are European languages other than English and French, there is a strong tendency to easily rely on European languages to establish an identity that unifies the land surrounded by the borders drawn irrationally by the

European powers. By using the language of the former colonial master as it is in the building of the nation, it aims to easily differentiate itself from other countries.

In Angola, in southwest Africa, Portuguese plays a major role in the formation of its people. The number of native Portuguese speakers has increased rapidly since the colonial period, and literacy and Portuguese are combined. One of the negative effects of this policy is that African countries whose official languages are English and French tend to neglect the inheritance of the original languages.

However, some are reflecting on the fact that they are seeking the axis of national formation only in the language of the former suzerain state. In Angola, a multilingual education policy that identifies the major Bantu languages as national languages and makes them educational languages is gradually bearing fruit. However, seeking the roots of national consciousness in Bantu languages may be viewed with caution because some of these languages are distributed across national borders, causing national instability.

To ease these tensions, there is a movement to seek the core of national identity in Khoisan languages, which were widely distributed in Angola before Bantu went south. The author analyses these discourses and discusses Angola's trial-and-error efforts to establish its unique multilingualism.

Chapter 3: Gebriel Alazar Tesfatsion

'Documentation of an Afar Traditional Conflict Reconciliation Speech'

Tesfatsion's chapter is a documentary study on a language called Afar, an Afro-Asiatic language of the Eastern Cushitic branch, spoken in the Horn of Africa. It is a documentation of spontaneous language use of the Afars in the communicative event of traditional conflict reconciliation. The purpose of his study is to capture and preserve the linguistic practices of the Afar people in the context of conflict resolution. The speech event documented is the recent case of reconciliation of the inter-clan conflict involving three families (*burra*) separating from their old clans to join another clan. To situate language use in its cultural context, the chapter first presents an overview of the overall traditional conflict resolution process of the

Afar people. This is followed by the transcription and translation of the speech. His study serves as corpora for future studies and practical needs such as language and cultural preservation.

Chapter 4: Daisuke Shinagawa
'Aspects of Linguistic Dynamism in Sheng as Kenyan Colloquial Swahili: Focusing on De-Standardisation and Re-Vernacularisation'

The multilingual situation is one of the most salient features in African society, which is ubiquitously observed not only at the societal level but also at the individual level. However, compared to the multilingualism discussed in the context of globalisation, be it as specific situations in other parts of the world or as a 'universal' value aimed to be achieved in the globalising world, actual situations in Africa seem to tell us a different story (cf. Lüpke and Storch 2013; Lüpke 2016; Mc Laughlin 2011; Zsiga et al. 2014, among others).

This chapter describes specific characteristics of African multilingual situations by focusing on current linguistic dynamism observed in colloquial varieties of Swahili, especially what is collectively labelled as Sheng, from structural as well as sociolinguistic perspectives. Two main points of discussion are as follows; (1) how the act of 'de-standardisation' as speakers' creative linguistic manipulation serves as a centrifugal force of structural change, and (2) how Sheng is being socially recognised as (resettled) 'vernaculars'. Shinagawa also argues that these dynamic processes work on the theoretical model of the 'African Potentials' especially by focusing on the mode of practical communication in multilingual situations in Swahili-speaking Africa.

Chapter 5: Sayaka Kutsukake
'Flexibility and the Potential of "African Multilingualism": A Case of Language Practice in Tanzania'

In Africa, multilingualism exists as a 'norm', and the notion of 'language' contrasts with that of European monolingual ideologies. However, many studies regarding multilingualism are still attached to the notion of language constructed in a formal European sense. This study believes that this aspect causes the language situation in Africa to be described and understood outside Africa as incomprehensively complex, and in many cases, inaccurate.

The language question in Africa seems to suggest that people are losing their identity, and they have developed fatalistic perspectives and attitudes towards their languages under systematic oppression, such as linguistic imperialism. However, people keep themselves attached to their languages and regularly show flexible and tolerant attitudes towards other languages rather than putting up resistance or expressing a desire to exclude these. This study describes the African sociolinguistic norm as an inclusive multilingual practice that enables meaning making for the whole community in this changing world.

Based on the fieldwork conducted by the author in 2015–2016, this study aims at making a distinction between the African view of language and the one in the European context by analysing the language attitudes and actual language practices in a village in Tanzania. Drawing on the framework of translanguaging, with a perspective of the multilingual norms in Africa, this study reveals how people in Africa mobilise a range of resources from their linguistic repertoires in a flexible manner.

Chapter 6: Shani Omari Mchepange and Mussa M. Hans

'Kiswahili Language and Its Potentiality for African Development'

Kiswahili language, since its origination on East Africa's coast many centuries ago, is progressing at an impressive pace. Due to its increasing number of speakers, the expansion of its scope as well as its elevated status, Kiswahili is spoken widely in the larger Eastern Africa region as a lingua franca. Apart from being a national and official language in various East African countries, Kiswahili also is one of the official languages in the Southern African Development Community (SADC). Likewise, Kiswahili is considered as one of the most widely spoken indigenous languages in Africa. The aim of this chapter is to examine Kiswahili language in order to uncover its potentiality for African development in its various sectors such as education, trade and economy, politics, diplomacy and culture. The chapter is based on Fishman's (1972) views regarding national languages and languages of wider communication in developing countries. The data for this study were collected by interviewing some Kiswahili speakers and professionals within the East African region and reviewing literature from various sources. The findings reveal that Kiswahili has a pivotal role to play in African development. The chapter gives some recommendations to ensure that African development is attained through the Kiswahili language.

Part II: Literature

Chapter 7: Keiko Takemura
'Swahili from the Perspectives of "Language" and "Literature"'

The United Republic of Tanzania (Tanzania), located in East Africa, is a country with more than 120 ethnic groups, but it chose Swahili, unique to the African continent, as its national language and official language. Among the languages used on the African continent, Swahili is quite a special case. Currently, except for English classes, language used for teaching all subjects at public elementary schools is Swahili. It is also the most frequently used language in newspapers, radio/television broadcasting and by public institutions, etc.

However, the linguistic status of Swahili is not definite. In secondary education and beyond, English is the medium of instruction. As globalisation is progressing in the 21st century, the recognition that African languages cannot compete in the world is spreading among Tanzanians. Many people are aware that they cannot get good jobs unless they have a high level of English proficiency. On the other hand, in the urban areas of Tanzania, the author would often hear conversations in Swahili and, when communicating with women who had little school education in the rural areas of the islands in Zanzibar, Swahili was her only option. By default, children who are supposed to receive public education also speak Swahili and not English. In other words, Swahili is the most frequently used spoken language. The author's experience of the problematic situation surrounding Swahili in Tanzania during the last 34 years, is that, although Swahili is used much more frequently than English, its status is not high.

What about the current status of Swahili as a written language? Especially when it comes to reading literary works, we have to say that there is a very harsh reality. People rarely buy or borrow books to read, so even if there are literary works written in Swahili, people who understand Swahili as their mother tongue or first language rarely read them. For example, not many Tanzanians can read the works of the writer Said Ahmed Mohamed who is relentlessly and energetically producing literary works in Swahili.

Still, the author is not pessimistic. Efforts are being made for the habit of reading books to take root, such as holding a Book Week in Tanzania and a project to build libraries in the villages of Zanzibar. At the same time, we should pay attention to the spread of online novels on social networking services (SNS). The author is also working on a project to translate Japanese picture books into Swahili and would like to deliver those picture books to children in East Africa, including Tanzania.

Chapter 8: Katsuhiko Shiota
'Cultural Transformation and the Reconstruction of Tradition in Yoruba Popular Music'

This chapter reinterprets how the Yoruba people of Nigeria create their own ethnic identity from the divided groups, incorporating foreign elements from the traditional culture in which their music travels to the groups. This chapter clarifies the process of being reborn as a new Yoruba popular culture.

Before the 19th century, a cultural diffusion pattern in which an advanced culture mainly brought from the Trans-Saharan trade was dispersed to rural areas through the developed country, Oyo. With the advent of European powers, however, a geopolitical composition gradually changed from the first stage to the next one. In Yorubaland of the 19th century, nations were fighting each other, but under the British colonial rule, they were united to one nation.

Although each region of Yoruba originally had traditional music, the court culture flowing in from Oyo mixed with the local music occurring in each area, so as to become localised in each region. When Yorubaland became a colony, in Lagos, the capital city, residents of various backgrounds brought in music resources and fused them in their way to create new urban music. Recording music activities by the recording industry began in the 1920s when popular music was already in place. Various genres depended on the culture, lifestyle and tastes of the audience at that time. Such popular music was different from traditional music. It was an entertainment for people whose community ties were weakened by urbanisation and a creation to reaffirm their new sense of belonging and identity.

In the 20th century, when the Yorubas' ethnic consciousness was established, the talking drum became touted as a star instrument of popular music as a representative element of the ethnic people. However, the talking drum had initially been a foreign element. As a result of its adaptation to traditional music over the years, it came to be regarded as part of extreme Yoruba culture. For the Yoruba people, access to tradition is more than just returning to the tradition. People living in their era select their traditional resources and integrate them with the new era's elements. The result is the skilful inheritance of tradition and the potential to keep their culture alive. This chapter considers that such a potential is the main reason why the Yoruba people continue to develop their culture without forgetting tradition.

Chapter 9: Haruse Murata
'Literature for African Children: Creation and Publication of Children's Books in French-Speaking West African Countries'

In West African countries using French as an official language, it is difficult for many authors to speak directly to African readers through their literary works because there are no fully developed publishing and distribution systems. However, the number of children's books published in the area has increased since the 1990s. One of the factors behind it was co-edition led by Beninese children's book publisher, Editions Ruisseaux d'Afrique. While it is difficult to publish books in each of the countries of the region, this publisher combined European knowledge with the experience and cooperation of African domestic publishers to run the co-edition. In this chapter Murata reviews the state of publishing in the region and highlights how this co-edition has been realised. It also studies the intention behind the co-edition to write about African society and culture, and thus develop children's self-consciousness. Finally, he examines some children's literature published by this co-edition.

Chapter 10: Maiko Kanda

'Writing from the In-between: Binyavanga Wainaina's Literary Practices'

The purpose of this chapter is to illustrate the writing practised by Binyavanga Wainaina as an example of African Potentials. This chapter defines 'African Potentials' as the coordinating capability in a multicultural situation. Historically, many African societies have maintained order in ethnic and cultural diversities. Its balance is not always stable but, rather, somewhat volatile. In other words, there could be a kind of flexibility depending on the time and situation.

Like his predecessors, Chinua Achebe and Ngũgĩ wa Thiong'o, Binyavanga, Wainaina pursued postcolonial issues. Achebe and Ngugi criticised the lasting colonial structure in a direct tone based on their ethnic affiliation. In comparison, Wainaina's literary attitude was more flexible for a practical result.

First, Wainaina created a new way of challenging Western stereotypes. *How to Write About Africa* dealt with the representation of the Other, whose issue is one of the main focuses for postcolonial literary criticism. However, Hamid Dabashi suggested that postcolonial critics have failed to deliver a decisive blow on this issue because they regarded the West as the only interlocutor. So did Achebe, dealing with Joseph Conrad's *Heart of Darkness*. Wainaina made a breakthrough by employing the ironic 'how-to' style of writing. It has become a literary platform today among people with a colonised background.

Second, in his memoir, *One Day I Will Write About This Place*, Wainaina explored a new concept of solidarity, not based on one's ethnic affiliation. Contrary to his Gikuyu family name, his first name after his maternal grandfather required him to consider the affiliation issue. It is entirely different from Ngũgĩ's statement as a Gikuyu novelist. Wainaina placed himself in the in-between space and elicited a new concept of solidarity, synchronic and polyphonic experiences by multicultural individuals with the same purpose. This concept was echoed in his focus on the LGBTQI+ issue in his last years.

Chapter 11: Fuko Onoda

'The Social Orientation of Kiswahili Poetry'

Achebe and Senghor once denied the effectiveness of 'art-for-art's sake' in Africa. Recently, Nyamnjoh also argued that, in African society, achievements by individuals become valuable only when they are done for collective interests. It can be said that, in Africa, art itself is not enough to be appreciated, rather, it is required to have a direct social impact.

There seems to be a close relationship between Kiswahili poetry and the society. An overview of the history of Kiswahili poetry makes us aware that the major changes in the poetry always coincide with important historical events such as foreign invasions or the achievement of independence. Besides, all these changes enable the poetry to have a more significant impact on the society.

In the society where art is required to have social orientation, art develops by seeking more efficient and powerful ways to appeal to the society, rather by pursuing its own innovation or novelty. Therefore, an expression that seems conservative to us, such as Kiswahili fixed verse, is the result of dynamic changes in response to social transition.

This chapter tries to highlight the social orientation of Kiswahili poetry by analysing the process of its change in accordance with the political background. The concept of 'social oriented art' discovered from the analysis of the local art activity in Africa may possibly propose the evaluation criteria of art differently from the West, and present universality of a non-Western origin.

Chapter 12: Francis B. Nyamnjoh

'Amos Tutuola as a Quest Hero for Endogenous Africa: Actively Anglicising the Yoruba Language and Yorubanising the English Language'

Everything moves – people, things and ideas – in predictable and unpredictable ways. Such circulation of things, ideas and people is not the monopoly of any group, community or society. Mobility or circulation leads to encounters of various forms, encounters that are (re)defining in myriad ways. If people, their things and ideas circulate, it follows that their identities, personal or collective, move as well, and through encounters with others, are constantly having to navigate, negotiate, accommodate or reject difference in an open-ended manner that makes of them a permanent work in progress. No mobility or interaction with others leaves anyone, anything or any idea indifferent, even if such interactions are not always equal and do not always result in immediate, palpable or tangible change.

This is the framework Nyamnjoh brings to his reflections on indigenous languages in Africa, their encounters, navigation and negotiation with colonial languages. He draws on the writings of Amos Tutuola, a writer who actively sought to Yorubanise English and Anglicise Yoruba, to argue that Africans have never been passive in their embrace, internationalisation, consumption and reproduction of European languages. If anything, just as they were able, long before encounters with Europe, to cultivate intelligibility from encounters between indigenous languages (hence the more appropriate term of endogenous languages), Africans have actively sought to Africanise European languages even when the intention by the colonising forces and their postcolonial continuities have been to settle for nothing short of deleting, reformatting and installing a whole new linguistic software in the African mind and social imaginary.

The chapter explores how Tutuola successfully employed his creative imagination in conversation with Yoruba folktales, to use and appropriate the English language to activate himself and his people through stories. He employed Yoruba as well, navigating between languages and worldviews, sharing African modes of thought in a colonial language, and promoting conviviality between different traditions and generations of being and becoming African. His focus on giving incompleteness a chance rather than embracing the extravagant illusion of completeness fuelled by spurious affirmations of superiority and autonomy speaks more to the logic of inclusion and less to that of exclusion and the violence of conquest and conversion. Through his creative appropriation of various influences in his life, African and European alike, Tutuola successfully stressed the need for conviviality between change and continuity, individual freedom and collective interest, tradition and modernity, Africa and the rest. Nyamnjoh asserts that Tutuola's writing especially poses a challenge to conventional assumptions about indigeneity and authenticity versus imports and hybridity, and forces us to rethink what really counts as 'indigenously African'.

3. Conclusion: What Does This Volume Aim For?

As can be seen from the titles and summaries of the various chapters, the purpose of this volume is to elucidate 'diversity' in the African continent. In Japan these days, 'diversity and inclusion' are often advocated. There, people question the traditional concept and existence of a modern nation, 'one race, one nation', and argue that 'diversity' should form the future society.

On the African continent, however, societies that have many different languages and cultures have long accepted, rejected, absorbed or transformed the differences, recognising that they are 'different from each other' in their daily lives. Africa's multicultural society has dealt with not only the language and culture of the African continent but also the language and culture of the European countries that became suzerains.

Of course, the African society has various negative thoughts that the suzerains planted during the colonial era. For example, the Bantu education policy of the apartheid era made people recognise, supposedly, that 'African languages are inferior languages'. Such negative thoughts cannot disappear overnight. Also, African countries' political economies are 'far behind' those of developed countries or Asian countries that should have been recognised as developing countries. Therefore, editors predict that there will be criticism that language and literature may not be useful for economic activity, and that such things may not make a living.

Nevertheless, people have passed down history to posterity by speaking and spinning it every day. Researchers, including these editors, must take a close look at the significant facts and understand the linguistic transformation and contact that are occurring on the African continent, and cultural and creative activities using those changing languages. The researchers must listen to the claims of the African people contained in the above activities. Doing so should, for the time being, lead us living in Japanese societies to illuminate this in Japan, which is by no means a monoethnic society. The editors and researchers state we must learn 'African Potentials' more than ever today. In this volume, we aim to portray the potential of diversity on the continent of Africa vividly.

Acknowledgements

This work was supported by JSPS KAKENHI Grant Number JP16H06318.

References

Bhabha, H. K. (1996) 'Unsatisfied: Notes on vernacular cosmopolitanism', in L. Garcia-Moreno and P. C. Pfeiffer (eds) *Text and Nation: Cross-Disciplinary Essays on Cultural and National Identities*, Columbia: Camden House, pp. 191–207.

Fishman, J. A. (1972) 'National languages and languages of wider communication in the developing countries', in A. S. Dil (ed.) *Language in Sociocultural Changes: Essays by Joshua A. Fishman*, Stanford: Stanford University Press, pp. 191–223.

Lüpke, F. (2016) 'Uncovering small-scale multilingualism', *Critical Multilingual Studies*, Vol. 4, No. 2, pp. 35–74.

Lüpke, F. and Storch, A. (2013) *Repertoires and Choices in African Languages*, Berlin: De Gruyer Mouton.

Mc Laughlin, F. (2011) *The Languages of Urban Africa*, London: Bloomsbury.

Nyamnjoh, F. B. (2017) 'Incompleteness: Frontier Africa and the currency of conviviality', *Journal of Asian and African Studies*, Vol. 52, Issue 3, pp. 253–270.

Wainaina, B. (2005) 'How to write about Africa', *Granta 92* (https://granta.com/how-to-write-about-africa/) (accessed: 4 February 2021).

────── (2011) *One Day I Will Write About This Place: A Memoir*, Minneapolis: Graywolf Press.

Zsiga, E. C., Boyer, O. T. and Kramer, R. (2014) *Languages in Africa:*

Multilingualism, Language Policy, and Education, Washington DC: George University Press.

Part I

Language

Chapter 1

Convivial Multilingualism as a Modern African Ethos: Cases of East African Non-Arab Arabophone Societies

Shuichiro Nakao

1. Introduction

Before starting our exploration of why (and how) African multilingualism should be appreciated as an expression of 'African Potentials' (Gebre et al. 2017; Ofosu-Kusi and Matsuda 2020), let us start with an introduction to a typical case of 'modern' monolingual societies. This may be perplexing to most of our African colleagues to whom I dedicate this chapter.

In such a society, a newborn child is exposed to the single vernacular of his/her nation. S/he can use it everywhere within the national borders, but hardly outside of them. Everything s/he reads is written in this language and it is difficult to find books in foreign languages in local bookshops or libraries (unless for use as ornaments). Everything s/he watches on TV – news, shows, animé programmes and even foreign movies – is also in this language. Schools offer a 'national language' curriculum over a period of about 12 years to teach how to write 'correctly' and read traditional literature from classic to modern. Also, the 'Foreign' (i.e., English) language is taught in school, which is thought to be quite useless in real life. If s/he is stopped by an alien and s/he does not have a good understanding of the 'foreign' language, s/he can simply run or try to open a translation application on a Smart Phone with a silent smile. This is the sociolinguistic reality lived by most of my Japanese kinsfolk native to a suburb of a Japanese megacity. This sociolinguistic pattern has been more or less prevalent in the West and the Far East, or roughly the Global North (or perhaps more widely) throughout the 20th century, in terms of the pursuit of linguistic nationalism.

In retrospect, it was only after the collapse of the Iron Curtain that such Northern monolingual societies faced the global rise of indigenous movements by linguistic minorities and the diversification of diversity, or 'super-diversity', to use Vertovec's (2007) term, caused by accelerating migration flows. It was in the 1990s that the 'language rights' of minorities were seriously considered when the United States enacted the 'Native American Languages Act of 1990', the Council of Europe adopted the 'European Charter for Regional or Minority Languages' (1992), Japan enacted the 'New Ainu Law' (1997, targeting the minority Ainu people) and UNESCO started to take the lead on worldwide 'endangered languages' projects. This 'one language, one people' scheme has a history of universal application, for example, to the deaf community (Furukawa-Yoshida 2015) or to African societies (Hieda 2002; Kurimoto 2002) in terms of creating language-based 'minority/ethnic groups' on the basis of 'mother tongue education' according to a universal model (Sunano 2009, 2012; Yoneda 2012).

Meanwhile, Northern linguists started to challenge traditional linguistic values, such as the dominance and nativism of English and monolingualism itself. American linguists developed the notions of 'World English(es)' and 'English as a Lingua Franca (ELF)' to acknowledge non-native English societies, while others criticised 'English imperialism'. The Council of Europe developed and promoted the novel notion of 'plurilingualism' (Council of Europe 2001) to foster experiences of linguistic *bricolage*, rather than targeting native-level acquisition of 'foreign' languages, in a pan-European context.[1] In the Japanese context, there have been several attempts to discover and cherish linguistic practices and the ethos and virtues of multilinguals and speakers of 'pidgin/creole' languages by men of literature. As a result, several concepts have developed such as 'creolism' (Imafuku 2003 [1991]), 'exophony' (Tawada 2003) and 'omniphone' (Kan 2005). Masahiko Nishi published *Beginner's Creole* (Nishi 1999), an interesting introduction to both the linguistic structures of Martinique French Creole and the ethos of *créolité* (Bernabé et al. 1993).

Nowadays, following a decade or two of investigations, linguists are noticing that fluidity and the mixing of languages are becoming more commonplace in international workplaces and daily contact situations in Northern megacities (Blommaert 2010; Pennycook 2016) and immigrants living there are developing new languages for their own sake (Nortier and Dorleijn 2013). In other words, multilingualism has not yet become a rooted tradition in the Global North and how to manage it in the era of globalisation has only recently become a real issue for its citizens. Northern researchers have just started to significantly recognise that the 'monolingual habitus', in other words, the monolingual way of thinking, pervades even in multilingual education (Benson 2014) and multilingual social security systems for immigrants (Blommaert 2010; Nakao 2012).[2]

In contrast to the Global North, modern sub-Saharan Africa is characterised by deep-seated traditions of everyday multilingual practices, where a single person deploys rich language repertoires, including his/her own 'ethnic' vernacular(s) and languages of wider communication. This reality was inexplicable to pre-1990s Africanists, who would first try to analyse it as an index of 'underdevelopment' or the distorted legacy of colonialism, while the success of Swahili as a 'national' language, especially in Tanzania, was judged as an exceptional 'miracle' of an African language (Miyamoto 2002). From another perspective, Africanists questioned why smaller African languages were not equally as endangered as those outside Africa (Kaji 2009).[3] These arguments were based on their Northern-centric analytic norms, where monolingualism was regarded as the default setting of 'modernity' (Sunano 2009, 2012). Recently, linguists have been acknowledging the similarity between the actual sociolinguistic situation observable in the Global South and what they are now pursuing in the Global North (Canagarajah 2009; Yoneda 2012) and investigations are beginning regarding how to adopt such a 'multilingual habitus' both in the Global South and the Global North by opening our eyes to the 'monolingual habitus' (Benson 2010, 2014). The African enigma must now be rephrased as: Why have African societies succeeded in achieving convivial multilingualism rather than reverting to robust monolingualism and what can we learn from it?

However, African multilingualism has never been manualised for application. If we wish to use it in the global arena of linguistic debates, we need interesting analyses of its underlying values and practices. Also, we must remember that African societies are never multilingual on equal terms, and it is not this chapter's aim to describe them all in general terms. We would have to specifically delineate what deserves to be labelled as the 'African' pattern of multilingualism to eventually develop and justify 'African Potentials' (Gebre et al. 2017; Ofosu-Kusi and Matsuda 2020). With these broader purposes in mind, this chapter focuses on African peoples' multilingual ethos expressed through their everyday languages and its potential value in the argument of African Potentials. We call the African pattern of multilingualism 'convivial multilingualism',[4] in line with Francis B. Nyamnjoh's arguments on incompleteness and conviviality as a currency of frontier Africans (Nyamnjoh 2017).

2. African Potentials in the Linguistic Margins of the Arab World

This chapter will draw on linguistic realities and ideologies expressed through metalinguistic discourses in three Eastern African communities lying south of Sudan: Mayu/Berta/Funj (western Ethiopia), urban South Sudanese (South Sudan) and Nubi (Kenya and Uganda).[5] In these societies, structurally simplified forms of Sudanese Arabic have been in continuous use for more than a century and a half for secular convivial purposes by those who self-claim non-Arab cosmopolitan identities.

Our choice of theme is partially based on the fact that Western languages such as English, French and Portuguese are popular too as second languages around the world, and the expansion of a dominant people's language as a centralised 'national' language can be seen in many multilingual societies around the globe. Such cases of linguistic practices are not necessarily advanced in the framework of 'African Potentials', as they could better be incorporated in another universal framework (e.g., ELF, plurilingualism, linguistic nationalism, etc.). On the other hand, Arabic is an extremely assimilative world language and, if one speaks it, one has the right (or sometimes the duty)[6] to claim 'Arab-ness'. There is expected to be no such non-'Arab' peoples who speak Arabic without being forced by the nation-state (i.e. as a national language) and there is almost none, except in Africa.[7] In this instance, our cases would represent those of a uniquely 'African' nature, not commonly found in other continents, which could offer a *raison d'être* to be an 'African Potential'.

Since our instances are not very well known, we need to briefly introduce them here:

The first one, the Berta/Funj ethnic group, is a loose confederation of Nilo-Saharan Berta-speaking peoples on both sides of the Sudanese-Ethiopian borderlands. In the past, they consisted of a significant portion of the Funj Sultanate (1504–1821), the first Islamic state in riverine Sudan, which was governed by heterogeneous non-Arab Africans, and this history makes them prefer 'Funj' as an auto-ethnonym to 'Berta', a derogatory term that has been common in academia.[8] Mayu is a dominant sect of Berta/Funj around Assosa, the regional capital of the Benishangul-Gumuz region of Ethiopia, defined by having mixed paternal Arab and maternal Berta origins. They are sometimes called *Waṭāwīṭ* ('bats') because of their fractured identity (González-Ruibal 2014). They are virtually all Sunni Muslims and an average Mayu person in Assosa would speak, besides the Mayu dialect of the Berta language, a local distinct variant of Sudanese Arabic (coined 'Benishangul Arabic' by Nakao 2017b) plus Oromo, Amharic and English as languages of wider communication. Despite the fact that Mayus are granted with Sunni Islam, Arabic and even a paternal (Sudanese) 'Arab' lineage, in the current era of identity politics, they promote their Berta/Funj identity but not an Arab one.[9]

In Sudanese history, Ottoman Egyptians defeated the Funj Sultanate in 1821 and started creating colonies in what is now South Sudan. African ex-slaves were recruited for the Egyptian army (*jihādiyya*), where an Arabic-based creole likely emerged (Nakao 2017a). After the Mahdist revolts, these African soldiers fled to East Africa and were employed by the British in their colonial army (later the King's African Rifles). During this period, a new ethnic group, Nubi, emerged. Although they have lost their ancestral languages in favour of a return to the creole Arabic (also called Nubi), their ancestral South Sudanese or other African ethnic groups have been retained as clans, such as 'Bari', 'Dinka', 'Zande', 'Lendu' (Congo), 'Tagalau' (Tegali of Sudan), 'Shegia' (a Sudanese Arab sect) and even 'Habashi' (Ethiopian). This has raised their awareness of their cosmopolitanism from the 19th century to the present day. This creolisation does not equate to linguistic homogenisation. Their descendants now live in East African towns and suburbs (e.g., Bombo near Kampala and Kibera in Nairobi), where they speak the Arabic creole, besides Swahili and English, plus the language of a locally dominant ethnic group. Like the Berta/Funj, practically all Nubis are Sunni Muslims, just like many Arabs and Swahilis, but they have never adopted an 'Arab' or 'Swahili' identity and they are quite proud to be different from them.

Back in South Sudan, the Arabic creole remained after the defeat of the Mahdists by the British and it spread among rural immigrants who were employed in newly created colonial cities like Juba, especially from the 1930s onwards (Nakao 2017a). This formed the core of Juba Arabic, a sister creole to Nubi, which has now become the most widely spoken lingua franca in the Equatoria region (in the modern sense, the southern half of the country). Some Ottoman-Egyptian *jihādiyya* and rural immigrants settled in a quarter called Malakia ('civilian quarter'), which became locally known as *buru lo tome*, 'elephant's stomach', since it swallowed people from every ethnic group from along the Nile (Nakao 2013). After the independence of Sudan in 1956, rural immigrants rushed into the town to expand it to the outskirts of Malakia and to form new generations who speak Juba Arabic as a native language. In this sense, Juba Arabic is a lingua franca-cum-creole (dubbed a 'pidgincreole' in modern creolistics) inherited from heterogeneous 19th century ex-slave soldiers by various modern South Sudanese peoples. Due to the Arab-Islamist policies implemented in ex-Sudan, Juba Arabic is sometimes stigmatised as the 'language of the *mundukúru* (Arabs with the derogatory nuance of 'slavers')' by the speakers themselves, but even after the independence of the state in 2011, it has remained widespread and, for example, most popular songs heard in Juba today are sung in it.

A monolingual-minded person would locate these three societies within the historical drift of the Arabisation of Africa anticipating complete assimilation, otherwise something that has not yet succeeded in it,[10] but such a biased interpretation and a wrong forecast are never justified. What we are determined to do here is to describe the reality and extract the underlying virtue. In Section 3, we will see how people conceptualise 'languages' and, in Section 4, we will see how people mitigate conceptualised 'languages' by hybridised language practices and, therefore, re-conceptualise the practice. This will reveal what Africans bear in mind when they act in a multilingual way.

3. There Are Two Types of Languages: The Conceptualisation of Languages[11]

Sudanese Arabic distinguishes two types of language, *lugha* and *ruṭāna* (Luffin 2003; James 2008; Lüpke and Storch 2013: 144; Mugaddam and Abdelhay 2013; Manfredi 2017).[12] In Khartoum, the term *lugha* is interpreted as a 'fully fledged language', typically represented by Arabic and English (and French, etc.), which are standardised and function as official languages, while *ruṭāna* means a 'gibberish', 'jargon', 'patois', 'dialect' or anything that is unqualified as *lugha*, such as secret jargons, slang, the incomprehensive 'languages' of the spirits in *zār* (spirit possession) cults and, among others, non-Arabic languages of African populations. The Arabic 'language' is called *al-lugha al-'Arabiyya*, but the Fur 'language' in Darfur is called *ruṭānat Fōr*.[13] Under the Arab-Islamist regime, *ruṭāna*s were regarded as a threat to 'national unity' and this stigmatisation was implemented through the media and also through public education (Mugaddam and Abdelhay 2013; Sharkey 2007; Mekki 2001).[14]

As such, Sudanese Arabic seems a racialistic language that automatically imposes an assimilatory effect on speakers – it is as much an 'incomplete baby' as Western modernity, one may be tempted to say (Nyamnjoh 2017). Non-Arab Africans, however, adopted the baby and raised hybridised Arabic varieties, in which these racialistic terms have gained different interpretations with a similar extension.

In the Benishangul Arabic of the Berta/Funj people, *lúk'a* (their rendition of *lugha*) refers to such languages as English and Arabic (including Written Arabic and spoken varieties like Benishangul Arabic), while *rut'áána* refers to any local languages and ethnic groups, such as Berta/Funj, Gumuz, Komo, Shinasha, Oromo and even Amharic, the *de facto* national language of Ethiopia since they consider it an ethnic language of the Amhara people. As a result, any African languages in the state are expressed on equal terms without any pejorative sense. In the second meaning of the word, *rut'áána* is the most common term for self-designating the 'Berta/Funj language' and its speakers.[15] When a Berta/Funj person calls to a group of his/her people, he/she usually says *'yaa rut'áána!'* ('O people of my language') with an affectionate tone.[16]

The term *lúk'a* is not a simple equivalent of Western concepts like 'lingua franca' or 'vehicular language' that are defined by their 'vehicular function' (Calvet 1981), i.e., inter-ethnic use, and has nothing to do with identity. The social domain of its use is largely limited to the Berta/Funj people and overlaps with the Berta/Funj language, while the urban *linguae francae* used in Assosa in the real sense of the term are Oromo or Amharic.[17] Mr A., a specialist in Berta/Funj language standardisation/education, and my teacher of the language, constantly referred to Arabic, a *lúk'a*, as 'the second language of the Berta/Funj people', namely the second important language they identify with, and Berta/Funj and Arabic education 'must develop side by side' (*laázim yit't'áwwaru jambu jámbu*).[18]

Why don't they just choose one? In partial answer to this enigma, González-Ruibal (2014: 190) clearly considers the Arabic language, together with the Islamic religion and Arab culture, as one of the 'objects of resistance against the hegemonic Ethiopian culture' to reinforce 'religious and political links with neighbouring Sudan and other Arabic countries, bypassing the state', which represents a 'transnational resource of legitimation – a kind of vernacular cosmopolitanism' (Bhabha 1996). To add to his explanation, we could locate the *rut'áána* in their linguistic expression of 'vernacular' cosmopolitanism. Unlike the 'global' cosmopolitanism that opts for assimilation, it is necessary to be 'conscious of the insufficiency of the self and the imperative of openness to the needs of others'

(Bhabha 1996). Owning a *rut'áána* is thus an important prerequisite for them to be cosmopolitan.

A similar change in meanings and attitudes is observable in Juba Arabic. Here again, any South Sudanese ethnic languages, from Dinka with millions of speakers to Tennet with some thousand speakers, are collectively called *rutân*, in contrast to *lúga* (a cognate of Sudanese Arabic *lugha*). Although South Sudan had been under northern Sudanese hegemony, the term *rutân* has lost its derogatory sense so that people can call Japanese and Italian *rutan Japanese* and *rutan Italian* to signal their 'ethnic' values, in the same way as *rutan Dinka* and *rutan Tennet* are used (although *luga Japanese* and *luga Italian* would be more common), which a Sudanese Arab would diplomatically not dare to say.[19] Although it is not a standardised language and many people now acquire it as a mother tongue, Juba Arabic is most often categorised as *lúga* with English – the official language of South Sudan, Arabic –the official language of ex-Sudan and Swahili – the official lingua franca of the East African Community of which South Sudan is now a part. In a conversation with Mr L, a South Sudanese friend of mine, he wondered why the word *rutân* had lost its derogatory sense and why *lúga* now includes languages like Juba Arabic, an unwritten, informal code of communication as opposed to the prototypical images represented by English and (Written) Arabic.[20] What could explain the change of criteria in terms of this categorisation?

It would be nonsense to ascribe politico-historical causes to this change, but we could interpret it as an expression of African people's philosophy. As Figure 1 shows, the two terms must be differently translated according to an Arab's or a non-Arab's view. The two meanings of *RUTANA* (*ruṭāna, rut'áána, rutân*) and *LUGHA* (*lugha, lúk'a, lúga*) represent the different cosmologies of Arabs and non-Arabs – the criterion of a *LUGHA* might be standard for Arabs, but for non-Arabs, it is emblematic of a language used for conviviality (Nyamnjoh 2017). A *RUTANA* is an 'in-group' language, which sounds 'gibberish' to Arabs, but for non-Arabs, it is their own most affectionate language, a source of pride in difference and a prerequisite of conviviality.

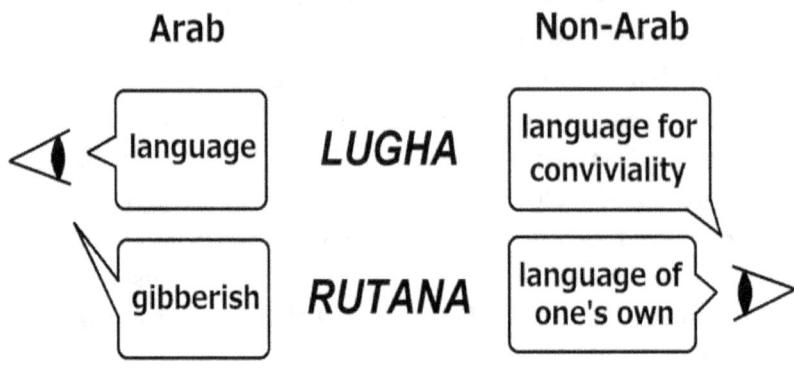

Figure 1. Arab and non-Arab views on the two types of 'languages'

The adoption and relocation of racialistic 'language' concepts is not limited to Benishangul and Juba Arabic, but perhaps quite widespread in Africa.[21] In Tanzanian colloquial Swahili, ethnic languages are called *kilugha* in contrast to *lugha* 'language' (e.g., English and Swahili). The prefix *ki-* seems etymologically a diminutive form with a derogatory meaning, although synchronically, this is not at all the case (Komori 2002; Maya Abe, personal communication). A Hausa dictionary lists two meanings for the word *yare*: 1. Dialect or language other than one's own. 2. Language (Newman 2007: 224). This could represent different cosmologies of native and (originally) non-native speakers. Mc Laughlin (2015) argues a similar polysemy of the word *làkk*, a Wolof word that can signal a range of meanings from 'speak a language fluently' to 'speak unintelligibly' (as a verb), reflecting the fact that Wolof has many non-native speakers. She further states that 'urban' Wolof speakers use the French term *langue* for European languages in contrast to *làkk* 'African languages' as a noun.

To embody this conceptualisation of a language with vernacular cosmopolitan attitudes, no one is supposed to be 'detribalised' when speaking a *LUGHA* as their only mother tongue or as a basis of their identity, even in Malakia, the oldest urban quarter in cosmopolitan Juba, often associated with 'detribalisation' (Kurimoto 2002; Nakao 2013). When a monolingual-minded person like me asked the question, a South Sudanese citizen from Malakia answered:

> Are we detribalised? No! Now you speak Juba Arabic and you are regular here in Malakia, but have you lost your tribe? I speak my *rutân*, and he [indicating his Malakian friend on his side] speaks his *rutân*, but we just speak Juba Arabic to get together. We have been friends since our childhood, and I must run to him if something happens to him. Because we are neighbours!²²

Lastly, Nubi, a 'creole' community that has lost its ancestral South Sudanese languages and now speaks Nubi as primary and English and Swahili as secondary identity markers, represents a more complex case. In Nubi, the word *rutân* has come to mean any 'language' including English, Arabic, Swahili, Nubi and Luo, and *lúgha*, a loanword via Swahili, is simply a synonym of *rutân* (Luffin 2003) or has a nuance meaning 'way of speech' (e.g., 'he speaks in a beautiful *lúgha*').²³ Yet Nubi speakers seem to make a distinction between the two concepts since the verbal form of the same root, *rútan* 'to speak an (ethnic) language' is not used for speaking English or Swahili. In a casual debate over multilingualism with Mr H., my Kenyan Nubi colleague, he used the English word *language* with a sense similar to LUGHA.

> I think multilingualism in Africa is an asset. ... Larger languages in the world [e.g., English] will open their society (**languages** *al kubâr fi dúnia dé bi fáta society tómon*). I think Tanzania, the 'sleeping giant', a country richer in resources, is economically poor perhaps because it is monolingual due to its *Ujamaa* policy. In my opinion, Kenyans can think of new ideas with open eyes thanks to our multilingualism. ... [However,] if we speak only English, we may feel the fear of being 'governed', as it is not my mother tongue. And we need Nubi as we do not want to become a Swahili – it is a target of contempt. ... Nubi is a minority language, but we never feel shame to speak it. We never hide our identity.²⁴

Their pride in being Nubi could be reconfirmed in their self-designation. In Mr H.'s words, 'They do not self-designate as Arabs due to speaking a variety of Arabic because, for us, Nubi is even above Arab. We could have identified as British since our grandparents fought for them and we have spoken English. But we never do so.'[25] This paradoxical case of Nubi – they are 'creolised' but still pluralistic – would support our claim that African multilingualism is not just the reality or a consequence of historical causes, but it has become an ethos or an embodied virtue.

It is also worth mentioning people's attitudes encountered during my fieldwork. The first time I started studying Juba Arabic, people's attitudes were apathetic. Some people I met in Juba suggested that I learn a *RUTANA* or the 'correct' (Written) Arabic, but not Juba Arabic. In contrast, my first opportunity to study Nubi was provided by Mr H. himself, who knew that I was specialised in Juba Arabic and invited me to Nairobi via an SNS. I thought that it would reflect the cultural difference between South Sudan and Kenya, but it probably did not. When I asked them to teach their colloquial Nairobi Swahili, he was apparently reluctant. For Nubis, Nubi was the *RUTANA* and Swahili was a *LUGHA*, as Juba Arabic was a *LUGHA* to South Sudanese.

These cases of conceptualisation and attitudes towards *LUGHAs* and *RUTANAs* could be representative of a humble expression of pluralistic ethos (i.e., the norm and the reality) in which non-native speakers have been aspiring to create a linguistic conviviality by appropriating a dominant people's language and dislocating its ethnocentricity. It protects people from one-way assimilation to the dominant language and culture and helps them to keep imagining a pluralistic world.

4. How Languages Mix: Realities and Conceptualisation of Language Hybridisation[26]

Another salient feature of African multilingualism is that the conceptualisation of the two types of 'languages' is mitigated by hybridising them in practice. This linguistic hybridisation would not only involve an intermixture of grammar and vocabulary but also often a simplification/reduction of the system. Here we interpret these hybridised practices as something deliberate, rather than attributing them to a lack of ability to keep them apart.

The Mayu dialect (M) of the Berta/Funj language has a great number of borrowings from Arabic. As a result, sometimes a Mayu Berta/Funj sentence seems to be a word-to-word translation of Benishangul Arabic (BA), as the next examples show.

(1) M. *maalêsh,*   *ali*   *t'áwwáláʔi*   *walá*   *shap'úthóó-ŋgó*   *addelefôn.*

       sorry   I   stayed.long   not   hit-to.you   telephone

   BA. *maaléesh,*   *ána*   *t'awwál-da*   *máa*   *darabda-léeg*   *ad-delefóon.*

       sorry   I   stayed.long-I   not   I.hit-to.you   the-telephone

       'Sorry, I did not call you for a long time.'

The M sentence exhibits the Arabic loanwords *maalêsh* 'sorry', *t'áwwala* 'stay long', *walá* 'not', *addelefóon* 'telephone' and the calqued phrases 'have not been doing' ('stayed long' + 'not' + past verb) and 'call on the telephone' ('hit' + 'telephone'). On the contrary, the BA phonology is characterised by two ejective consonants which no other Arabic variety attests, as well as the lack of 'emphatic' consonants and the voicing contrast (e.g., *t* vs. *d*, *s* vs. *z*) shared in most Arabic varieties (Nakao 2017b). M and BA also share tonal features, such as high tone levelling (HLH → HHH), as (2) shows.

(2) M. *k'óli* 'eat' + *máré* 'they' → *k'óli-máré* 'they eat'

       thá 'in' + *Itóbia* 'Ethiopia' → *thá Ítóbia* 'in Ethiopia'

   BA. *az-zána* 'the year' + *dá* 'this' → *az-záná dá* 'this year'[27]

       fíi 'exist' + *shunú* 'what' → *fíi shúnú* 'what happened (what is there)?'

These features make M and BA sound similar to each other and one might wonder if they are simply a single language with two sets of vocabulary (and morphology). This impression could be confirmed by the next examples (3a–d), where M *sha* and BA *ashan* exhibit similar polyfunctionality to mark (a) reason/purpose clause, (b) reason phrase ('for that reason'), (c) manipulative clause and (d) quotation clause. Since the cognate Sudanese Arabic form *'ashān* is used exclusively for (a) and (b), their function in BA could be a result of the influence of M, while M *sha* seems to exhibit phonological intermixture with BA *ashan*, because it can alternate with an older form *tha*. The only exception is the last example (3e), where only M marks a complement of the verb *s'úllá* 'be called' with *sha* as a preposition, but BA cannot use *ashan* in this construction (here marked as *ashan).

(3) a. M. *maabí p'ishiga áŋ* **sha** *arraʔiiz p'eriɲí tha Asóósa.*

BA. *annáaz mabzuut'iin* **ashan** *arraʔiiz jáay le Asóósa.*

'People are happy **because** the president is coming to Assosa.'

b. M. **sha** *shúgo ɲinéŋ shibílóógálí albún.*

BA. **ashan** *gída ishdaréed albún.*

'**For** that (reason), I bought coffee beans.'

c. M. *maabí íshiʔí* **sha** *bak'á ádó árraʔiiz.*

BA. *annáaz ábu* **ashan** *arraʔiiz má yáji.*

'People refused **so that** the president will not come.'

d. M. *maabí k'alóóʔí bá* **sha** *arraʔiiz p'eriɲí thálé.*

BA. *annáaz gáálu* **ashan** *arraʔiiz jáay hína.*

'People said **that** the president is coming here.'

e. M. *maabálé s'úllá* **sha** *Boorid.*

BA. *azzóol dá bigul-lééhu (***ashan**) *Ázad.*

'This man is called (**as**) Lion.'

There could be more than one way of interpreting this slight difference in the grammar of *sha/ashan*, but here we consider it as indicative of deliberate hybridisation, rather than differentiation, of the two languages (i.e., M and BA have not yet completed the assimilation of the grammatical system in this point, rather than the speakers are deliberately differentiating between the two only on this point).

Juba Arabic (JA) and Nubi are classical examples of 'simplified' varieties of Arabic (Nakao 2017a), while Sudanese Arabic (SA) is a variety of colloquial Arabic like Egyptian, Syrian and Iraqi dialects which share their basic morphophonology with Written Arabic. For example, the SA word *ruṭāna* (4a) has a peculiar 'emphatic' *ṭ* pronounced with the tongue bent like a plate, which is replaced by a simple *t* in JA/Nubi. When this word is compounded with a modifier noun (4b), it is suffixed by *-t* in SA, while JA/Nubi only changes the tone. The verbal form of this root in SA is either *raṭan-* (4c, d) or *-rṭun* (4e, f) according to the tense-aspect and marked by a subject person affix (*-ta*, *-i-* and *-a-* and the modal marker *b(i)-*). In JA/Nubi, the verbal form is *rútan*, derived by a tonal shift, and it lacks inflections for the tense-aspect or subject person.

(4)   SA.   JA. = Nubi

a. *ruṭāna*   *rutân*   'a RUTANA'

b. *ruṭānat dēnka*   *rutan dínka*   'Dinka language'

c. *(hu) raṭan*   *úwo rútan*   'he spoke a RUTANA'

d. *(ana) raṭan-ta*   *ána rútan*   'I spoke a RUTANA'

e. *(hu) b-i-rṭun*   *úwo bi-rútan*   'he speaks a RUTANA'

f. *(ana) b-a-rṭun*   *ána bi-rútan*   'I speak a RUTANA'

In the 1980s, linguists claimed that JA was losing such features under the influence of the dominant SA, regarding JA simply as a process of Arabicsation (Nakao 2017a). In reality, as my data from South Sudanese informants born after 1990 reveal, it did not. JA has remained almost the same as Nubi, largely conserving the state of the Arabic creole which emerged before 1890,[28] for roughly more than a century and a half.

Again, there is evidence to analyse that the two varieties were deliberately kept apart. First, many urban South Sudanese in Juba can speak, in addition to JA, SA (with a South Sudanese accent). This language is most typically used to converse with someone from northern Sudan, but rarely among those born and bred in Juba, and if one unintentionally does so, one would instantly be corrected (Nakao 2017a). Second, the main influence from SA to JA is observed in the lexicon, where SA words have gradually replaced older ones (preserved in Nubi). As such, we could conclude that JA has symbolically retained its simplified structures in preference to the lexicon.

(5)
SA.	JA.	Nubi	
lē	*le*	*na*	'to, for'
bambē	*bambé*	*kiyáta*	'sweet potato'
digin	*dígin* (rare/archaic form: *nyékém*)	*nyékém*	'chin'
shaʿar	*sáar* (rare/archaic form: *sûf*)	*sû*	'hair'
záraʿ	*zára*, *kúruju* (same frequency)	*kúruju*	'to cultivate'
ghāba	*gába*, *kibira* (same frequency)	*kibira*	'forest'
gōs	*dángá*	*adángá*	'bow'
ḥanak	*bángírí*	*bángírí*	'jaw'

Lastly, Nubi again represents an extreme case. Nubi is an Arabic creole born from the contact between South Sudanese languages and SA, and its speakers are all speakers of Swahili, another important language born from the contact between African Bantu language(s) and oriental languages including Arabic. What is more, Nubi is heavily influenced by Swahili, and their Swahili – here we term NS (for Nairobi/Nubi Swahili) – in turn shares many features with Nubi (Nakao 2019b).[29] As examples in (6) show, Nubi *fí* and NS *iko/-ko* 'be, exist' share the same polyfunctionality, with usages deviating from either JA and Standard Swahili (SS).

(6) a. Nubi *fí*   shunú bára? (= JA.)
     NS.   *iko* nini   inje? (≠ SS. *kuna nini nje.*)
           exist what out
     'What is out there?' (existence)

    b. Nubi *fí*   yôm   tá-ba-áruf. (≈ JA.)
     NS.   *iko* siku   u-ta-jua.   (≠ SS. *siku moja utajua.*)
           exist day   you-will-know
     'One day you will know.' (indefinite marker)

    c. Nubi *án-fí* ma   hóma hári. (≠ JA. *ána indu húmma sedîd.*)

	NS.	*ni-**ko***	na	homa	kali.	(≠ SS. *ni-na homa kali.*)
		I-exist	with	fever	severe	
		'I have (literally 'I am with') a strong fever.' (possessive)				
d.	Nubi	*án-**fí***	séme.		(≠ JA. *ána séme* or *ána kwês.*)	
	NS.	*ni-**ko***	poa.		(= SS.)	
		I-exist	fine			
		'I am fine.' (predicative copula)				

What is more, modern Nubis speak Nubi, Swahili and English non-separately. Often their speech cannot be categorised as a single language, but a mixed code. As shown in the following examples (spontaneous data), in (7a), the speaker switches from English to Swahili and to Nubi in a single noun phrase and a verbal form. In (7b), the Swahili infinitive prefix *ku-* is borrowed into a Nubi sentence to form a calque of the English auxiliary verb 'have to'. In (7b), English words are freely used in Nubi syntax, and in (7d), Nubi and English words seem to be embedded in a Swahili sentence, but these sentences often co-occur in a single utterance. What could we call this language?

(7)	a.	*we can do [some practice*		*ya*	*[ku-agára]].*
		we can do some practice		of	to-read
		English		Swahili	Swahili-Nubi
		'We can do some practice of reading.'			
	b.	*ná-[éndis*	*ku]-gên*		*faltá.*
		we-[have	to]-sit		down
		Nubi-[Nubi	Swahili]$_{English}$-Nubi		Nubi
		'We have to settle down.'			
	c.	*time*	*kalâs*		*expire.*
		time	already		expire
		English	Nubi		English
		'The time has expired.'			

d. *lábda*   *sabâ*   *u-ta-come.*

   maybe   tomorrow   you-will-come

   Swahili/Nubi Nubi   Swahili-Swahili-English

   'Maybe tomorrow you may come.'

Nubis call this language 'Nubi's *sheng*' (*shéŋ ta Núbi*, here I intentionally spell it with a small letter). This is an adoption of the term 'Sheng', which is nowadays defined as the colloquial variety of Swahili spoken in urban Kenya and characterised by frequent code-mixing with English (as its alleged etymology, a contraction of *Swahili-English* is implied) and loanwords from local languages (Shinagawa, this volume; Githiora 2019). The use of such super-hybridised linguistic code and calling it an '(ethnic) *sheng*' might be prevalent in Kenya, as suggested by the words of a Kenyan youth, 'There is Kikuyu Sheng and Dholuo Sheng, and so on' (quoted by Githiora 2019: 91). We could compare this conceptualisation of linguistic hybridisation with recent terms coined by modern linguists such as 'translanguaging', 'polylingual languaging', 'metrolingualism', etc. (Pennycook 2016), which means that urban Kenyans are as keen as these scholars as regards linguistic thinking.

The hybridisation of languages in Africa is, of course, a widespread practice as seen in other chapters of this volume, and we will refrain from providing a long list of the associated literature. Of course, there must be many unnamed practices or languages that deserve investigation. It is, however, important here to reconfirm that analysing the structures and functions of such practices in an objective framework is inadequate and we would have to build upon an interpretative framework to creatively approach African multilingualism.

5. Conclusion

In this chapter, we investigated how we can approach convivial multilingualism in Africa in terms of African Potentials. For this purpose, we focused on conceptualisations and linguistic structures/practices of African Arabic speakers and interpreted them as expressions of African peoples' philosophy, rather than simply being descriptive. Through the argument, it was suggested that, despite the great tradition of analysing language in terms of identity, whether it be national, ethnic or anything else, it is of course never the only theme non-elite frontier Africans think about. What people may imagine by language is not always a community, but a universe consisting of many different components. Our cases presented here could indicate African peoples' casual aspirations for convivial pluralism, which never envisage assimilation as a scheduled future.

Such an approach would be 'incomplete' from the nomothetic linguistic viewpoint, yet it would be helpful to answer some African sociolinguistic enigmas from the point of view of the virtue of multilingualism. For example, why people speak so many languages even beyond necessity, why such a fluid multilingual situation could be established as a more-than-a-century-long tradition, why people are so proud of their own 'minority' languages while they are keen to speak languages of wider communication and why they deliberately mix the 'languages' they themselves conceptualise. Although our argument was at the cost of ignoring possible developmental arguments, it has not only the potential to de/re-construct the general discipline of language (Lüpke and Storch 2013) but also contribute to a wider, convivial scholarship (Nyamnjoh 2017).

Endnotes

[1] The CEFR (Council of Europe 2001: 4–5) distinguishes 'plurilingualism' from 'multilingualism', where they define 'the knowledge of a number of languages, or the co-existence of different languages in a given society'.

[2] To give an ironic example, in 2013, the Special Broadcasting Service (SBS) in Australia launched radio broadcasts in the Dinka language, belonging to the largest ethnic group of South Sudanese refugees. Of course, the South Sudanese Civil War erupted in the same year due to the tribalised violence started by the president, Salva Kiir, a Dinka. SBS should have chosen a local variant of Arabic, a lingua franca in the country, whose speakers' numbers have never been captured in statistical surveys of

'mother tongues' of refugee communities (Nakao 2012). In a similar case, Blommaert (2010) gives an example of a Rwandan refugee, whose status was not justified because he could not speak Rwandan, the idealistic 'mother tongue' of the refugees.

³ UNESCO's *Atlas of the World's Languages in Danger* (Moseley (ed.) 2010) lists Walloon in Belgium (600,000 speakers) and Sardinian in Italy (1,300,000 speakers) as 'definitely endangered'. The same applies to Narim in South Sudan (3,623 speakers) and Khwe in Namibia and Botswana (5,000 speakers), i.e., the speakers of these languages may feel roughly the same level of language loss.

⁴ This concept could be a norm, paraphrastically expressed as: 'Every person must take good care of his/her "ethnic language", while in public, s/he is supposed to speak a neutral "dominant language" to maintain conviviality'. The most significant feature when compared to Northern norms would be a prerequisite that a dominant language must be appropriated, but to not let it assimilate different peoples as a single cohesion.

⁵ This chapter is based on my fieldwork in South Sudan (2009–2013), Uganda (2014–2015), Kenya (2014–2019) and Ethiopia (2017–2019).

⁶ To quote the words of an influential 20th-century Arab nationalist, Sati al-Husri (Dawisha 2003: 72): 'Every Arab-speaking people is Arab. Every individual belonging to one of these Arabic-speaking peoples is an Arab. And if he does not recognise this, and if he is not proud of his Arabism, then we must look for the reasons that have made him take this stand. It may be an expression of ignorance; in that case, we must teach him the truth. ... He is an Arab regardless of his own wishes'.

⁷ Interesting exceptions are some Aramaic-speaking Christian and Mandaean minorities in Turkey and Iran, although what matters to their identity most is religion, rather than language.

⁸ As James (1977) explicitly demonstrates, 'Funj' is used as the autoethnonym by heterogeneous Nilo-Saharan groups in the region (Berta, Uduk, Gumuz, Komo, etc.). Each group does not share the coherent extension of the term. My Mayu informant excludes Uduk, Komo and so on, but includes the Guba sect of Gumuz within the range of their common 'Funj' identity and the list of Funj peoples changed every time we conversed.

⁹ Interview with Berta Council members, Assosa, 14 September 2017. Since the 2000s, the Education Bureau of the Benishangul-Gumuz Region and the Summer Institute of Linguistics (Ethiopia branch) have started developing various local languages of the region (Nakao 2017b).

¹⁰ Actually, linguists in the 1980s often regarded Juba Arabic simply as a diffusion of Arabic within an Arab nation-state (Calvet 1981) or the development of a local colloquial Arabic in parallel with the Arabisation of Egypt and the Levant in the early Islamic period (Versteegh 1984). See Section 4.

¹¹ Written and Sudanese Arabic are transcribed according to the Library of Congress romanisation. Juba Arabic, Nubi and Benishangul Arabic are transcribed according to Nakao (2017a, 2017b) (with the modification of the letter <š> as sh and the glottal stop as ʔ). For Berta/Funj, we modify two letters of the standard orthography according to the International Phonetic Alphabet for readability (e.g. orthographic <q> as ʼ or ʔ, <ñ> as ŋ or ɲ).

¹² The cognate term *riṭāna* 'non-Arabic language (e.g., Persian and Greek)' also appears in classical texts in Written Arabic (*al-fuṣḥā*), although it is rare in the modern standard language. Chadian Arabic *riṭāna* or *ratīn* signal any non-Arabic languages including English and French, inheriting the original meaning (Luffin 2003).

¹³ To simplify the argument, here we neglect the fact that colloquial Arabic varieties are called *dārijiyya* (or *ʻāmmiyya*) in contrast to *al-fuṣḥā*, the standardised written Arabic.

¹⁴ To quote the words of the late Yousif Kuwa Mekki, one of the most significant Nuba leaders, 'Until the time of secondary school I used to feel that I was an Arab, because I was taught that! ... Up to now this inferiority complex makes a lot of Nuba feel that they don't belong to the Nuba race. They feel ashamed of what is called "Nuba"' (Mekki 2001: 31).

¹⁵ There are also specific terms such as *ndú Barthó/Álfuuɲú* 'mouth (language) of Berta/Funj'.

¹⁶ Fieldnotes, Assosa, 15 March 2019.

¹⁷ During my stay in Assosa, the only instance of the apathetic 'vehicular' use of Arabic was observed when I introduced a Sudanese Uduk student to a group of Berta/Funj people (Fieldnotes, Assosa, 15 September 2017).

¹⁸ Interview with Mr A. in Assosa, 12 September 2017.

¹⁹ See also Manfredi (2017).

[20] Interview with Mr L. at Toyonaka, Osaka, Japan, on 22 August 2020.

[21] To my own knowledge, apart from Africa, Tok Pisin, an English-based pidgincreole and a lingua franca in Papua New Guinea, has a similar expression, *tok ples* 'ethnic language', which is contrasted with *Tok Inglis* 'English' and *Tok Pisin* itself.

[22] Fieldnotes, Juba, 22 September 2013. In reality, there are old Malakian citizens who do not speak their 'ethnic' language, but people tend to consider it as a marginal, personal matter.

[23] Fieldnotes, Nairobi, 5 September 2019.

[24] Fieldnotes, Nairobi, 5 September 2019.

[25] Fieldnotes, Nairobi, 3 September 2019.

[26] The data introduced here are based on my aforementioned fieldwork in Juba, Assosa and Nairobi from 2009 to 2019.

[27] Benishangul Arabic also went through grammatical simplification, such as the lack of gender concordance for inanimate nouns. In this construction, Sudanese Arabic would use *di* 'this (feminine singular)' to agree with *as-sana* 'year (a feminine noun)', instead of *da* 'this (masculine singular)', i.e., *as-sana di* 'this year'.

[28] The only difference in these constructions is that Nubi has developed optional 'contracted' forms of subject pronouns, such as **ó-bi-rútan** (= **úwo bi-rútan**), **án**-*bi-rútan* (= **ána** *bi-rútan*).

[29] Similar constructions seem common in Sheng (Githiora 2019: 91).

Acknowledgements

This study is based on my talks prepared for two conferences of the African Potentials project (Nakao 2018, 2019a). I am grateful to Katsuhiko Shiota, Fuko Onoda and Keiko Takemura for personal discussions on earlier drafts, and my African colleagues for inspiring me with the main ideas of this chapter. This work was supported by JSPS KAKENHI Grant Number JP16H06318, JP18KK0009 and JP19K13160.

References

Benson, C. (2010) 'How multilingual African contexts are pushing educational research and practice in new directions', *Language and Education*, Vol. 24, Issue 4, pp. 323–336.

─────── (2014) 'Adopting a multilingual habitus: What North and South can learn from each other about the essential role of non-dominant languages in education', in D. Gorter, V. Zenotz and J. Cenozet (eds) *Minority Languages and Multilingual Education: Bridging the Local and the Global*, Berlin: Springer, pp. 11–28.

Bernabé, J., Chamoiseau, P. and Confiant, R. (1993) *Éloge de la créolité*, Paris: Gallimard.

Bhabha, H. K. (1996) 'Unsatisfied: Notes on vernacular cosmopolitanism', in L. Garcia-Moreno and P. C. Pfeiffer (eds) *Text and Nation: Cross-Disciplinary Essays on Cultural and National Identities*, Columbia: Camden House, pp. 191–207.

Blommaert, J. (2010) *The Sociolinguistics of Globalization*, Cambridge: Cambridge University Press.

Calvet, L.-J. (1981) *Les langues véhiculaires*, Paris: PUF (Presses universitaires de France).

Canagarajah, S. (2009) 'The plurilingual tradition and the English language in South Asia', *AILA Review*, Vol. 22, Issue 1, pp. 5–22.

Council of Europe (2001) *Common European Framework of Reference for Languages: Learning, Teaching, Assessment*, Strasbourg: Council of Europe.

Dawisha, A. I. (2003) *Arab Nationalism in the Twentieth Century: From Triumph to Despair*, Princeton: Princeton University Press.

Furukawa-Yoshida, Y. (2015) 'Reconsidering linguistic ideology: A case study of communication among deaf children in Kenya', *Journal of Nilo-Ethiopian Studies*, No. 20, pp. 17–31.

Gebre, Y., Ohta, I. and Matsuda, M. (2017) 'Introduction: Achieving peace and coexistence through African Potentials', in Y. Gebre, I. Ohta and M. Matsuda (eds) *African Virtues in the Pursuit of Conviviality: Exploring Local Solutions in Light of Global Prescriptions*, Bamenda: Langaa RPCIG, pp. 3–37.

Githiora, C. (2019) *Sheng: Rise of a Kenyan Swahili Vernacular*, Suffolk: James Currey.

González-Ruibal, A. (2014) *An Archaeology of Resistance: Materiality and Time in an African Borderland*, Lanham: Rowman and Littlefield.

Hieda, O. (2002) 'Created "languages", cases from Eastern Africa (Kenya, Ethiopia)', in M. Miyamoto and M. Matsuda (eds) *Social Change in Modern Africa: Observing Dynamism of Language and Culture*, Tokyo: Jinbun-shoin, pp. 220–235 (in Japanese).

Imafuku, R. (2003 [1991]) *Creolism*, Tokyo: Chikuma-shobō (in Japanese).

James, W. (1977) 'The Funj mystique: Approaches to a problem of Sudan history', in R. K. Jain (ed.) *Text and Context: The Social Anthropology of Tradition*, Philadelphia: ISHI (Institute for the Study of Human Issues), pp. 95–133.

────── (2008) 'Sudan: Majorities, minorities, and language interactions', in A. Simpson (ed.) *Language and National Identity in Africa*, Oxford: Oxford University Press, pp. 61–78.

Kaji, S. (2009) 'Language and society in Africa', in S. Kaji and Y. Sunano (eds) *Language and Society in Africa: Lives in Multilingual Situations*, Tokyo: Sangensha, pp. 9–30 (in Japanese).

Kan, K. (2005) *Omniphone: Poetics of 'The Symphony of the World'*, Tokyo: Iwanami-Shoten (in Japanese).

Komori, J. (2002) 'Language choice in a multilingual society: A case of Ukerewe, Tanzania', in M. Miyamoto and M. Matsuda (eds) *Social Change in Modern Africa: Observing Dynamism of Language and Culture*, Tokyo: Jinbun-shoin, pp. 170–193 (in Japanese).

Kurimoto, E. (2002) 'English, Arabic and Juba Arabic: Language, education, politics and identity in Sudan', in M. Miyamoto and M. Matsuda (eds) *Social Change in Modern Africa: Observing Dynamism of Language and Culture*, Tokyo: Jinbun-shoin, pp. 74–92 (in Japanese).

Luffin, X. (2003) 'L'évolution sémantique du terme *ritāna* dans les parlers arabes soudano-tchadiens', *Annales Aequatoria*, Vol. 24, pp. 159–177.

Lüpke, F. and Storch, A. (2013) *Repertoires and Choices in African Languages*, Berlin: Mouton de Gruyter.

Manfredi, S. (2017) 'The construction of linguistic borders and the rise of national identity in South Sudan: Some insights into Juba Arabic (*árabi júba*)', in R. Bassiouney (ed.) *Identity and Dialect*

Performance A Study of Communities and Dialects, London: Routledge, pp. 138–163.

Mc Laughlin, F. (2015) 'Can a language endanger itself? Reshaping repertoires in urban Senegal', in J. Essegbey, B. Henderson and F. Mc Laughlin (eds) *Language Documentation and Endangerment in Africa*, Amsterdam: John Benjamins, pp. 131–152.

Mekki, Y. K. (2001) 'Things were no longer the same', in S. M. Rahhal (ed.) *The Right to Be Nuba: The Story of a Sudanese People's Struggle for Survival*, Asmara: The Red Sea Press, pp. 25–35.

Miyamoto, M. (2002) 'Ecological history of language and Society: An introduction to studies of African language and society', in M. Miyamoto and M. Matsuda (eds) *Social Change in Modern Africa: Observing Dynamism of Language and Culture*, Tokyo: Jinbun-shoin, pp. 24–52 (in Japanese).

Moseley, C. (ed.) (2010) *Atlas of the World's Languages in Danger, 3rd edition*, Paris: UNESCO Publishing.

Mugaddam, A. H. and Abdelhay, A. K. (2013) 'Exploring the sociolinguistic profile of Tima in the Nuba Mountains of Sudan', in T. C. Schadeberg and R. M. Blench (eds) *Nuba Mountains Languages Studies*, Cologne: Rüdiger Köppe Verlag, pp. 297–324.

Nakao, S. (2012) 'Southern Sudanese Arabic in diaspora: The present state and language policy in Australia', *Journal of Kijutsuken (Descriptive Linguistics Study Group)*, Vol. 4, pp. 101–121 (in Japanese).

—————— (2013) 'A history from below: Malakia in Juba, South Sudan, c. 1927–1954', *Journal of Sophia Asian Studies*, No. 31, pp. 139–160.

—————— (2017a) 'A grammar of Juba Arabic', unpublished doctoral dissertation, Kyoto University.

—————— (2017b) 'Notes on Benishangul Arabic (1)', *Studies in Ethiopian Languages*, Vol. 6, pp. 21–43 (in Japanese).

—————— (2018) 'Dynamics of Arabic in Northeastern Africa: Convivial multilingualism', *9th 'African Potentials' Project Meeting*, Kyoto University, Kyoto, 16 June 2018 (in Japanese).

—————— (2019a) 'African plurilingual tradition and conviviality: Lessons from Non-Arab Arabic-speaking communities in Eastern

Africa', *International Symposium on African Potentials and the Future of Humanity*, Kyoto University, Kyoto, 27 January 2019.

——————— (2019b) 'Swahili influence on Nubi (Arabic creole): An update from Kibera', *International Workshop Sociolinguistic Perspectives on Variation in Swahili: New Approaches to the Study of Language and its Social Context in East Africa*, Johannes Gutenberg University Mainz, Mainz, 30 November 2019.

Newman, P. (2007) *A Hausa-English Dictionary*, New Haven: Yale University Press.

Nishi, M. (1999) *Beginner's Creole*, Tokyo: Kinokuniya-shoten (in Japanese).

Nortier, J. and Dorleijn, M. (2013) 'Multi-ethnolects: Kebabnorsk, Perkerdansk, Verlan, Kanakensprache, Straattaal, etc.', in P. Bakker and Y. Matras (eds) *Contact Languages: A Comprehensive Guide*, Berlin: Mouton de Gruyter, pp. 229–271.

Nyamnjoh, F. B. (2017) 'Incompleteness: Frontier Africa and the currency of conviviality', *Journal of Asian and African Studies*, Vol. 52, Issue 3, pp. 253–270.

Ofosu-Kusi, Y. and M. Matsuda (2020) 'Introduction: The contemporary world and African Potentials', in Y. Ofosu-Kusi and M. Matsuda (eds) *The Challenges of African Potentials: Conviviality, Informality and Futurity*, Bamenda: Langaa RPCIG, pp. 1–12.

Pennycook, A. (2016) 'Mobile times, mobile terms: The trans-super-poly-metro movement', in N. Coupland (ed.) *Sociolinguistics: Theoretical Debates*, Cambridge: Cambridge University Press, pp. 201–216.

Sharkey, H. (2007) 'Arab identity and ideology in Sudan: The politics of language, ethnicity, and race', *African Affairs*, Vol. 107, Issue 426, pp. 21–43.

Sunano, Y. (2009) 'Language problems in Africa: Legacies of colonialism', in S. Kaji and Y. Sunano (eds) *Language and Society in Africa: Lives in Multilingual Situations*, Tokyo: Sangensha, pp. 31–63 (in Japanese).

——————— (2012) 'Prologue: Rethinking multilingualism', in Y. Sunano (ed.) *Rethinking Multilingualism: Comparisons of Multilingual Situations*, Tokyo: Sangensha, pp. 11–48 (in Japanese).

Tawada, Y. (2003) *Exophony: Travels outside Mother Tongues*, Tokyo: Iwanami-Shoten (in Japanese).

Versteegh, K. (1984) *Pidginization and Creolization: The Case of Arabic*, Amsterdam: John Benjamins.

Vertovec, S. (2007) 'Super-diversity and its implications', *Ethnic and Racial Studies*, Vol. 30, Issue 6, pp. 1024–1054.

Yoneda, N. (2012) '"Multilingualism" of European origin and multilingual situations in Africa', in Y. Sunano (ed.) *Rethinking Multilingualism: Comparisons of Multilingual Situations*, Tokyo: Sangensha, pp. 118–141 (in Japanese).

Chapter 2

Socio-Linguistic Dynamism among Languages: Sketching from Angola as a Frame of Reflection[1]

Satoshi Terao

1. Introduction

In Angola, in February 2002, a mopping-up operation by the 'Popular Front for the Liberation of Angola' (MPLA) resulted in the death of Savimbi, who was the chairman and leader of the 'National Union for the Total Independence of Angola' (UNITA). This was an anti-government group that had long and stubbornly resisted the MPLA which had been in power since the country had gained independence. In April of the same year, the remnants of UNITA, who had lost President Savimbi, signed a Memorandum of Understanding known as the Luena Ceasefire Agreement with the MPLA, finally putting an end to the civil war.

However, during the civil war and after independence, more than 300,000 lives were lost. The after-effects of the civil war, such as the remaining minefields, are still obvious. About one quarter of the country's population, or about five million people, became concentrated around the capital, Luanda. This was primarily to escape the war, and the slums known as *musseques* continued to expand. Even now, the redistribution of wealth from underground resources, such as oil and diamonds, remains stagnant and inequalities in the social structure have not been addressed.

Since Angola's independence, the political stability and economic upturn in the country have provided opportunities for the implementation of policies that have been advocated as the 'idea of founding a nation'. In particular, the government values measures for national integration, which it was unable to carry out for a long time in the midst of the civil war which continued to incite ethnic or tribal conflict in the country. In constructing its theory of national integration, the government paid a lot of attention to the existence of the Bantu languages and described them as *línguas nacionais* (national languages of Angola, hereinafter referred to as the 'national language'). However, there has been no detailed discussion about why these languages have become important within the framework of national integration.

First, by examining how languages have been treated in Angola in the past, we will investigate the background of the language policy that the government is trying to implement.

2. Angola as a Multilingual Society

Angola is a republic in southwestern Africa in the southern hemisphere. It has a long coastline facing the South Atlantic on the west, and it is bordered by the Democratic Republic of the Congo (formerly Zaire, capital Kinshasa) to the north and northeast, Zambia to the southeast and Namibia to the south. Across the Zaire (Congo) River lies an enclave of Angola called Cabinda to the north, bordering the Republic of Congo (capital Brazzaville) on the north and the Democratic Republic of the Congo on the south and east. With a land area of 1,256,700 square kilometres, it is slightly larger than the Republic of South Africa (1,221,037 square kilometres). Furthermore, it is the second largest country in Africa south of the equator after the Democratic Republic of the Congo (2,345,410 square kilometres).

It is not easy to explain the characteristics of the Angolan people and the languages spoken by them. If using a 'racial concept' to 'classify' the people living there, there would have been the *negro* and the *branco* in Portuguese, some of whom were Portuguese colonists during the colonial period, or 'mixed blood', referring to those who had both as ancestors. These were called *mestiço* or *mulato* in Portuguese and lived in large cities such as Luanda. The country was also home to a few ethnic Indians (people of Indian descent, mainly Gujarati merchants) and Cubans and their descendants (people who were sent as soldiers during the revolutionary war and the civil war).

Except for these latter two groups, most people are classified into 'ethnic groups' which are categorised according to the linguistic classification adopted by European linguists, Christian missionaries and anthropologists, or a term not used by Westerners to refer to themselves, *tribo* which is a discriminatory concept. This taxonomic concept is commonly referred to in Angola as *grupo etno-linguístico*, i.e., 'linguistic ethnic group'.

In line with the position taken during the period of Portuguese rule, they were classified into the nine groups as listed below. This was enacted in law in the latter half of the 1970s, immediately after independence. Sometimes, this involves a different way of interpreting the original term, 'linguistic ethnic group'.

The nine languages are as follows: (1) Kikongo, (2) Kimbundu, (3) Umbundu, (4) Lunda Kokwe (Chokwe or Cokwe), (5) Nganguela, (6) Nyaneka-Umbi (Humbi), (7) Herero (Helelo), (8) Oshiwambo or Oshikwanhama and (9) Khoisan.

Although these group names basically correspond to the language names, Khoisan actually refers to a group of languages traditionally spoken by people called *bosquímanos* ('Bushmen' in English), which includes many variations. ('Khoisan languages' is a term used in comparative linguistics in various languages, hereinafter referred to as languages). The other groups belong to the 'Bantu languages' and are described later.

Concerning the classification of (1) to (3) above, i.e., Kikongo, Kimbundu and Umbundu, it has been confirmed that these groups were distributed in the northwestern part of Angola, where development and linguistic research were relatively advanced. Also, the organisation that led the civil war gained a raison d'être by these various languages highlighting and agitating the differences between the groups.

On the other hand, with regard to (4) to (8), language research itself has not progressed very much. This is for various reasons, for example, languages (6) to (8) are distributed in the region along the southern coast of Angola where the population is small due to drought. In the cases of (4) and (5), the development of the infrastructure in the inland region of eastern Angola is falling behind. Therefore, there has not been much progress in language research, and not only the range of distribution, but also the language names, the names of the ethnic groups and the number of languages are not constant.

Therefore, they are not classified (deterministically), but are often classified.

3. Portuguese Colonial Policy and Angola

In 1482, six years before Bartolomeu Dias reached the Cape of Good Hope, and 16 years before Vasco da Gama had 'discovered' the routes between India and Angola, the Portuguese navigator, Diogo Cão, reached the northern coastal waters of Angola, currently downstream of the Congo (Zaire). Colonisation in Angola began in 1575 with the Portuguese, Paulo Dias de Novais, who settled with approximately 700 others along the coast of present-day Angola. In the following year, Luanda (spelled Loanda until the early 1920s) was developed as a colonial city and has been the capital of Angola ever since.

The colonists arriving in Angola initially used the *capitania* system of *sezmaria* (land sales), as they did in Brazil, but this was abandoned as early as the 17th century. Instead, the country became a slave supplier to sugarcane plantations that were first established on the island of São Tomé in the Gulf of Guinea and then introduced into Brazil. Portugal effectively maintained control of the coastal areas until the latter half of the 19th century when the allied Western powers began a full-scale entry into southern Africa. The Portuguese established trading houses, some of which were fortified. These were dotted along the coastline and used as a base for trade with the hinterlands, such as the inland areas where the slave trade was one of the main operations. The interior regions were governed by the rulers of the so-called 'Kingdom of Negro' or, more precisely, 'a kingdom formed by a group of Bantu speakers', such as the Kingdom of Congo, which had existed before the Portuguese started their activities.

This volatile situation continued as the Kingdom of Congo invaded in 1665 and ruled the entire region until the following year. However, at the end of the 17th century, a smallpox epidemic broke out among the 'negros' and armed resistance towards the Portuguese weakened. As a result of this military control of the inland kingdom, the Portuguese influence in the northwestern part of Angola reached 500 kilometres inland. However, the activities of the Portuguese were far removed from colonial management, and their interest was limited to the acquisition of slaves. As a result, the 'Bantu kingdom' groups were Christianised and they were maintained as puppets in the machine of the Portuguese slave trade, creating a structure of dual governance. In 1721, the Kingdom of Portugal passed a law monopolising the slave trade, which enriched the royal family, but made Angola less attractive to the Portuguese public.

Thus, Angola continued as the most convenient source of slaves because of its short distance from Brazil. It was used to quickly secure the labour force that was needed for the Portuguese royal family to carry out its colonial policy in Brazil. In this sense, Angola can be said to have been a 'Brazilian colony'. Between 1765 and 1769, approximately 14,000 Angolan community residents were transported, in other words 'exported', to Brazil as slaves (Marques 1981: 160). An estimated two million black slaves travelled from the African continent between 1700 and 1820 (Marques 1981: 137). For this reason, in the Nordeste region of northeastern Brazil, where sugar cane plantations were actively developed, especially in the southern region around the present state of Bahia, the Bantu languages of Angola remain as well as Yoruba languages. This term refers to the languages spoken by slaves brought from the northern Gulf of Guinea, north of present Angola. There are many terms in common in these languages, especially in fields such as cooking and religious ceremonies. After all, from the point of view of the slave trade, the fact remains that there was a more active trade between the colonies, namely between Brazil and Angola, than between Angola and Portugal. Cultural interaction is a by-product of these human exchanges.

However, the role of Angola as a colony and slave supplier to Brazil underwent a fundamental transformation in the first half of the 19th century. This is due to the fact that Brazil became independent in 1822. In addition, the Portuguese government officially abolished the slave trade in 1836. With the independence of Brazil, Angola became the largest overseas colony of the Kingdom of Portugal, at least in terms of area. In fact, its agricultural productivity and abundant resources placed it at the centre of Portuguese colonialism.

However, the Portuguese royal family had not yet conducted full-scale colonial management in Angola. Even before Angola became independent, the Portuguese royal family was financially dependent on Brazil, and Angola was left behind in terms of its economic development because it lacked the financial and human resources to provide the infrastructure to support development. This is reflected in the 19th century estimates of the proportion of 'white' and 'mixed blood' in colonial Angola (Bender 2004: 71). According to these estimates, in 1845, 'white' people accounted for 0.03 per cent of the population, while 'mixed-race' accounted for only 0.01 per cent. In 1900, the percentages were only double that, at 0.06 per cent and 0.02 per cent, respectively. Also noteworthy was the high illiteracy rate among Portuguese settlers in the 20th century.

So what languages were used for trade in the hinterland of the coastline where the Portuguese had travelled for a long time under the auspices of the colony? At least in present northwestern Angola, from the mouth of the Congo (Zaire) River to Luanda, the two Bantu languages, Kikongo and Kimbundu, appear to have intermingled at times. In the Kingdom of Congo, which had been dominant in the region even before the arrival of the Portuguese, Kongo had been used as the main language. However, when the Kingdom of Congo declined and became a puppet of the Portuguese, and then became only a figurehead, Kimbundu, which was distributed south of the Kongo Kingdom, became powerful, although it was still influenced by Kikongo. Aside from the fact that only a few Bantu speakers learned Portuguese as an intermediary language to use with Portuguese merchants, it is thought that Kimbundu was used as an intermediary language in the hinterlands. Vansina shows that slaves setting out from Luanda were taught the Kimbundu language no matter where they came from when they were loaded onto ships (Vansina 2001: 273–274).

In the latter half of the 19th century, when the world powers colonised Africa and the so-called 'African partition' was just around the corner, the Portuguese government at last started to focus on

'Angola as a colony'. At first, however, the Portuguese plan was too much even for its own national strength, and it was repeatedly interfered with by more powerful countries. A case in point is the initiative by the Portuguese government known as the 'Rose Map' (1877) and the ultimatum from the UK in 1890 which resulted in a real 'rosy illusion'. The 'Rose Map' initiative was an attempt to secure a Portuguese colony that would link present-day Angola and Mozambique, traversing south-central Africa from the Atlantic Ocean to the Indian Ocean. For Britain, securing this territory across Africa by connecting Cairo and Cape Town was not negotiable, and the Portuguese government's idea was ignored.

Considering the international situation at that time, this development was to be expected, but the treatment from England, with whom Portugal had been friendly for a long time, caused public opinion in Portugal to boil over. However, Britain and other European powers could not be countered by force. The Portuguese, concentrating on their nostalgia for their past maritime kingdom, tended to be idealistic rather than having practical colonial policies. As a result, Angola and Mozambique were recognised as Portuguese territories between the end of the 19th century and the beginning of the 20th century and became a buffer zone for the partition of Africa by the great powers. However, full-scale colonial policies were still not being implemented in either country, and measures for the residents of the territories, including in the domain of education, remained very limited.

A notable measure relating to language education in Angola during the first half of the 20th century was Decree No. 77, promulgated in December 1921 by the Governor-General of Angola, Norton de Matos (1867–1955). Article 1 of this law permits the compulsory education of the Portuguese language and the prohibition of foreign language education in missionary activities. Article 3 permits the use of the language of 'natives' only as a spoken language in the official doctrine (introduction to catechism and the Christian faith) as a supplement during the period of the basic education of Portuguese. It also prohibits the use of the 'native' language in any form including publications in the official doctrine [paragraph (1)]. It prohibits the use of religious texts written in languages other than Portuguese except for those containing the word 'native' as an alternative translation of Portuguese [paragraph (2)], and it states that the word 'native' should be limited only to introductory education (in public schools) to prevent abuse among indigenous people and to make an effort for a prompt transition to Portuguese (1867–1955).

Norton de Matos was reputed to be a liberal and well-informed person. In 1949, he ran for president himself, criticising the presidential system that was under the control of Prime Minister Salazar, who led a dictatorship at the time (although he withdrew his candidacy before the election day). However, in the colonies, the policy was to rely on the Christian Church to carry out an explicit assimilation policy with the indigenous people. In other words, it is clear from this decree that even a person who was regarded as 'enlightened' followed the negative and unregulated 'neglectful colonialism' of the Portuguese government, which stated the 'disdain of indigenous people and the neglect of education'.

It may be an irony that Portugal's apathy has kept Angola in a state of underdevelopment, thus contributing to the preservation of its native culture. However, in areas where access is relatively easy, Roman Catholic and Protestant missionaries engaged in turbulent battles, and this is also a cause of today's conflicts.

In the 1950s, as independence movements gained momentum across the African continent and international opinion grew in support of independence, the Portuguese government tried to carry out its colonial management in a visibly formal manner. It also tried to develop a theory to justify its actions, in order to maintain the classic colonial dependence established by selling its low-quality, high-price industrial products to underdeveloped colonies.

With this momentum, the Portuguese government vigorously promoted emigration from mainland Portugal where the surplus of labour force had become worse. It sought to develop its infrastructure, agriculture and mining industries, in order to shake off the infamy of 'neglectful colonialism'. It also tried to introduce a logic emanating from Brazil about the justification of the Portuguese colonial system. This is known as *Luso-tropicalismo* or 'Luso-tropicalism'.

A critical examination of the details of 'Luso-tropicalism' is for another occasion, but the theory originated from a backlash against social Darwinian and eugenic discourse in Europe and the USA. This discourse was instigated by concepts such as 'the social development of Brazil is hindered by mixed-race populations' and even such notions as 'a flexible and dynamic Brazilian society was born of the mixture of diverse ethnic groups and Portuguese people who did not cling to mixed blood'. This concept was also known as 'racial democracy'.

The concept was first used by a Brazilian, Gilberto Freyre (1900–1987). However, the ideas that form part of the concept do not directly apply to Portuguese African colonies such as Angola, which are not as mixed-race as Brazil. The problem involved revising 'Luso-tropicalism' as a pretext to suit the actual situation of the Portuguese colonies.

Freyre himself became an active theorist in justifying Portuguese colonial possessions. His book *Portugal and the Tropics* (Freyre 1961) is a clear expression of his attitude and gives advice to the Portuguese. In this book, which is subtitled 'Proposals on the Portuguese way of integrating cultures different from indigenous and European cultures in a new structure of civilisation—Luso-tropicalismo', he presents a methodology which affirms that the current status of all Portuguese territories, based on the qualities of the Portuguese, are at a stage where a policy of colonialism can be established leading to a 'Brazilian mixed society' in the future. Based on this concept, he attempted to introduce the notion of 'integration' which in reality forced Portuguese African colonies, such as Angola, further towards Portugal. These were called 'Portuguese Overseas Prefectures' in those days. It goes without saying that Portuguese was regarded as an important element of this integrated philosophy.

This book was published in 1961, a year after the 'African Year', when many countries in Africa gained independence. However, it may have been too late for the Portuguese colonies to suppress their desire for independence with a hastily formed theory of dominance.

After the War of Liberation, which started in 1961, the dictatorship in Portugal collapsed in 1974 leading to independence in November 1975. Since the beginning of the War of Liberation, however, the anti-Portuguese guerrilla groups were not huge; the MPLA, the 'National Liberation Front of Angola' (FNLA) and UNITA, based on the respective ethnic groups of Kimbundu, Bakongo and Obimbundu, acted according to their separate declarations and corresponding support. Before and after independence, the conflict between these organisations became more intense, and a civil war broke out. However, the capital, Luanda, was under the control of the MPLA, which continued to rule in the form of a one-party dictatorship without being able to control the entire country. The MPLA, with the support of the Soviet Union and Cuba, was a political party that promoted communism from the start, and the name of the country after independence reflected this as it was called the 'People's Republic of Angola'. However, with the collapse of the Soviet Union in the 1990s and a lack of support, the MPLA swiftly changed its party policy in 1992. It changed its Constitution to steer the country towards a multiparty parliamentary democracy, and changed its name to the 'Republic of Angola'.

How does the political elite steer policy decisions? In linguistic terms, many people in Angola are members of the Bantu-speaking population. However, some of the Portuguese settlers and their descendants, including the *mestiços*, speak Portuguese, and many are native speakers. Portuguese was spoken by 20 per cent of the population in 1990 (Cuesta 1990: 15).

The spread of Portuguese as a language used in education was a result of it being used in elementary education in urban areas and, also, the Portuguese government declared it the official language of education after independence. However, the government's efforts in the domain of education were limited, and the compulsory education system after independence was far from consistent due to the civil war and other disorders. Under Portuguese colonial policies, educated 'natives' who could read and write Portuguese were classified as *asimilado(s)/civilizado(s)*, i.e., 'assimilated or civilised people' and the other 'natives' were known as *indígena(s)*, i.e., 'savages' and were left to their own devices. This policy created a social division that distinguished between 'knowledgeable people' and 'illiterate and ignorant people' among Angolan citizens. This disparity happened even before Angola became independent, and it is still a barrier to the spread of Portuguese. The political elite at the heart of the Angolan government and political party, the MPLA, mainly comprises the former 'assimilated people' or their descendants. They identify as *mestiços*, and their native language is often Portuguese.

On the other hand, due to the influence of the mass media, mainly around coastal urban areas, Portuguese is becoming popular as a medium of communication in everyday life outside of the elite class. Consequently, Bantu languages have a strong influence on usage and vocabulary. Languages range from being minor, in other words considered as a Creole language, to being used more often due to exposure through education.

4. The Future of Angolan Identity

In the face of adversity as mentioned above, how to establish *Angolanidade*, which translates as 'Angolanity' or 'Angolanness', has become a very important issue in Angola today.

Angolanidade represents an opportunity to transform and rebuild the 'Luso-tropicalism' that the Portuguese dictatorship used as a justification for continuing colonial rule, as mentioned previously. However, this alone is no more than a rehash of colonialism. The key is to establish Angola as an externally persuasive 'national state' and, above all, to establish the Angolan identity in a way that will convince the population.

In terms of *Angolanidade*, Angolan people need to integrate linguistically with Bantu speakers who form the majority of Angolans. However, we must remember that Angola's civil war was indeed a struggle between different Bantu forces. Bantu languages spread throughout southern Africa, crossing the border of Angola and resulting in the division of the great powers into African states. There is a 'Pan-Bantu' that connects the Bantu mindset and, in some cases, threatens the stability of Angola.

In other words, when incorporating Bantu into *Angolanidade*, it is necessary to understand the advantages and disadvantages of the fragmented separation between Bantu speakers and 'Pan-Bantu', which includes Bantu consciousness, and then to integrate this throughout Angola. The question is what kind of concrete framework should be created to promote this coordination.

An example of this is a newspaper article from 4 October 2007 entitled 'A true Angolan? Who are you talking about?' by Wa-Zani, a columnist at *Jornal de Angola*, a daily newspaper published in the capital, Luanda. In this article, it was explained how at first, when the Portuguese, Vasco da Gama and Bartolomeu Dias, discovered the Cape of Good Hope in 1498, 'Bantu' had not yet arrived. Father Asúa Altuna (1993), in 'Bantu culture' argues that these people only reached a place in the south of the African continent at the beginning of the 17th century. Interestingly, at almost the same time, the Dutch East India Company was founded in 1621 and Cape Town was founded by Jan van Liebeck in April 1652.

Then, the article questioned the use of Bantu as a symbol of authenticity in southern Africa, arguing that Bantu had the same historical background as Caucasians, who tended to be seen as aggressors and, therefore, were excluded from being part of the national identity.

The reality is that much of sub-Saharan Africa – central and southern Africa – was inhabited by the Pygmeu. Today, most live in what is now the forest area of the Democratic Republic of the Congo and, in Angola, they are scattered throughout the southern region, south of 14 degrees south, an area now also occupied by the 'Bantu'.

The article goes on to ask what we Angolans want to say when we talk about 'inherent' Angolans in the context of 'pure', 'genuine' or 'orthodox'? Perhaps the oldest living representatives of the Angolan people are the mobile hunter-gatherers who are now living in isolation in the population? If the authenticity of Angolans is to be discussed, it is doubtful that only the Khoisan in the south deserve this legitimacy. However, today, are genuine and indigenous Angolans registered as voters? They have a right to be Angolans. However, it is difficult to get their names on voting cards. This is because it was always difficult to write one's name in a registry office of the town hall in order to procure an ID card. They were never counted in the category of 'assimilated human beings' during the colonial period, and do they count even now? Then the article concluded by proposing a peaceful and balanced establishment of *Angolanidade*.

According to the above discourse, it is difficult to be registered as an Angolan due to the fact that Khoisan speakers are mobile people and they have a low level of education. However, if the argument of who is a 'true Angolan' is to be pursued, only Khoisan speakers are applicable in terms of being an 'ethnic minority'. This leads to a debate regarding what constitutes a 'true Angolan' and discourages excessive self-assertion among Bantu speakers. These factors have led to tensions and animosities that potentially contributed to the civil war.

It seems that Bantu speakers are deliberately counting the date of arrival in Angola as far south as they are concerned. In any case, this is meaningless for Bantu speakers, who have no great difference in their origins or historical background, and can easily fall into a sort of selfishness (so-called 'tribalism') and quarrel with each other. In order to mitigate this, and to establish a strong *Angolanidade*, it is necessary to pay attention to Khoisan speakers, which is a different element of *Angolanidade*.

This is similar to the perspective often used by Latin American countries, which became independent prior to Africa in the 19th century. The Aztecs and the Mayas of Mexico and the Tupi of Brazil are examples of indigenous peoples who were used to enhance the national identity and 'ethnicity' even though their descendants were socially excluded. For example, in Mexico, the present state has inherited the glory of civilisation created by the Mayas, and especially the Aztecs, as indigenous people.

In the case of Brazil, although the Tupi have become an ethnic minority and speakers of minority languages from the past, and they are not really classed as a 'civilisation', there is a trend of 'Tupi Mania' that considers them to have certain original characteristics of which they should be proud. This Brazilian concept of 'Tupi Mania' is similar to the aforementioned notion of focusing on Khoisan speakers.

5. Trends in Angolan Language Policy

As discussed so far, the Angolan government has become increasingly involved in language policy in recent years due to the end of the civil war and also the political and economic stability as a result of oil production. This section summarises these trends.

After approval by the Parliament of the Republic of Angola, the *Lei de Bases do Sistema de Educação* (Basic Act on the Education System, 13/01, 31 December 2001) was promulgated. Article 9 is devoted to 'Language', following Article 8 the 'mandatory system', which clearly states that primary education is compulsory (for six years as opposed to four years as before). The text is as follows:

1. Education in schools shall be delivered in Portuguese.
2. The state promotes and ensures education in the national languages (*línguas nacionais*) for human, scientific, technical, material and financial purposes.
3. Without being bound by point 1, education can be provided in the national languages, especially in the field of adult education.

The present Constitution of the Republic of Angola (2010) for the first time makes provision for an official language, Portuguese, as stated in Article 19.1, 'the official language of the Republic of Angola is Portuguese'. In the next section of the same article, there is mention of 'other languages in Angola' as follows: 'The state shall value and promote the study, teaching and use of other Angolan languages, in addition to the main international languages of communication' (Article 19.2). Article 21, which starts with the wording, 'The fundamental tasks of the Angolan state shall be', continues with various (17) 'fundamental tasks of the state', and at section n., mentions: 'To protect, value and dignify Angolan languages of African origin, as part of the cultural heritage, and to promote their development, as living languages which reflect national identity'.

It seems that Angola has carefully referred to the introduction of national languages into the education system in its legal documents. In fact, according to the 'General Characteristics and Education System of Angola and Its Education System' which is a report on educational system reform prepared by the Ministry of Education in accordance with above educational law, both the primary education curriculum and the first secondary education curriculum contain the following text at the beginning:

Angola is located in southern Africa where Umbundu, Kimbundu, Kikongo and other national languages are spoken, such as Chokwe (Tchokwe) and Ngangela (N'gangela). It is a multilingual (wording *plurilinguístico*) country, where Portuguese is the official language and the language of communication among Angolans.

Formal education takes place in Portuguese, while there is still debate at government level about the possibility of including national languages in the curriculum.

A few months after the promulgation of the 'Basic Act on the Education System', it was only after Savimbi's death in battle that peace was realised and language policies began to take shape. Currently, the national language policy in Angola is overseen by the Institute of National Languages (ILN: *Instituto de Línguas Nacionais*). This institute has been developing recommendations and programmes for language education using the Angolan government's national languages. Its presence has intensified since its inauguration in 2005, when its current representative, the linguist, Batumene Kukanda, was inaugurated as the representative of the *Centre International des Civilisations Bantu* (CICIBA), formerly the 'Centre International Bantu Civilisations'. It is worth noting that Kukanda, while mindful of the negative effects of lexical borrowing, suggests that the Portuguese vocabulary should be used to increase the vocabulary of the national languages.

With a focus on '*Angolanidade* Construction Based on National Languages', Kukanda is in an important position in terms of mapping out the language policy in Angola by seeking to utilise the cultures of both Pan-Bantu and Portuguese. Furthermore, in order to promote the introduction of the languages in the field of education, at the ILN, Kukanda has taken the lead and is currently promoting the unification of the orthography of each language.

As a result of these efforts, primary education in national languages was introduced in 2007 in parts of Angola, following teacher training for education in national languages in 2005 and educational trials in national languages in 2006. This was organised by the National Institute of Investigation and Schooling Development (INIDE: *Instituto Nacional de Investigação e Desenvolvimento*

Escolar) and the Department of Educational Bureau of Angolan Ministry of Education. Depending on the region, six languages have been selected as educational languages: Kikongo, Kimbundu, Umbundu, Chokwe, Nganguela and Kwanyama. In 2007, 4,500 first-year students participated. For example, in Huila City, where Umbundu is the selected language, 15 Umbundu language teachers were trained, and in 2007, approximately 500 first-year elementary school students at two suburban elementary schools began to learn to read and write Umbundu.

During the pilot phase, two publishers in the Republic of South Africa, including Longman (a subsidiary of the London-based educational publishing company, Pearson), a publisher with experience in developing multilingual teaching materials with headquarters in Cape Town, were commissioned to undertake such tasks as teacher training and the development of teaching materials for children and teachers. In addition, in autumn 2008, the organisations of Pearson/Longman and Molteno, a language policy contractor with headquarters near Johannesburg, have started a project to distribute textbooks to children with the aim of expanding educational opportunities in national languages in 2009. In addition to the above, a total of seven languages, including Nyaneka, have been selected as target languages. In July 2008, journalists and teachers fluent in the target language gathered at Longman's office in Cape Town, South Africa, to examine the details of the textbook. In 2009, textbooks for the first and second years of elementary school were distributed to eight of Angola's 18 prefectures.

Augustinho Neto, the writer and first president of Angola, gave a historic speech on Angola culture on 8 January 1978, which is regarded as 'Culture Day'. On this day in 2008, in the southern city of Namibe, which marked the 30th anniversary of Culture Day, the Minister of Culture, Cardoso Boaventura Cardoso, mentioned the start of education in national languages and said, 'Each language must shape the elements of peaceful coexistence and the link between global and local.' He went on to say, 'It occupies a strategic position in the fight against extreme poverty and famine, such as the significant growth of literacy and primary education, and the acquisition of knowledge and competitiveness in the labour market, and contributes as an element of social integration.'

The Third National Language Conference was held in Huambo, midwestern Angola (Formerly Nova Lisboa [New Lisbon]), from 15–17 October 2008, to summarise the progress of the national language programme. At the end of the meeting, a communique entitled, 'In all rural areas of Angola, education in national languages should be compulsory in primary, secondary and higher education' was issued, accompanied by the following proposals.

- Education in national languages should be conducted in accordance with scientific research already undertaken, with officially approved writing laws, and with content developed in line with the realities of Angolan culture.
- In order to promote education in national languages, it is important to increase the number of teachers and those in charge of teacher training.
- In all national languages, efforts must be made to bring the writing system into line with the current situation and harmonise it.
- Important legal systems such as the Constitution, the Political Parties Act and the Declaration on Human Rights should be translated into national languages.
- The National Language Basic Law should be enacted as soon as possible.

Meanwhile, in March 2008, an international conference on the theme of 'National Language Policy and the Role of Languages with Limited Cross-Border Language/Distribution' was held in Johannesburg, with representatives from Angola attending from the ILN such as Kukanda. This was the first international conference for Southern African countries to discuss language policy. Cooperation in language policy across the borders in southern Africa is undoubtedly becoming stronger.

6. Conclusion

Angola has finally emerged from 40 years of civil war, including the 30 years of civil war since its independence. With the help of an expansion of resources that started some time ago, Angola is finally establishing its economic base. On the other hand, it has only just begun to seek ways to ease ethnic conflicts that have been ongoing since before independence, and achieve some form of national reconciliation to accomplish 'nation building'.

In these circumstances, in order to resolve ethnic conflicts and integrate individuals as 'Angolan people', it has become a major challenge to establish *Angolanidade* as a principle of integration. The state itself, which is called 'Angola', is a result of the division of the country into colonies by powerful countries, and a realistic *Angolanidade* is based on this historical background. At the same time, there needs to be a delicate balance of three issues: (1) selfishness among those who make up each 'linguistic ethnic group' which is often known as 'tribalism'; (2) 'Pan-Bantu' which crosses the southern half of Africa; and (3) 'Luso-tropicalism' which was advocated as a principle of integration by the Portuguese colonial rulers.

Whether we follow the logic of 'the act of speaking a Bantu language', which is the biggest factor governing the identity of groups, or the logic of coexistence between various cultures, which is the pillar of 'Angolan', the premise is the existence of 'national languages'.

In other words, it can be said that identifying local languages as 'national languages' and making them educational languages contributes to the construction of *Angolanidade* according to the following three points: (a) the recognition of each language as a 'national language' can serve as a symbol of breaking away from the narrow-minded patriotism of belonging to a 'linguistic ethnic group'; (b) all of the languages falling under the auspices of 'national languages' are Bantu languages, and 'Pan-Bantu' can be incorporated as a way of providing links between these speakers; and (c) by juxtaposing 'national languages' with Portuguese, which has the monopoly as the medium of public communication, a structure can be created to support the uniqueness of Angola, in other words, *Angolanidade*, by overhauling the only official language that supports the traditional 'Luso-tropicalism'.

In this way, 'national languages' are expected to be catalysts to coordinate between the different group identities and their various personalities, such as 'patriotism', 'Pan-Bantu' and 'Luso-tropicalism' and to produce *Angolanidade*. However, these languages have long experienced discrimination and disdain as 'vernacular and indigenous dialects' on the part of European colonial administrations and urban residents, including 'negros', who spoke European languages (mainly Portuguese). It is not easy to recover a strong identity in these circumstances. For this reason, a 'Pan-Bantu' connection with countries other than Angola where Bantu is spoken is also necessary to improve the image of Bantu in this country. Among the languages included in the 'national languages' are those which are distributed across neighbouring countries, such as Kikongo (in DR Congo and Congo-Brazzaville) and Herero (Helelo) (in Namibia). These languages have the potential to encourage international cooperation in the development of educational materials and the promotion of 'patriotism' in education.

It should also be noted, however, that such pressure may give one language an advantage and could introduce the concept of a higher and lower status between each 'national language'. Just as the FNLA conducted guerrilla activities under the guise of 'Congolese supremacy' in the past, there is a risk that 'Pan-Bantu' will break away from the notion of *Angolanidade*. It could overwhelm the concept and become out of control within the framework of the nation. Indeed, it should be noted that in recent years, multilingual education in 'national languages' has been based on the know-how and organisational power of South African companies.

Furthermore, as stated in the ILN, there is an urgent requirement to fix the writing system in each national language for the purpose of education. However, it goes against the belief of respecting linguistic diversity to quickly adapt the linguistic situation in Angola, where a variety of languages are still alive. There is also a possibility that people will become marginalised in terms of language under such rapid change.

In this respect, attention should be paid to what kind of language policy the Angolan government will formulate and implement in the future.

Many languages are spoken in Angola as well as in Mozambique, Guinea Bissau, where Portuguese is officially spoken on the African continent, and Mbini (the continental part of the Republic of Equatorial Guinea), where Spanish is the official language, but interest in and research into these languages is lagging behind that of English-speaking and French-speaking countries.

In order to overcome this disparity and promote regionally balanced studies in sub-Saharan Africa, it is essential to understand the linguistic situation in Angola, which accounts for the largest area in sub-Saharan non-English and non-French regions.

Endnotes

1. This chapter is based on Terao (2009) and has been totally revised and brought up to date.

Acknowledgements

This work was supported by JSPS KAKENHI Grant Number JP16H06318.

References

Asúa Altuna, Raul Ruiz de (1993) *Cultura Tradicional Banto (2. ed.)*, Luanda: Secretariado Arquidiocesano de Pastoral

Bender, G. J. (2004) *Angola sob o Domínio Português: Mito e Realidade*, Luanda: Editorial Nzila.

Cuesta, P. V. (1990) 'O ensino do português enquanto língua segunda em Angola', *Angolê: Artes, Letras, Ideias*, Vol. 1, pp. 15–18.

Freyre, G. (1961) *O Luso e o Trópico*, Lisboa: Comissão Executiva das Comemorações do Quinto Centenário da Morte do Infante D. Henrique.

Marques, A. H. de Oliveira (1981) *Portugal: The World's Textbooks on History, Vol. 2 (Translation of História de Portugal, Lisbon: Editorial Palas, 1972–73, 3 Vols)*, Tokyo: HoLP Shuppan Publications (in Japanese).

Terao, S. (2009) 'The trial of a multilingual policy in Angola', *Journal of Intercultural Studies, Kobe University*, Vol. 32, pp. 33–66 (in Japanese).

Vansina, J. (2001) 'Portuguese vs Kimbundu: Language use in the colony of Angola (1575– c.1845)', *Bulletin des Séances / Mededelingen der Zittingen*, Vol. 47, Issue 3, pp. 267–281.

Chapter 3

Documentation of an Afar Traditional Conflict Reconciliation Speech[1]

Gebriel Alazar Tesfatsion

1. Introduction

The Afar language is not acutely lacking in descriptive language resources. Dictionaries of the language are available: an English–Afar dictionary (Parker 2006); an Afar–English dictionary (Parker 2009); an Afar–French dictionary (Morin 2012); a polyglot Afar–English–French dictionary (Parker and Hayward 1985); and an Italian–Afar dictionary (Derchi 1895), among others. The language also has comprehensive grammar described in *A Generative Grammar of Afar* (Bliese 1981) and the thesis titled '*L'afar: description grammaticale d'une langue couchitique (Djibouti, Erythrée et Ethiopie)*' (Kamil, 2015). Studies in different grammatical components of the language abound: Reinisch (1885, 1886, 1887); De Charency (1877); Colizza (1887); Colby (1961, 1970); Luc (1967); Hayward (1974, 1976); Bliese (1976a, 1976b); Parker (1979); Morin (1986); Hayward and Corbett (1988); Fulmer (1991, 1997); Simeone-Senelle (2007); Simeone-Senelle and Kamil (2013); Hara et al (2019) and so on. There have also been attempts at studying the oral traditions of the language in such works as Balehegn (2016), Hailemichael (1995) and Muauz and Saleh (2017). What the language lacks in is documentation of speakers' actual language practices in natural speech contexts. This chapter is a contribution to that end. It is a documentation of the linguistic practices of the Afar in the context of customary conflict reconciliation. It differs from the above linguistic works in that it goes beyond the lexical descriptions provided in dictionaries and the morpho-syntactic analysis of descriptive linguistic studies. Instead, it situates the language in its actual social context.

Documentation regarding actual, spontaneous language use in a social context is important. The UNESCO Ad Hoc Expert Group on Endangered Languages (2003: 16) identifies the amount and quality of 'transcribed, translated and annotated audio-visual recordings of natural speech', in addition to the presence and quality of dictionaries and grammar references guides, as a measure of the urgency for such documentation.

The language use of the Afar people is an interesting case in point. Existing studies on the Afar people reveal that they value language eloquence in public discourse and that they are gifted as regards language. Reda (2011) states:

> The Afar people are known for their efficient communication skills and institutions. They are well versed and articulate in expressing their views in a disciplined manner, often consolidating their arguments using carefully selected idiomatic expressions and proverbs (2011: 423).

In another study, Reda (2013: 69) re-affirms this by saying, 'Afar elders speak with a rhetoric of influence occasionally supported by wonderful proverbs, parables and stories.'

Earlier studies underline the importance of language in society as well. Ayele (1997) and Siseraw (1996) contend that oratory is central to power and prestige in the social politics of the Afar people. According to them, their society bestows power on those who are endowed with greater oratory abilities, irrespective of their wealth.

One area where the efficacy of language use can be seen in Afar social life is during conflict resolution. Abebe (n.d.) underlines:

> Within indigenous conflict resolution, it is important to present the case in well-articulated language with amicable manner since verdict is subjective which forward from the value judgement of the judges and the conflicting parties saying [sic].

Reda (2011: 427) echoes this: 'The tradition of settling disputes or peace-making is often consolidated with well-articulated proverbs and sayings.' While these studies provide evidence of effective language use in Afar social discourse, there have not been any documentary and descriptive studies on the actual language practice. This chapter aims to capture and preserve the linguistic practices of the Afar people in the context of conflict resolution. It takes the recent reconciliation event of the inter-clan conflict that took place in Adekwa, a subzone of Dallol in the Afar region of Ethiopia (Figure 1), on 1 September 2019.

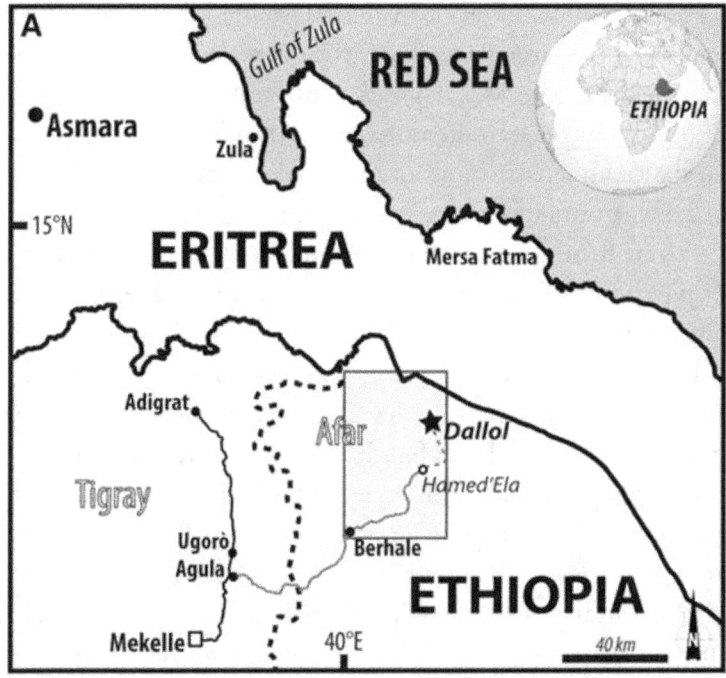

Figure 1. Study area (adopted from Cavalazzi et al. 2019)

This chapter has four sections. The first section forms the introduction to the study. This is followed by a section providing background information on the Afar people, their social structure, customary conflict resolution and reconciliation. The third section provides the transcription and translation of the speech. Finally, this chapter offers a brief commentary on the speech.

2. Background

2-1. Afar

The Afar, also referred to as Adal, Adali, Oda'ali, Teltal and Dankali by neighbouring people, are a Cushitic ethnic group in Africa. They inhabit an area known as the Afar triangle between northeastern Ethiopia, southeastern Eritrea and northern Djibouti. This area of land, which is about 150,000 square kilometres, is mostly hot, dry and arid. A large part of the region is desert with an average annual temperature of 34.5 degrees centigrade and it receives only 100 to 200 millimetres of rain annually (Cumming 2016). Due to the lack of a national census in all the countries where the Afar reside, their accurate population size is not known. However, they are estimated to be around 2.5 million (Abdellah 2018: 25). Most of the Afar people practise transhumant pastoralism with a few others depending on fishing.

Almost all of the people are Sunni Muslims with only a few Christian believers. Islam is believed to have come to the region through Arab merchants from Saudi Arabia around the 9th century.

The Afar people speak a language which is also called the Afar language. It is an East Cushitic language of the Afro-asiatic phylum. The language is classified under the Lowland East Cushitic branch along with such languages as Saho, Somali and Oromo. It is closely related to the Saho language. The Afar language has four dialects: Northern Afar, Central Afar, Aussa and Baadu (Ba'adu) (Lewis 2009: 121).

2-2. The Social Structure of the Afar People

The social structure of the Afar people, like most tribes in the region, is based on a patrilineal system.

The social structure of the Afar is 'highly segmented' (Reda 2011: 425). Piquet (2001: 8) states that there are 'more than 100 clan families'. A clan, known as *kedo* or *mela*, forms the basis of the 'elementary socio-political structure' in Afar society (Rahem 2001: 156). There is strong solidarity among the members of a clan (Getachew 2001). Each member of the clan is responsible for any crimes committed by members and they share both the punishment and compensation. A clan is led by a clan leader called *kedo abba*. The authority of *kedo abba* is hereditary and it often passes on to the eldest son. A clan leader is both the administrator and the chief of justice of his clan. *Kedo Abba* is his title, meaning supreme leader, while *mekabantu* (*mekabon* pl) is the title of the chief of justice of the clan. Clan leaders are held in high esteem among the Afar, as can be understood from their proverb, '*Issi amoita hamita hamita kedo ke daar akak makime garbo aysuk mataisa*', which translates as 'A forest through which a river has ceased to run and a tribe even slightly unfaithful to its leader are both on the decline'.[2] Under him, the clan leader has a council of village elders called *baro idola* who assist him in administrative and judicial matters. The Afar are a gerontocracy in that older people hold positions of power and lead the people. The leader also represents his clan in inter-clan matters.

A clan is made up of several sub-clans called *gullub* or *dahla*. The sub-clans are led by a leader referred to as *gullub abba*.

The Afar social structure has an age set-based system which is 'a system in which members are recruited to sets based roughly on their chronological age, either at birth or at some form of initiation (often circumcision)' (Lowenthal, 1973: 12). The age set-based system of the Afar is called *finaa* or *fimaa*.[3] Village elders and the concerned clan leader recruit young people who are born or circumcised around the same time, who possess physical strength and who are of good character and embody cultural values, among other criteria into a *fimaa* (Kassa 1997). The size of a *fimaa* ranges from twelve to one hundred depending on the size of the clan. Special care is taken to make the age groups representative of the different sub-clans and lineages in the clan. *Fimaa* also has its own leader called *fimaa abba*. This title is also hereditary, and passes on to the younger brother. The purpose of *fimaa* is to serve as the executive body of the society. Hence, '[t]hey are expected to work in collaboration with elders of the clan and [the] clan head' (Kassa 1997: 10).

The basic unit of social structure is the family, known as *burra*. Family in Afar often comprises an extended family including grandparents, parents, siblings and their children (Talachew and Habtewold, 2008: 106).

2-3. The Afar Justice and Conflict Resolution System
2-3-1. General Note on the Customary Justice System

The Afar have developed a strong and elaborate conflict resolution system during their existence. This system has enabled them to resolve their day-to-day disputes and kept them intact as one society. Muauz Ghidey Alemu (Muauz 2013) classifies the system as *Qadda*, *Mada'a* and *Mablo*. *Qadda* refers to the whole tradition of the Afar, of which conflict resolution is one, while *Mada'a* is the customary law. *Mablo* means the act of mediation, negotiation and arbitration.

Central to the Afar conflict resolution system is the customary law known as *Mada'a*. The law is oral and has been passed from generation to generation through word of mouth. *Mada'a*, to the Afar, is a book of life. It instructs them on how to best live their lives in every way and how to clear up conflicts in their communal life. In the Afar society, the elderly, who are knowledgeable about the traditional laws, play a significant role in resolving these conflicts. The title *Makabantu* (*Makaban*, pl.) is conferred upon these persons. This title is also given to the clan, sub-clan and family leaders when they are called upon to preside over conflict mediation.

Mada'a has two parts to it: *Afare* and *Adale*. The former is a set of laws concerning conflicts involving only Afars, while the latter pertains to situations between Afars and non-Afars. The Afar see the need to develop a separate set of laws to regulate their interaction with other neighbouring tribes. Five types of *Mada'a* are used among the Afar. These are Bur-Ali Mada'a, Buduto Bedih Mada'a, Afki Eki-Ma'd Mada'a, Bedoita Melah Mada'a and Debnek-We-imih Mada'a (Abdellah 2018: 54). These *Mada'a*s, which are practised among the various clans in different parts of the Afar region, are fundamentally the same. The distinction lies in the nature and severity of the punishments for the different crimes. The context of place is believed to be the reason for these variations. For instance, in regions where goats are not in abundance, the punishment could take the form of having sheep instead or fewer goats.

Mada'a divides crimes and transgressions into four based on the part of the body used to commit the wrongdoing. These are *gaba* (hand), *iba* (leg and/or foot), *araba* (tongue) and *samo* (genitalia).

The Afar justice and conflict resolution system is restorative in nature. The purpose of the justice system is not to punish the transgressor for their crime per se but to restore the harmony that has been disrupted as a result of the conflict. When a person commits a transgression, the whole clan shares in the punishment. A person who commits murder, for instance, is sentenced to pay by offering 100 camels (Reda 2011: 40) and it is beyond the capabilities of the transgressor to meet the sentence. Hence, the whole clan contributes and pays the fine. Similarly, any compensation is also shared among the relevant clan. Hence, a person is part of the whole and vice versa.

The Afar take conflict resolution seriously and seek to resolve issues at once as they believe the peace and harmony of the whole community could be in danger if the resolution is deferred. Those engaged in the dispute could take justice into their own hands and seek to harm one another and their respective families. There are numerous instances where the failure to resolve a murder case immediately has resulted in a blood feud which has continued for generations. The Afar are known to pile stones upon the tomb of the murdered as a sign that they were killed by the hands of a fellow being. The tombs are known as *Waydal* (see Figure 2). This serves as a reminder for the living for years, often instigating guilt among the

Figure 2. A Waydal in the cemetery in a place called Marka (Photo courtesy of Seid Ali Abdu)

relatives due to their inaction and prompting them to seek revenge.

Hence, the Afar, mindful of how conflicts can escalate into violence and feuds for years, which can jeopardise the peace and harmony of the whole community, endeavour to find instant, just resolutions for all the parties involved.

2-3-2. Mi-ino teke: A Peace-Making Step

An Afar conflict resolution is an elaborate process that is said to take from a day to months and, in some cases, years. The whole process is described in detail in the book *'Med-a: Ye Afar hizb ye bahl hig sine sre-at'* (Abdellah 2018: 108–118).

As mentioned, the Afar customary conflict resolution system is restorative in nature. The restorative justice system goes beyond settling the conflict and seeks to restore the social harmony disrupted by the conflict through a reconciliation process. The modern state legal system closes after finding out who has committed the crime and meting out the punishment it deems proportional to the severity of the crime. However, there is another crucial step to the process in the customary system. The Afar believe that simply meting out a punishment to the transgressor is not enough in itself as it will not restore harmony. One party might, for instance, feel that the punishment does not make up for their loss and this might encourage them to take revenge. In other words, the resolution process up to the point of punishment and compensation might leave a bad taste in the mouths of the disputants. As there is no way of knowing how the ruling has affected the concerned people in emotional terms (Abdellah 2018), the Afar see the need to conduct what can roughly be translated as a 'peace-making session' to allow the involved parties to let go of hard feelings, forgive one another and make peace. This peace-making session is called *mi-ino teke*. The *makabon* and *baro idola* (village elderly) speak to the disputants and everyone concerned in a language that appeals to their sense of brotherhood and oneness, forgiveness and love and is adorned with traditional proverbs and sayings. Through this, it is believed that negativity and ill feelings are washed away and harmony is restored.

After *mi-ino teke*, the final closing step is *fatiha*. The event finishes by reciting the Quranic chapter, *Al Fatiha*. After *fatiha*, the case is closed.

This chapter does not purport to study language in the whole *mablo* procession. The focus of this study is on the penultimate step in the elaborate process of the Afar traditional conflict resolution called *mi-ino teke*. This is the peace-making step held after the verdict has been given. It is the most important step as the purpose of the whole process is to restore peace and harmony.

2-4. A Brief Background to the Speech

This section gives a brief background to the conflict situation in question. The conflict reconciliation declaration event, known as *obba* in the Afar language, pertains to the inter-clan conflict involving three families, *bura*, namely Minifire, Balussuwa and Semaye. The cause of the conflict is that these families wish to separate from the clan they had been part of to join another clan. This has important implications in the Afar clan system for two reasons. First, the separation of a lineage from a clan in order to join another creates an imbalance in the socio-politics of the clans as the size of a clan is a measure of its power. Second, in the clan system, every clan member shares in the punishment and takes responsibility for the compensation for crimes committed by any member of the clan. Hence, the secessionist group owes the clan the compensation it had paid for the crimes its members had committed in the course of its existence. On account of the gravity of the case, the concerned families had not stated their request outright. Instead, the request to break away from their old clan and join a new one had been going on for some time through clandestine contact with clan leaders of respected, neutral clans. Subsequently, the formal conflict resolution process had been going on for some time. The conflict reached its final resolution with the declaration of the conflict reconciliation event held on 1 September 2019, from which the documented speech is taken. Although conflict reconciliation was reached, the original clans rejected the reconciliation, and the litigation is going on to date.

The event took place in Adekwa, in a subzone of Dallol in the Afar region of Ethiopia. There were hundreds of Afar men in attendance from all parts of the Afar region, including ones from Eritrea and Djibouti on account of the gravity of the matter. In the event of the declaration of reconciliation, Afar elders gave several speeches. This chapter has chosen to present one of these speeches.

3. The Speech

May peace be upon you (*Islamic Greeting*).

assalamu ʕaleikum

(*Audience*): May peace be upon you too.

(*Audience*): wa ʕaleikum assalam

It is wonderful that you are rejoicing.

uŋkwaʕ ruffa: inte:nim

(*Audience*): Bless you.

(*Audience*): maʕa:ne ɡei

The three brothers because of whom we are gathered here, your wish has materialised. I am happy that you are rejoicing.

asido:ha saʕalai akel warissa ha:ak suɡe:ni faɖak suɡte:nim sinih bihha inte:h uŋk'aʕ ruffa: inte:nim

(*Audience*): Bless you.

(*Audience*): maʕa:ne ɡei

I also rejoice for you. Secondly, what I (would like to) remind you before we get into (our) talk: (It is like) the proverb of the man who said all the camels are the offspring of (the camel called) Gulli. From what I have been hearing here, you were saying, 'We still have not found the two brothers.' I wish to leave you with a reminder to keep up the search for the two brothers.

anu ka:du ruffa si:nih aɖhe nammajtah kassi:samaha ja:bat hulna:mak duma ɡa:li inki:h ɡu:li dailo ijje numih missilaha akel abbuk suɡe-tijak namma saʕala:ja ɡe:kak nani lino:h aɖhuk suɡtem wo: namma saʕala ɡorrisa:nah arahat haita:nam sin kasi:seh habam faɖa

'Speak when there is something to be said, not because you have to' goes an Afar saying. Those who have spoken before me have said everything that has to be said.

jab ra:ʕawak ja:bana ikkah jab anu ra:ʕe mali:h inta ʕafar missila-hai ja:be mari ɡaba akak kale:h [personal name] ja:bak ɡaba kal-e:h jab akak muluj-e:h

[Personal name] has finalised the speech. The talking has come to a conclusion then.

It is like the proverb of the man who said, 'the *kassou* players have retired (to their places), the talk has ended'. What has to be said was already said the afternoon of the day before yesterday. There must have been lots of resistance and exhaustion along the way, but you have come through it all. Hence, I congratulate you.

kassoʊ⁴ orb-eːh jab rogoːgeh jab ambaːhin harrak ɡaba kaleh j-eneːh manɡo ɡeɖe kalite keː manɡo taʕabi edde jen kaː imːai wohuku amo ɡeɖak baɡul ɡahhak inteːnimih kaːdu uŋk'aʕ siːnik aɖhe

Thirdly, these people are liable for the same things; they pay the same blood price. An attack on one is an attack on all. They die for one another and kill for one another. They pay a bereavement gift as one family and they have the same ribs. They have one enemy and one love. They have one land. They have learned that they are people who despise the same thing.

sidohaitoːhu amari iŋki bar jalleh bar akak jaːnam biːllu iŋki barjalleh lak mudak harai muda jakeːh ittah rabaːh ittah ʕidaːh iŋki kura leːh iŋki kabbuːda leːh iŋki naʕboita leːh iŋki kahanu leːh iŋki baːɖɖo leːh iŋki-m janʕibe mara j-e-kke-miːj noːbbeh

That! let the sky hear! Let the land hear! Let the ignorant hear! Let the jinn hear! Let humanity hear! Let the fool hear! These people have become one and we shall henceforth refer to them as *this* people: Minifire, Bal-ussuwa and Semaye, three brothers.

tohu ʕaran j-aː-bb-ai baːɖɖo t-aːbbai ɡuddaʕi jaːbbai ɡuddaʕi taːbbai ɡinn-i jaːbbai dʒinsi jaːbbai duʕur jaːbbai ta mari iŋkitto jekkeh to maraːi aɖhenno minifirei balʕussuwai keː seːmaje sidoːha saʕalaːj

The prudent among them have been tracing their descent, counting

tu taːɖaɡo amo keːnik loːwak suɡteːh ʕumar ibn kataːb abuːsa heads, knowing that they descended from Omar Katab. They also knew who they mixed with. However, they have not gotten to know each other until now. It has become clear that out of indifference, they did not seek each other although they had always known each other.

These relatives, thus knowing that they were born together, however, out of indifference, thought that if each family could support itself, why they wanted each other, and they did not care to re-establish a bond with their lineage.

If we may ask why they now, all of a sudden, wish to do so—we should not accuse them of clannism or clannishness. The reason they have now been able to value their lineage and seek each other is because knowledge and wisdom have progressed. They have sought each other in their newfound knowledge and wisdom. Because this is an example to other communities, I give great thanks to you for this step.

These three brothers, Minifire, Semaye and Bal-ussuwa, we have witnessed that they have become three stones of the hearth. Those who are here in person have heard and those who are elsewhere have heard. Through the Afar representatives from the five zones,

kinnim ama:tuk suɠe:nih aka raden mara ka:du aɖaguk suɠe:ni ka:du asa:ku sitta mabaritinno:nui mahaɖi akkalewai ko: rada ijje:nihi:j habai dari:na:nah itta lo:wite:wa:k suɠeni:m tumbbullije:h duma:k itta a:ɖaguk suɠe:nih

aramad sittah aba:kuk suɠem aɖaguk suɠɠa ijjen waʕdi habaidarina:naha kulli buɖa is du:deksa maha titta fanɖa:h janamaha itta lo:witenih masuɠino:nui

asa:ku itta akah lo:wite:nim maha:j innu tekeki kedi:minnu ke:nik mannai itta akah lo:wito:nu du:denim ʕimlimi tatre:h kas tatre:mih sabbataha kulsa le ɠadda si:nih ɠahisa:h aɖhe

asido:ha saʕal minifire:j se:maje:j ke: balʕussuwa sido:ha ɖikanɖik teke:h iŋki baju ke: iŋker aba tekkemi iŋkih no:beh akkel tanim to:beh ɠe:rikkel tanim to:beh ʕafar raka:kai ka:du ko:na zo:nuk jable mari jani:h ja:bbe mari aiti ede le:h huɠɠane warado:dih kulsa le ɠadda ɠahsa:h

all the Afar people have their eyes and ears on this event. I give thanks to the neighbouring subzones.	
All we have left to do now is to sacrifice a sheep to commemorate the declaration. All the Afar people have now heard this. Everything God has created on the surface of the earth and under the sky have also heard.	tawai nek raʕtemi obbah idda elle rabtaːmak kalih imik ɡaba kalleh tah iŋkih ʕafar ummatta toːbbeh jalli jaxluqemi aːrdiː baɡu-l ʕaran ɡuba-l iŋkih toːbbe
I thank you for listening to me.	jo aŋkaħiseːnimih ɡadda ɡeja

4. Brief Commentary

The speech was given at the declaration of the inter-clan conflict reconciliation event held in Adekwa, in a subzone of Dallol in the Afar region of Ethiopia, on 1 September 2019. The speaker was one of the elders called forward to give a declaration speech called *obba* in the Afar language. The speech lasted around four minutes in length.

The main cause of the conflict is that two 'families' claim that they do not belong to the clan they had been part of for so many years, but belong to another clan, a claim, they contend, they have come to understand after consulting with the knowledgeable elderly among them. Hence, the purpose of the talk, apart from the declaration, is to re-establish the appropriateness of the decision to grant the families separation from the clan they had been part of and join their new clan family, even though it was at the expense of upsetting the clan they had separated from. The four-minute talk was structured to address this.

From the outset, the speaker is keen to emphasise the completion of the process that had been going on. He quotes another Afar proverb to get this message across: '*kassʊ orb-eːh jab roɡoːɡ-eh ijj-e numi-h missilaha*'. It means *kassʊ*[5] performers have retired to their homes; the talking has ended. *Kassou* is a traditional song sung by men to 'express a grievance against another [clan]'. Hence, the message is that just as *kassou* performers leave when they receive a proper answer to their grievance, so too the conflict that has brought them there has come to a proper resolution. He describes the moment that has brought them there as a moment of celebration, depicting the act as brothers coming together, congratulating the people of these groups, and declaring that he was rejoicing for them.

He is aware that the big clan from which two of the three groups have split resent the reunion. (The reasons for their resentment are discussed in Section 2-4). As a result of this awareness, he shrewdly quotes the traditional Afar proverb, '*gaːli inkiːh guːli dailo*'. The proverb, which translates as 'All camels are the offspring of one camel', captures the tenet of the Afar people's social psychology, i.e., people of the same clan are essentially siblings.

He then underlines the oneness of the families using the rhetorical device of repetition. The repetitive phrase structure is 'iŋki … leːh', i.e., 'one … have'. The speech lists the things that binds the families together: *bar, kura, kabbuːda, naʕboita* (enemy), *kahanu* (love), *baːddo* (land). This repetition culminates in the statement '*iŋki-m janʕibe mara j-e-kke-miː-j n-oː-bbeh*', which translates as 'We have learned they have become people who despise the same thing'. This essentially means they have become like one person.

Having pronounced their oneness, the speaker declares the reconciliation. He uses hyperbole when he starts to proclaim, '*tohu ʕaran j-aː-bbai baːddo t-aː-bbai*' (Translation: 'Then let the sky hear! Let the earth hear!'). Hence, he bestows grandeur on the event in announcing that the three families are part of a union by asking the sky, the earth, the demons, humankind, fools and the ignorant to bear witness.

In the next section of the speech, the speaker refutes any doubts about the motif of the union. He implies that the union is not a calculated move with any ulterior motives, but that the families have acted upon what the wise among them have always known, that they are descendants of the mythic ancestor, Omar Katab. The reference is to the Afar myth, the *Harel Mahis,* according to which a section of the Afar people, called the Asaimara, descended from an Arab. This, however, has been refuted by scholars as there are no substantial linguistic, cultural or historical relations between the Afar and the Arabs according to Lewis (1994), as quoted in Hassen (2011). He attributes the fact that they could not unite due to indifference on the part of the three families. He then poses the question that he assumes is in the minds of the aggrieved clans: why now? After hesitating for a moment, he contends that they have found their conviction through the progression of knowledge and wisdom that the age they live in has afforded them. This answer earns him an ovation from the crowd.

With that, the speaker returns to the subject of the oneness of the three families. He likens their unity to becoming three stones in the hearth. The use of the metaphor of the three stones is to signify that when they were separated, they were dysfunctional and, in their unity, they regain their harmony.

He ends his speech with a pronouncement of the declaration. The speaker proclaims that the Afar people in attendance and those not in attendance, through representatives from all parts of Afar land, have all heard about the reunion of the three families. He reinforces the declaration with the hyperbolic statement that every creature on the face of the earth bears witness to the reunion of these families.

In this light, the peace-making discourse carries greater significance than the simple resolution of the specific conflict that has brought them together. It also offers a discussion on the impending challenges to the social organisation that has kept them together thus far and is now beginning to fall apart.

Endnotes

[1] Audio-visual recording and consent for this study was obtained from my informant, Jamie Adem, during my field trip in Ethiopia, from 9–25 September 2019. Of the many speeches delivered by elders in the event, one speech is chosen for the presentation. The four-minute speech has been meticulously translated into English.

[2] Proverb and translation taken from Parker (1971: 286).

[3] *Finaa* and *fimaa* seem to be dialectal variants. *Fimaa* is used in this chapter following Abdellah (2018).

⁴ i. evening singsong.

ii. song of accusation and defiance.

iii. A challenging song [sic] – if one clan has a grievance against another, it may sing its challenge which is answered by the other group's song.

(All definitions of words endnoted henceforth are taken from Parker and Hayward (1985) unless specified otherwise).

⁵ See endnote 4.

Acknowledgements

The fieldwork for this chapter was done as part of the research project 'Documentation and Description of Ethiopian Languages: Towards a social innovation'. I thank Professor Hideyuki Inui, head of the project, for graciously allowing me to do my fieldwork under this project. I have benefited a lot from the guidance of my academic advisor, Professor Jun Ikeda and the support of my senior classmate, Shogo Hara. I am also grateful for the feedback and comments I received from the reviewer, Professor Daisuke Shinagawa. This work was supported by JSPS KAKENHI Grant Number JP16H06318.

References

Abdellah, A. (2018) *Med-a: Ye Afar hizb ye bahl hig sine sre-at*, Addis Ababa: Ethiopia Justice System Institute and Afar Bureau of Culture and Tourism, pp. 25–118.

Abebe, A. (n.d.) 'Conflict and conflict resolution process among Afar, Northeast Ethiopia',
(https://www.academia.edu/18082660/Afar_people_and_their_conflict_resolution_process) (accessed: 7 January 2021).

Ayele, G. (1997) 'Conflict over land use: Pastoralism, commercial and state agriculture: The case of the Afar', in K. Fukui, E. Kurumoto and M. Shigata (eds) *Ethiopia in Broader Perspectives: Proceedings of the 13th International Conference of Ethiopian Studies, Kyoto, 12-17 December 1997, Vol. II.*, Kyoto: Shokado, pp. 358–377.

Balehegn, M. (2016) 'Ecological and social wisdom in camel praise poetry sung by Afar Nomads of Ethiopia', *Journal of Ethnobiology*, Vol. 36, No. 2, pp. 457–472.

Bliese, L. (1976a) 'Afar', in M. Bender (ed.) *The Non-Semitic Languages of Ethiopia*, East Lansing: African Studies Center, Michigan State University, pp. 133–165.

―――― (1976b) 'Proportional relations and synchronic developments in 'Afar morphology', *Folia Orientalia*, Vol. 17, pp. 41–50.

―――― (1981) *A Generative Grammar of Afar*, Dallas: Summer Institute of Linguistics.

Cavalazzi, B., Barbieri, R., Gómez, F., Capaccioni, B., Olsson-Francis, K., Pondrelli, M., Rossi, A. P., Hickman-Lewis, K., Agangi, A., Gasparotto, G., Glamoclija, M., Ori, G. G., Rodriguez, N. and Hagos, M. (2019) 'The Dallol geothermal area, northern Afar (Ethiopia) – An exceptional planetary field analog on earth', *Astrobiology*, Vol. 19, No. 4, pp. 553–578 (https://doi.org/10.1089/ast.2018.1926) (accessed: 2 January 2021).

Colby, J. (1961) *Danakil grammar (Lessons 1-16)*, Asmara: Red Sea Mission Team.

―――― (1970) 'Notes on the northern dialect of the "Afar language"', *Journal of Ethiopian Studies*, Vol. 8, pp. 1–8.

Colizza, G. (1887) *Lingua afar nel nord-est dell'Africa*, Vienna: A. Hoelder.

Cumming, V. (2016) 'This alien world is the hottest place on Earth', *BBC*, 15 June 2016 (http://www.bbc.com/earth/story/20160614-the-people-and-creatures-living-in-earths-hottest-place) (accessed: 12 January 2018).

De Charency, H. (1877) 'Grammatical notes of the Dankali language', *Bulletin de la Société Philologique 216*.

Derchi, F. (1895) *Dizionario e frasario italo-dancalo*, Rome: Società Geografica Italiana.

Fulmer, S. (1991) 'Dual-position affixes in Afar: An argument for phonologically-driven morphology', in A. Halpern (ed.) *The Proceedings of the Ninth West Coast Conference on Formal Linguistics*, Stanford: CSLI (Center for the Study of Language and

Information), Stanford University, pp. 189–203.

——— (1997) 'Parallelism and planes in optimality theory: Evidence from Afar', Doctoral thesis, University of Arizona.

Getachew, K. N. (2001) *Among the Pastoral Afar in Ethiopia: Tradition, Continuity and Socio-Economic Change*, Utrecht: International Books, in association with OSSREA.

Hailemichael, A. (1995) 'A thematic analysis of the Afar camel folk literature: An ethnography-of-communication approach', *Journal of Ethiopian Studies*, Vol. 28, No. 1, pp. 1–22.

Hara, S., Alazar, G. Suzuki, K. and Ikeda, J. (2019) 'Notes on Afar verbal morphology', *Studies in Ethiopian Languages*, Vol. 8, pp. 1–19.

Hassen, M. (2011) 'Indigenous governance among the Southern Afar (ca.1815–1974), Ethiopia', *Ethiopian Journal of the Social Sciences and Humanities*, Vol. 7, No. 1-2, pp. 1–26.

Hayward, R. J. (1974) 'The segmental phonemes of 'Afar', *Bulletin of the School of Oriental and African Studies*, Vol. 37, pp. 385–406.

——— (1976). 'Categories of the predicator in 'Afar with special reference to the grammar of radical extensions', Doctoral thesis, University of London.

Hayward, R. J. and Corbett, G. G. (1988) 'Resolution rules in Qafar', *Linguistics*, Vol. 26, No. 2, pp. 259–279.

Kamil, H. (2015) 'L'afar: Description grammaticale d'une langue couchitique (Djibouti, Erythrée et Ethiopie)', Doctoral thesis, Institut National des Langues et Civilisations Orientales.

Kassa, G. (1997) 'A note on the Finaa (Fimaa) institution among the pastoral Afar of the Middle Awash Valley, North Eastern Ethiopia', *Journal of Ethiopian Studies*, Vol. 30, No. 2, pp.1–26 (https://www.jstor.org/stable/41966070) (accessed: 19 January 2020).

Lewis, I. M. (1994) *Peoples of the Horn of Africa: Somali, Afar, and Saho*, London: Haan Associates for the International African Institute.

Lewis, M. P. (2009) *Ethnologue: Languages of the World* (16th edition), Dallas: SIL International.

Lowenthal, R. (1973) 'Tharaka age-organization and the theory of age-set systems', Doctoral thesis, University of Illinois.

Luc, F. (1967) *Grammaire 'Afar*, Djibouti: Randa.

Morin, D. (1986) '*Typologie grammaticale du couchitique: Le cas de l'afar et du somali'*, Doctoral thesis, Université Sorbonne Nouvelle.

─── (2012) *Dictionnaire afar-français*, Paris: Karthala.

Muauz, G. (2013) 'The Mada'a and Mablo of the Afar: Customary system of conflict transformation', *Wollo University Annual Research Proceeding*, Vol. 2.

Muauz, G. and Saleh, M. (2017) 'On the poetics and politics of the Afar Kassow', *Eastern African Literary and Cultural Studies*, Vol. 3, Issue 1, pp. 19–39.

Parker, E. (1971) 'Afar stories, riddles, proverbs', *Journal of Ethiopian Studies*, Vol. 9, No. 2, pp. 219–287 (https://www.jstor.org/stable/41967477) (accessed: 19 January 2020).

─── (1979) 'Prerequisites for an adequate lexicography of 'Afar', Doctoral thesis, University of London.

─── (2006) *English-Afar Dictionary*, Springfield: Dunwoody Press.

─── (2009) *Afar-English Dictionary*, Springfield: Dunwoody Press.

Parker, E. and Hayward, R. (1985) *An Afar-English-French Dictionary*, London: School of Oriental and African Studies, University of London.

Piquet, F. (2001) *Even After Good Rains, Afar Pastoralists Remain Vulnerable, Report on Afar Region*, Addis Ababa: UN–Emergencies Unit for Ethiopia (https://reliefweb.int/sites/reliefweb.int/files/resources/609C7A905DEFCF1185256AF60061F79D-undp-eue_eth_30oct.pdf) (accessed: 18 February 2019).

Rahem, K. (2001) 'Haral Mahis et les Afar, importance d'un mythe dans les positionnements sociaux et les stratégies de pouvoir', *Annales d'Éthiopie*, Vol. 17, No. 1, pp.151–174 (https://www.persee.fr/docAsPDF/ethio_0066-2127_2001_num_17_1_996.pdf) (accessed: 21 December 2019).

Reda, K. (2011) 'Social organization and cultural institutions of the Afar of Northern Ethiopia', *International Journal of Sociology and Anthropology*, Vol. 3, No. 11, pp. 423–429 (http://www.academicjournals.org/IJSA) (accessed: 19 January 2020).

─── (2013) 'Peace-making from within: The tradition of conflict resolution in Northern Afar, Ethiopia', *Ethiopian Journal of the*

Social Sciences and Humanities, Vol. 9, No. 1, pp. 57–77 (https://www.ajol.info/index.php/ejossah/article/view/90018) (accessed: 23 January 2020).

Reinisch, S. L. (1885) 'Die Afar-Sprache [pt. 1]', *Sitzungsberichte der (Kaiserlichen) Akademie der Wissenschaften zu Wien, Philosophisch-Historische Klasse*, Vol. 111, pp. 5–112.

────── (1886) 'Die Afar-Sprache [pt. 2]', *Sitzungsberichte der (Kaiserlichen) Akademie der Wissenschaften zu Wien, Philosophisch-Historische Klasse*, Vol. 113, pp. 795–916.

────── (1887) 'Die Afar-Sprache [pt. 3]', *Sitzungsberichte der (Kaiserlichen) Akademie der Wissenschaften zu Wien, Philosophisch-Historische Klasse*, Vol. 114, pp. 89–168.

Simeone-Senelle, M. (2007) 'Les relatives en afar', halshs-00343529 (https://halshs.archives-ouvertes.fr/halshs-00343529) (accessed: 7 January 2021).

Simeone-Senelle, M. and Hassan Kamil, M. (2013) 'Agreement in 'Afar', *43th Colloquium on African Languages and Linguistics*, Leiden: Leiden University.

Siseraw, D. (1996) 'Person and society among the pastoral Afar of North East Ethiopia', Master's thesis, Addis Ababa University.

Talachew, G. and Habtewold, S. (2008) 'Customary dispute resolution in Afar Society', in A. Pankhurst and G. Assefa (eds) *Grass-Roots Justice in Ethiopia: The Contribution of Customary Dispute Resolution*, Addis Ababa: Centre français des études éthiopiennes, pp. 93–106 (https://books.openedition.org/cfee/471?lang=en) (accessed: 23 January 2020).

UNESCO Ad Hoc Expert Group on Endangered Languages (2003) 'Language vitality and endangerment', *International Expert Meeting on UNESCO Programme Safeguarding of Endangered Languages*, Paris, 10–12 March 2003.

Chapter 4

Aspects of Linguistic Dynamism in Sheng as Kenyan Colloquial Swahili: Focusing on De-Standardisation and Re-Vernacularisation

Daisuke Shinagawa

1. Introduction: Multilingualism in Africa and Convivial Linguistic Practices

With almost one third of the world's languages spoken on the continent of Africa (Eberhard et al. 2019),[1] linguistic diversity is one of the most salient features of the area. Multilingualism can be observed everywhere, not only in urban areas where politically and economically prestigious official languages play a critical role in upward social mobility, but also in rural settings where people usually speak a lingua franca, be it regional, national or international. This enables wider communication across ethnic boundaries, besides the use of their mother tongue (cf. Bokamba 2015; Zsiga et al. 2014, among many others).

This 'usual' situation in the African context, however, has been viewed differently depending on varying perspectives and at different times in history. From the point of view of colonisation and post-colonial nation building, the multilingual situation, or the existence of multiple languages, was generally seen by policymakers as an obstacle to national unity (cf. Whiteley 2017 [1971] (ed.); Mazrui and Mazrui 1985),[2] just as in 19th century Europe where, the legitimation of a standardised national language was an essential part of the nation building process, which in turn became a threat to minority languages. However, in the late 20th century, when the endangerment of linguistic diversity attracted global concern (cf. Krauss 1992; Dixon 1997), linguistic diversity and stable multilingualism[3] as an ideal societal state, embracing multiple languages in a community, became a 'universal' value of the globalising world, e.g., as seen in the Resolution adopted by the UN General Assembly on 16 May 2007:

(1) The General Assembly, ... [r]ecognizing also that **genuine multilingualism promotes unity in diversity** and international understanding, and recognizing the importance of the capacity to communicate to the peoples of the world in their own languages, including in formats accessible to persons with disabilities (UN general assembly 2007, emphasis added).

Accordingly, international organisations and authorities to date have been making various efforts to preserve and revitalise minority languages as well as to advocate the linguistic rights of speakers' communities (Figure 1. See also Mosely 2010, Skutnabb-Kangas 2002). Africa is not an exception in terms of being influenced by this global trend of multilingualism, e.g., explicit statements regarding the basic linguistic rights of indigenous languages[4] in many of the constitutions of African states which were reformed around the turn of the present century would be regarded as its clear reflection.

While the introduction of the 'universal' value of multilingualism into African countries apparently seems to be a rational decision made by nation states of the globalising world of the 21st century, we should notice the fact that the concept of multilingualism discussed so far was developed in the context of the late 20th century of the Western world, where minority languages were, and even still are, systematically under threat of linguistic dominance by standardised national languages (cf. Crystal 2000; Romaine 2002; Kraus and Grin 2018). This is sharply different from the usual situations in Africa where indigenous languages are less threatened, partly due to the insufficient systematic implementation of national language policies (cf. Brenzinger 1992). In this sense, the introduction of a Western-oriented multilingual policy to African contexts can be regarded as an acceptance of ready-made concepts that are neither rooted in nor expected to apply to the African reality. In other words, multilingualism 'has been a social reality in most of Africa from time immemorial' (Mansour 1993: 123) regardless of the political commitment of national language policies or the acceptance

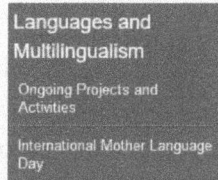

Figure 1. UNESCO's website on 'Languages and Multilingualism'
(http://www.unesco.org/new/en/culture/themes/cultural-diversity/languages-and-multilingualism)

of the global movement initiated by international authorities.

Then, how can we describe and characterise the actual state of multilingual situations in Africa? The basic stance of this chapter is to ponder the question from the perspective of 'conviviality', a term originally developed by Illich (1973) and later adopted by Nyamnjoh (2017) as a critical concept characterising 'African potentialities'. According to Nyamnjoh (ibid: 263), the concept of conviviality is defined as the 'recognition and provision for the fact or reality of being incomplete' and the term 'incompleteness' is adopted as a key concept differentiating it from Eurocentric modernity[5] that tends to 'privilege neat dichotomies and dualisms'. This dualistic view, in turn, can be regarded as a logical background to the 'categorial' view of language, as well as the so-called 'standard language culture' (Milroy and Milroy 1997; Lüpke 2016: 39), both of which seem to sharply contrast with people's understanding and actual practice performed in the context of multilingual situations in Africa.

Based on this understanding, the present chapter attempts to describe actual linguistic dynamism observed in varieties of Kenyan Swahili, with a particular focus on Sheng, a collective label for Kenyan colloquial Swahili varieties originating from an urban mixed code (cf. Spyropoulos 1987; Abdulaziz and Osinde 1997; Ferrari 2004; Bosire 2009; Githiora 2018, among others). The remaining sections are organised as follows: in Section 2, some background concepts to the subsequent discussions will be introduced. In Section 3, we will investigate structural aspects of the linguistic dynamism found in Sheng and discuss its grammatical fluidity, mainly by referring to the data provided in Shinagawa (2019), where we will focus on 'de-standardised' features of Sheng. In Section 4, we will investigate the sociolinguistic dynamism reflected on the social recognition of Sheng, which is observed in materials publicly accessible online or those obtained through the fieldwork I conducted in 2019 mostly in Nairobi. In this section, the focus will be on 're-vernacularisation' as a sociolinguistic process of potential diversification. Section 5 will conclude the chapter with a further discussion on what this dynamism suggests to us in terms of a more practical understanding of multilingual situations in Africa from the perspective of conviviality in linguistic practices.[6]

2. Conceptualisation of Language and (In)Completeness in Language Ideology

Before presenting the data and analysis, we will briefly summarise some key concepts crucial to the following discussion. As mentioned above, conviviality, as a key concept used to describe and analyse the linguistic dynamism observed in actual multilingual settings in Swahili-speaking Africa, contrasts sharply with the ideology behind Western-oriented multilingualism. In this section we will take a further look at the ideological background behind this contrast by focusing on the linguistic standard as a sociolinguistic concept as well as distinctive views on the conceptualisation of language.

2-1. Standard Language Ideology and the Categorial View of Language

As pointed out by Lüpke (2016), Western type of multilingualism can be regarded as based on the foundation of a 'standard language culture'.

> (2) In Western societies, the prevailing standard language culture is based on fictional monolingualism and maximal language separation and on prestigious standard varieties enforced through powerful language management mechanisms (Lüpke 2016: 39).

As explained by Milroy (2007: 133), in a standard language culture, people's attitude to languages is dominated by standard language ideology, which is based on the supposed existence of standard forms of language, and by which people 'believe that their attitude to the standard to be common sense and assume that virtually everyone agrees with them'. While standard languages[7] in general fulfil values such as correctness, authenticity, prestige and legitimacy (Milroy ibid: 134–135), among them the notion of (or consciousness of) correctness is crucial in this context as it is inevitably related to 'completeness', which counteracts with a key concept of conviviality.

On the other hand, it is important to note that there is a specific view of the conceptualisation of language behind this ideology. A standard language, or language standardisation as a process, is only possible with the idealisation that languages are mutually distinctive semiotic system. As mentioned by Lüpke (2016: 41), multilingual settings in the Western world are generally characterised as having 'tiered bilingual configurations (and division of labor of codes in them)', where languages are structurally and functionally differentiated from one another and socially stratified. This type of conceptualisation of language, which also provides the basis for the 'fictional monolingualism' mentioned in (2), can be referred to as the 'categorial view'[8] of language, which regards a language as an independent, mutually disjunctive and concrete system in that a standard variety should be distinguished from any other non-standard varieties.

2-2. Bantu Noun Classification and the Relative View of Language

Apart from the 'categorial' view of language, which can be regarded as a logical background on which the Western view of multilingualism is based, there is a contrasting view of the conceptualisation of language that can be easily observed in actual linguistic practices in African multilingual settings, i.e., language is regarded as part of cultural representation characterising a specific ethnic group such as the arts, styles, customs, etc. shared in the speakers' communities.

This rather abstract but flexible view of language can be regarded as rooted in the core systematic feature shared exclusively in Bantu languages as well as in a number of other groups of African languages, i.e., the noun class system as an ontological categorisation reflecting the collective knowledge of their worldviews. For example, it is generally understood that class 7 in the Bantu nominal classificational system is a typical class deriving language names. However, cl. 7 marker *isi-* in Zulu, for instance, substantially denotes any cultural entity that is identifiable to ethnic groups and language is only part of it (Bailey 1995: 34). This suggests how languages, or more precisely 'vernaculars' in this context, are recognised by people 'languaging' Bantu languages in their daily lives. Just as any traditional 'ethnic' knowledge is interpreted flexibly from time to time to fit contemporary contexts, as traditional customs may keep changing their surface realisation by communicating and interacting with different values and systems introduced from outer groups, and even as individual ethnic identity can fluctuate between different groups through one's life course, what is tagged by cl. 7 prefix as a name of a language can be regarded as more flexible, fluid, and sometimes a more mutually inseparable entity than the 'categorial' language characterised as a mutually independent speech code.

It should also be noted here that this flexible view of language appropriately captures the dynamic aspect of language contact. Contrasting 'language as a system' (corresponding to the categorial view) with 'language as practice' (the relative view), Mufwene (2017) explains as follows:

(3) Although speakers communicate by applying morpho-syntactic strategies they have developed or learned, **they can also adapt them to new situations or innovate new ones**. Systems emerge from repetitions in the practices of individual speakers, which converge into communal norms from the mutual accommodations speakers make to each other's ways of expressing meanings. This implies that the culture-specific ways of packaging information and the associated worldviews are not immutable' (Mufwene 2017: e204, emphasis added).

As discussed in Section 3, structural fluidity is one of the most salient features of Kenyan colloquial Swahili including Sheng. Thus this 'relational' view is regarded as an appropriate conceptualisation of what is happening in the actual situations in multilingual settings of our concern.

2-3. Development of an 'Incomplete Lingua Franca' and (Re-)Vernacularisation

Given the naïve understanding of the standard language ideology that is grounded on the categorial view of language, every one of the community members is considered to be a 'native' speaker with a comprehensive competence in at least one of the languages spoken in the relevant society. While in the multilingual situations where standard language ideology has little practical privilege (see 2-1) and people recognise language as part of their cultural representation (see 2-2), no one could be a 'pure' speaker of a single 'standard' language. Rather, they are seen as active players in simultaneous multilingual communication, i.e., positive actors of translanguaging (García and Wei 2014).

Sheng is actually a syncretic linguistic code with a grammatical basis from colloquial Swahili (functionally equivalent to 'Kenyan Swahili (KS)' in (6) below), which has been developed in such a multilingual situation where grammatical 'correctness' has no practical role to play in the practice of communication, as Githiora (2018) explains:

(4) It was abundantly clear that producing grammatically "correct" Standard Swahili or English sentences in either language through translation was practically impossible for most respondents. "Bilingualism" is the result of contact between two communities of practice, but it does not necessarily mean having native-like control of two separate languages; in reality, no one but the idealised, fictional "native speaker" knows their language absolutely (Githiora 2018: 5).

Thus Githiora (ibid: 11, 33–34) points out that Sheng speakers often make 'errors' of spelling such as *ngari* instead of *gari* 'car' or *nyubani* instead of *nyumbani* 'at home, household', but these 'errors', which are linguistically regarded as a typical instance of phonological adaptation to their native system,[9] are nothing but a paraphrase of 'deviation from the norm of Standard Swahili'. Where standard language culture has no practicality, this kind of incompleteness is just one possible form of communication created in the multilingual ecology.

What should be noted here in relation to 'incompleteness' is the labels vernacular[10] and vernacularisation[11] as a process for a language (especially vehicular lingua franca) to be used as a vernacular, i.e., a non-standard variety used in more informal and intimate domains for group-internal communication. According to Calvet (2006) after Manessy (1994), this term is also used to indicate a further process which can lead to a language becoming an identity marker of the speakers and their community.

(5) 'Vernacularisation' in Manessy (1994) as cited in Calvet (2006: 110)
a. [*V*]*ernacularization* is a phenomenon that consists of manifesting in the form of a language that shifts from a communicational function to one that proclaims identity.
b. The set of phenomena that are produced when a collectivity of speakers becomes clearly aware of the bonds that exist between its members, the interests that unite them and their common expectations to such a degree that the collectivity is led to singularise itself by its linguistic behaviour.

Githiora (2018) argues that while there is no doubt that the most widespread vernacular in the sense stated above is colloquial Kenyan Swahili (KS) as a collective label for non-standard varieties, Sheng is also recognised as such in certain situations or communities.

(6) Indication of the re-vernacularisation of Sheng (Githiora 2018: 34, 44, emphasis added)
 a. Vernacular influenced Swahili (KS) is associated with uneducated speakers, and the rural or urban poor. Despite the lesser prestige afforded to KS, it is high ranking on the affective filter because it projects speakers as 'ordinary *mwananchi* [nation]' or 'salt of the earth' Kenyan, and **Sheng too identifies the speaker as one of 'us'** – *masafara* (sufferers, proletariat).
 b. KS and Sheng are the real speech codes in the streets, inside the households, in shared, close-knit treatments known as 'plots' (*ploti* in Swahili, *tiplo* in Sheng), in mass politics and popular culture.

As discussed in 4-2, it is confirmed that Sheng is currently becoming more like a vernacular in the sense stated above, though it was regarded more as a language of inter-ethnic bridging and it represented the hope for a symbolic language of national unity, at least before the politically induced ethnic divide happened in 2007. Based on these concepts, in the next section, we will discuss the structural aspect of dynamism observed in Sheng.

3. Dynamism in Linguistic Structures

Linguistic fluidity has been understood as a salient feature[12] of the so-called urban youth languages which emerged in urban centres as a typical African multilingual situation (Kiessling and Mous 2004; Nassenstein and Hollington [eds] 2015). While such fluidity is most frequently observed at lexical level through relexification from languages, it can also be attested at different levels of grammar. In this section we will have a further look at such grammatical fluidity based on the grammatical description of the strategies used to construct relative clauses in Sheng (Shinagawa 2019).

3-1. Preliminaries

Sheng's structural fluidity, or hybridity, at phonological and morphological levels can be summarised as in Table 1 (based on Shinagawa 2007: 122–123), which clearly shows that contact-induced hybridity is brought about not only by introduction of specific forms from local ethnic languages (e.g. the nominal suffix *-o* that is parallel to the morphological template attested in e.g. Luo, the verbal suffix derived from historical *-*ag* in Bantu, etc.), but also by introducing linguistic processes such as devoicing at intervocalic (non-postnasal) positions (i.e., as an areal-typological feature) or simplified class agreement (as a typical feature induced by language contact).

3-2. Syntactic Hybridity and Fluidity: Relative Constructions in Sheng

While this kind of phonological and morphological hybridity has been frequently mentioned and described in the literature (Mbaabu and Nzuga 2003; Ferrari 2004; Bosire 2009, among others), there have been few investigations regarding the syntactic fluidity of Sheng. In one of these rare attempts, Shinagawa (2019) investigated the structural variation of relative constructions attested in a text corpus and argued that there emerges a unique syntactic pattern. The two most salient features include (i) the loss of StS relativiser *amba-*, which Myers-Scotton (1979: 120) reports as a preferred strategy in (70s) KPS, and (ii) the substitutional use of the adnominal possessive marker *enye-* 'having'. These are illustrated in (7).[14]

(7) *kwa sababu... I think   mimi   tu   the only person*
    because...   I think   INDP$_{1SG}$ just the only person
    mw-enye na≠fany-a   i-le   kitu   na≠fany-a
    1-having SM$_{1SG}$.PRS≠do-FV 9-DEM.R 7.thing SM$_{1SG}$.PRS≠do-FV
    'Because, I think I'm the only person (in the country) who does what I do' (Shinagawa 2019: 132).

Table 1. Summary of phonological/morphological manipulation (cf. Shinagawa 2007)[13]

Characteristics		Possible source of influence	Examples
Phonology	Metathesis/Pig Latin	Jargonistic	Sh *kimbeko* 'cup' < StS *kikombe* (/ki.ko.mbe/)
	Devoicing of voiced (non-prenasalised) obstruents	(NE) Bantu	Sh *msee* 'friend, guy' [m̥se(:)] vs. StS *mzee* 'old/respected person' Sh *mase* [mase] < KCS *maze/madhe* < Eng *mother*
Nominal morphology	Shortening with -*o*	Nilote/Luo	Sh *fiso* {fis-o} < (StS *fizikia*) < Eng *physics* Sh *kibaro* {ki-bar-o} < StS *kibarua* 'day labour(er)'
	Derivational use of *ma-* and *ka-*	Bantu	Sh *masee* {ma-see} 'best friend(s)' < StS *mzee / wazee* Sh *kahatisi katoko* {ka-hatisi ka-toko} 'a small piece of story'
Verbal morphology and morphosyntax	Regularisation of irregular forms	Contact-induced simplification	KCS *kuja* {ku-j-a} 'Come! (imperative)' < StS *njoo*, cf StS *kula* {ku-l-a} 'Eat!' etc.
	Simplified concord	Contact-induced simplification	KCS *watu mingi, magari mingi* vs. StS *watu wengi* 'many people', *magari mengi*, 'many cars'
	Lack of applicative forms	Contact-induced simplification	Sh *Nunua masiwa wakeni* vs. StS *Nunulia wageni maziwa* 'Buy milk for guests'
	Imperfective marker *-ag*	Bantu	Sh *ningependeko* vs. KCS *ningependaga* vs. StS *ningependa* 'I would like'

It is confirmed in (7) that the word *mw-enye* plays a role of relativising the following clause *nafanya ile kitu nafanya* '(lit.) I do the thing that I do' to the head noun *the only person*, which refers to the speaker himself, i.e., this *-enye* functions as a subject relativiser. On the other hand, there is a clear tendency that the object relative is mostly expressed by the remote demonstrative, which is illustrated as *i-le* in (7). It should be noted that this distributional tendency, i.e., *-enye* relativises a subject, while *-le* is used as an object relativiser, is almost consistent throughout the corpus. Also, there is a significant tendency that null forms, i.e., those lacking any segmental relative marker, are attested in the context of relativising a subject of stative predicates, while synthetic marking with a verbal relative marker, which is morphologically more complex than other forms, is only used in temporal adverbial clauses (as templatic expressions) in limited ways. The following is the illustration of typical examples of such forms: a remote demonstrative as an object relative (8), a null expression as a stative subject relative (9), and a temporal adverbial clause with a verb-internal relative marker (10), all of which are quoted from Shinagawa (2019).

(8) *si   hao   ni   wa-le   wa-see*
NEG.COP DEM.M$_2$ COP 2-DEM.R 2-guy
u-li≠kuw-a   u-na-ni≠ambi-a
SM$_{2sg}$-PST≠be-FV SM$_{2sg}$-PRS-OM$_{1sg}$≠tell-FV
'Ain't they the guys you were telling me about?'

(9) *ku-li≠let-w-a   ma-basi i-na≠it-w-a   mang'oro*
SM$_{17}$-PST≠bring-PASS-FV 6-bus   SM$_9$-PRS≠call-PASS-FV mang'oro
'The buses called Mang'oro were introduced.'

(10) *Hao   watu   wa-li-po≠anz-a*
DEM.M$_2$ 2.person SM$_2$-PST-RM$_{16}$≠start-FV
ku≠imb-a   wa-li≠kuw-a   wa-me≠pend-an-a
15≠sing-FV SM$_2$-PST≠be-FV SM$_2$-PERF≠love-RECIP-FV
'When those guys started to sing, they had loved each other.'

The syntactic patterns of relative marking constructions observed in the corpus are summarised in Table 2. Again, a crucial point here is that while the strategies are hybrid in that the converted use of demonstratives can be seen as a grammatical replication from indigenous Bantu languages, while the null forms are generally attested in contact languages etc., the corpus also shows clear syntactic regularities, i.e., hybridity does not necessarily mean randomness.

However, it should also be noted that the 'regularities' are not necessarily shared with neighbouring Swahili varieties or even in 'subdialects' of Sheng. For example, though *-enye* is actually used as a relative marker in various contact Swahili varieties (especially those spoken in DRC, cf. Nassenstein 2015; Nassenstein and Bose 2016), its syntactic distribution is not identical among different varieties (see Shinagawa 2019 for more details). Moreover, according to Nakao (2018), in another sub-variety of Sheng spoken by the Nubi people settled in the Kibera area of Nairobi, *-enye* is actually used even in non-subject relative constructions, as in *kitu chenye unataka* 'The thing (*kitu*) that (*chenye*) you want (*unataka*)'. So, not only the hybridity but also the syntactic fluidity can be clearly observed even across different varieties that are collectively labelled as Sheng.

This structural fluidity, which may be regarded simply as an irregularity in the 'categorial' view of language (2-1), can be understood as a dynamism that creates language-internal typological microvariation. On the other hand, from a sociolinguistic perspective such as the 'sociolinguistics of mobility' proposed by Blommaert (2010), this fluidity can be described as a 'natural status' of vernacular languages and makes Sheng a vibrantly productive communication code as a (re-)vernacularised speech code. In the next section, we will discuss how this mechanism of vernacularisation takes place in society by tracing the diachrony of people's social recognition about Sheng.

Table 2. Focus of occurrence of major relativisation strategies in terms of syntactic properties of head nouns (Shinagawa 2019)[15]

		S-Pa	S-Be	S	A	O-Po	O	Obl	L	T
Null		←	┄┄	┄					┄	┄
Marked by	RM-V		↕	↑	↑		↕		┄	↑
	DEM		↕				↕			
	-enye		┄	↑		↑				

The most frequent strategies adopted for a specific syntactic context are marked by bold lines, while the strategies marked by a dotted line are attested at least once in the context in question; e.g., the most frequent strategy adopted in the relative constructions headed by an agentive subject (A) is -*enye*, while RM-V, which is marked by a dotted line, is attested at least once in the corpus.

4. Dynamism in Social Recognition

As has been pointed out in Kiessling and Mous (2004), there seems to be a typical 'developmental process' regarding the sociolinguistic functions that African urban youth languages (AUYL) tend to follow, which in turn form an essential part of the social recognition of such languages. According to Kiessling and Mous (ibid: 313–334), many AUYL including Sheng play a role of expressing antisocial group identity as an 'antilanguage' (Halliday 1978), reflecting the fact that they are used in 'urban', i.e., 'street' settings, which may easily evoke the image of resisting the existing norms in their initial stage of development. However, this identity may not necessarily be immutable. By reversing the old norms and creating new values, the young generation, as speakers of AUYL, may develop their identity into one aimed at reforming society, i.e., what is termed as 'project identity' by Castells (1997), and the language they speak may be recognised as representing such an identity.

On the other hand, AUYL as a mixed urban code spoken by people with various linguistic backgrounds serves the function of bridging ethnic boundaries. This communicative function, together with the resistance identity towards the neo-colonial power that inherited the political system and was grounded on the ethnic divisions enforced by the former colonial regime, may lead to the language being recognised as a symbol of national unity. This scenario, which may be applicable to the development of many other AUYL, can be generalised as in (11).

(11) a typical process of functional transition of AUYL (cf. Kiessling and Mous 2004) antilanguage > rebel language > inter-ethnic bridge > national identity marker

In the following, we will discuss how this process can be applied to the development of Sheng before the ethnic divide as a result of the political conflict, and how it is being de-contextualised especially in terms of its political profile in the process of overcoming the social crisis.

4-1. From 'Antilanguage' to 'National Identity Marker'

It is broadly understood that, as with the general tendency regarding the development of AUYL generalised in (11), Sheng, too, emerged as an urban youth code with an under-dog type of speakers' identity in the post-colonial Nairobi, as described in Spyropoulos (1987).

(12) [I]t was associated with a particular socio-economic group consisting of migrant labourers, as well as Kikuyu ex-Mau Mau detainees and their relations, school drop-outs and the like. Within the socio-economic structure of the society, these people were at the lower end of the hierarchy. However, since then the use of Sheng has filtered upwards, ... its association is no longer limited to one specific section of the population (Spyropoulos 1987: 130).

As spreading over geographical (from Eastleigh to Westlands), societal (from the lower end to more upwards in terms of the politico-economic hierarchy), and generational boundaries, Sheng has become an emblematic speech code representing the city of Nairobi and the youth living there. This metropolitan nature, in turn, came to be perceived as a symbol of uniting people from different ethnic backgrounds.[16]

This image of inter-ethnic bridging is thoroughly reflected in various works of contemporary art created around the turn of this century, e.g., as shown in the following passages from an interview article by Binyavanga Wainaina, where he was talking with the hip-hop artists Kalamashaka about their new song entitled *Moto* 'fire', the lyrics of which are written in Sheng.

(13) Excerpts from 'Interview with Kalamashaka' by Binyavanga Wainaina (Wainaina 2003).
    a. 'Chorus[17]: let the fire burn, let the fire get them, the fire that burns inside our hearts surprise them. **Fire, fire let it announce a revolution** ...'
    b. I ask them [Kalamashaka], 'Are you guys advocating **revolution?**'

c. Joni: 'People from this side of Nairobi are going to that side of Nairobi to listen to Kalamashaka. **This revolution is not about violence, it's about being conscious of who you are**. That is what our new song (*Moto*) is about. So now, for the first time, young people from all classes are listening to our message. Have you ever seen a Nairobi like that? From Westlands, Lavington, they're hearing that message. And they give you feedback' (Wainaina 2003: 54, emphasis added).

It is important to note that not only is the inter-ethnic image of Sheng manifested in the conversation, but this image is repeatedly associated with 'revolution', which in turn evokes the image of 'rebels' fighting with existing authorities. As Shinagawa (2012) mentions, the term 'rebel language' was repeatedly used to refer to Sheng by young Nairobians,[18] reflecting two layered images of Sheng, i.e., the rebellion to the political/neo-colonial power by uniting people of different ethnic backgrounds, as well as to the sociolinguistic norms of Standard Swahili.

As stated in (13), the 'revolution' is also aiming to overturn the existing norms and values that constitute people's identity (i.e., 'being conscious of who you are'). It is in this context that Sheng can be symbolised as a language of national unity; e.g., Mbaabu and Nzuga (2003) have rightly pointed out this direction.

(14) Sheng does not only give them [the youth] national identity, but it is also a language which they can manipulate. Maybe, the hope of a truly national language lies in Sheng and its contribution to standard Kiswahili (Mbaabu and Nzuga 2003: ii).

So far, we have confirmed that a general tendency for the transition of social functions and/or images observed in AUYL formalised in (11) can also be typically applied to the development of Sheng. However, the situation changed drastically after the political crisis caused as a direct result of the presidential election held in late 2007, leading to the so-called post-election violence (PEV).

4-2. The De-Contextualisation and Re-Vernacularisation of Sheng

Not to mention other social disasters caused by PEV, what it meant to Sheng the most was that it deprived the speakers of their typical sociolinguistic domains in which they could use the language, when inter-ethnic communication itself became a social risk (cf. Muraya 2015). It should, however, be mentioned that it is rather ironic that avoiding the use of Sheng proves that the language had, by then, truly become a language of bridging ethnic boundaries.

This period of disruption caused by PEV, in turn, seems to make a critical impact on Sheng's social function and hence its social image, especially in terms of its political aspects. This change in social image can be observed in the various works created by Well told story (renamed as Shujaaz Inc. in January 2020),[19] a communications research and production company officially launched in 2010, which is famous for 'Sheng-speaking' media products including a popular magazine called *Shujaaz* and its related multimedia content (Figure 2).

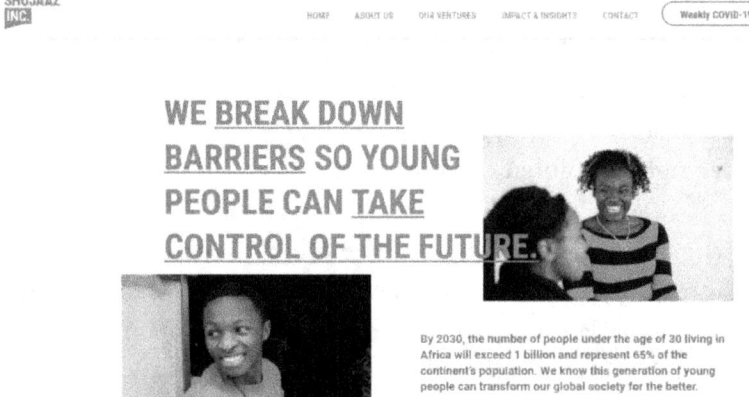

Figure 2. A snapshot of Shujaaz website
(https://www.shujaazinc.com/ [accessed on 20 June 2020])

In an interview session with some staff members in September 2019,[20] it was told that the founding aim of the company was to build a sober media that helps to motivate youths to improve their lives after PEV, i.e., PEV is thus regarded as having critically influenced the channels of public communications, especially those used by youths. At the same time, there was no language except Sheng that could be chosen as a media of communication when the country was recovering from the social calamity. Having gone through this process, however, Sheng is no more a symbol of political debate such as inter-ethnic 'revolution' in the sense that Kalamashaka and Wainaina were discussing in the pre-PEV era. Sheng is no longer a language used to fight against colonialism or tribalism ('ukabila' in Swahili). Rather, it has become more like a language that unites small and immediate communities, based on which people are living their daily lives. In this sense, it can be said that Sheng is becoming more associated with a sense of social class division rather than ethnic boundaries, as well as with economic activities rather than political alliances. What was impressive in the conversation with them was that Sheng is becoming symbolic of a language of small business such as 'chamaaz' and 'merry-go-round', which is autonomous but loosely-organised groups of people sharing immediate aims in their economy. These stories regarding Sheng's social image and function in the post-PEV era seem to point to the fact that Sheng is becoming depoliticised and more localised.

(15) The social function of Sheng is tending more towards:
    a. protecting societal (class) unity rather than fighting with 'ukabila'
    b. 'good governance' of small, immediate communities rather than nationwide 'resistance'
    c. 'economic activities' rather than 'political debates'

It may be worth mentioning that this depoliticised nature of Sheng is also reported in a non-Nairobi variety of Sheng by Rüsch (2016), where she observes that 'Sheng ya kijaka (Luo-Sheng)' shows less resistant/anti-identity features than 'typical' Sheng does. However, as shown in the above conversation, it seems rather convincing that the Sheng in Nairobi, consisting of the most 'typical' varieties, is also following the trend of depoliticisation. As also mentioned above, one of the important consequences of this de-contextualisation of Sheng's political profile is that it is becoming more associated with use in immediate, small-scale communities. This process has parallels with 'vernacularisation' mentioned in 2-3., where sociolectal divergence,[21] rather than convergence, tends to occur. In other words, it is likely that this kind of social situation can be a fertile ground for the creation of not only lexical but structural variations of Sheng discussed in 3-2, especially if such communities are characterised by a common ethnic/linguistic root. In this sense, the dynamic relation between structural fluidity and the 're-vernacularisation' process in small-scale communities (cf. Lüpke 2016) will be quite an interesting field for further research from a perspective of interdisciplinary investigations consisting not only of linguistics but of urban sociology and anthropology.

4-3. Parallels in the Music Scene[22]

Interestingly, but quite naturally at the same time, the depoliticisation process discussed in 4-2 is also reflected in current trends in Sheng-related music. As briefly mentioned in 4-1, the first-generation artists of Kenyan 'Gengetone' hip-hop, including Kalamashaka, released many songs with 'political seriousness' (Peck 2018: 112) in the lyrics, as Clark and Koster (2014) point out in the following:

(16) In Kenya, Kalamashaka released the politically charged song 'Tafsiri hii' (translate this) in 1997. ... Kalamashaka established themselves as a politically conscious group early on (Clark and Koster 2014: xv).

While this line of political consciousness was succeeded by fellow artists or followers such as Nameless, Mashifta (Kitu Sewer and G. Wiji) and Ukoo Fulani Mau Mau etc., the mainstream trend gradually shifted to a 'more commercial and more fun' direction as society started to recover from PEV. The smash hit of the song called *Wamlambez* ('Let them lick him/her') by Sailors_254, one of the leading groups representing the current scene of 'Genge Beat', and the comments made in reaction by the authorities, which is nothing to do with any political significance, may be regarded as unsurprising consequences of this trend (Figure 3).

Figure 3. A snapshot of tweets by Dr Ezekiel Mutua, Chief Executive of Kenya Film Classification Board, on Wamlambez

Again, the depoliticising process, or de-contextualisation process from the previous images, seems to be clearly observed in the current dynamism of Sheng and its related phenomena. The crucial consequence of this trend seems to lead Sheng to be used in more local, small-scale communities. This 're-vernacularisation' process, in turn, serves as the background for Sheng to create more internal linguistic diversity through the process of 'de-standardisation', which may be regarded as a practical 'norm' of colloquial communication in multilingual Africa.

5. Conclusion: For Further Discussions on Linguistic Dynamism and 'Conviviality'

In this chapter, we have discussed the linguistic dynamism currently observed in Kenyan colloquial Swahili, especially in Sheng as one of the varieties that can be traced back to the urban youth speech code which emerged in post-colonial urban Nairobi. The key features we have discussed are summarised as follows.

(17) Key features observed in structural and recognitional aspects of Sheng:
   a. The structural aspect: 'de-standardisation' by making use of linguistic materials and processes available in the multilingual settings as a centrifugal force of structural hybridity and fluidity.
   b. The sociolinguistic aspect: 're-vernacularisation' especially through de-contextualisation of its political profile that once Sheng manifested as its core identity.

To conclude this chapter, it may be worth providing some provisional ideas on the interrelationship between the linguistic dynamism we discussed here and the perspective of 'African potentiality'. As discussed in 2-1, unlike the Western view of multilingualism that presupposes a categorial view of language, the languages spoken in multilingual settings described in this chapter are usually unaffected by the standard language ideology, and people are able to cope with the situation without a political commitment to enforce the standard language culture.[23] This situation is in sharp contrast to European contexts where linguistic dominance is contested in the form of standard (prestigious) versus non-standard (less prestigious, i.e., 'accented'), which, in turn, may result in a schematic imbalance between the dominant and the dominated. In the multilingual situations we have examined in this chapter, however, such a dichotomy seems to have little significance.

In that sense, the process of structural de-standardisation, and the vernacularisation, which may be paraphrased as 'de-standardisation of the sociolinguistic status' can be regarded as striking characteristics of multilingual communication highly contrastive to the situation dominated by the standard language culture. Moreover, it can be said that it is this dynamism that upholds the creative multilingual contact not only with socio-economically prestigious languages (practically English in most East African countries) but also with any non-prestigious speech code. If we are right in thinking that these practices and processes are nothing but centrifugal movement from the (imaginary) completeness, the linguistic dynamism discussed here may rather be regarded as a direct realisation of communicative aspects of 'African potentiality'.

Endnotes

[1] e.g., *Ethnologue* (22nd edition, Eberhard et al. 2019) gives the number of 2,140 for living languages spoken in Africa out of the total of 7,111 world's languages.

[2] On the other hand, in the last years of colonial era, the shift of langue use to ethnic languages can be regarded as a result of the strategy of ethnic insulation by the colonial power; e.g., in Kenya, the Swahilisation of the Kikuyu people, the majority and the leader of the Mau Mau emergency (1952–1960), was 'partially arrested … under the pressure of counter-insurgency techniques inaugurated by the British'. (Mazrui and Mazrui 1985: 15)

[3] This is an intended paraphrase of 'genuine multilingualism' stated in (1), which seems to be somewhat an idealised situation where minority languages coexist in harmony with dominant, socio-politically prestigious languages.

[4] Most of the constitutions also refer to the promotion and protection of the linguistic right for sign languages and braille, following the statement in (1).

[5] 'Eurocentric or western modernity – a modernity of here and now … – is often choreographed, packaged and marketed as the only modernity worthy of recognition, representation, reproduction and globalisation' (Nyamnjoh 2017: 254).

[6] For a conceptual discussion on the 'convivial multilingualism', see Nakao (this volume).

[7] As claimed in Lüpke (2016: 40), another critical aspect of the standard language is that it is formed as a result of reification. Thus, what is discussed as 'de-standardisation' in this chapter may be paraphrased as 'unintentional devaluation of the reified standard'.

[8] See also a similar view in Blommaert's (2010) explanation of 'sociolinguistics of distribution' as a classic Labovian paradigm based on the Saussurean synchrony, where language is conceptualised as a 'fixed' system.

[9] This type of nasal effacement of nasal cluster is typically observed in the pronunciation of native speakers of languages without phonological contrast of voice in obstruents, causing post-nasal voicing of voiceless obstruents, which is broadly attested in Kenyan Bantu languages, as Hyman

(2003: 50) mentions Nande JD42, Kikuyu E51 and Bukusu JE31c as languages with post-nasal voicing.

[10] As in Macaulay (2001: 420), this term has been used in the literature in quite a polysemic way. The typical features that the term indicates include; (i) non-standard, (ii) unwritten (i.e., no official orthography is provided), (iii) non-official, and (iv) colloquial, the last of which is a core concept used here. Though Macaulay states the last usage is 'less clearly defined', we understand that Labov's (1970: 46) statement about the term as 'the style in which the minimum attention is given to the monitoring of speech' is included as part of characteristics of what the term indicates.

[11] Note that this term can be used with a different definition in the area of language policy and language education, e.g., in Kamwangamalu (2013: 545) vernacularisation is defined 'as the use of an indigenous language in the higher domains, such as the educational system', which is logically rather opposite to what is discussed here.

[12] This kind of hybridity is by no means a unique feature only attested in the so-called contact languages. Rather, one of the main points in the following discussion is that practically all the 'vernacular' languages, by definition, are open to be influenced by other languages spoken in the same multilingual situation.

[13] Abbreviations used in the table include; KCS: Kenyan Colloquial Swahili (a general term for vernacular varieties including those spoken since colonial era such as 'Kenyan Pidgin Swahili' (Heine 1979) or more general 'Upcountry Swahili' (Myers-Scotton 1979), which provide Sheng with its grammatical basis), Sh: Sheng, StS: Standard Swahili.

[14] Abbreviations in the glossing line basically follow a general convention of Bantu linguistics as follows; 1, 2, 3 ... noun class numbers, DEM.(M/R): demonstrative (middle/remote), FV: final vowel, INDP: independent pronoun, OM: object marker, RM: relative marker. Remaining others are as conventionalised in the Leipzig Glossing Rules (Comrie et al. 2015).

[15] Abbreviation of syntactic environments (the head noun's grammatical relation to a relative verb); S-be: Subject of copulative verb, S-Pa: Subject of passive verb, S: (non-Agentive) Subject, A: Agentive Subject, O-Po: Object possessed by Subject, O: Object, Obl: Oblique, L Locative, T: Temporal (for L and T, either semantic or syntactic). The number of occurrence of each strategy in each syntactic environment [counted in the

corpus based on the text data from the 'Sheng Interview'; ambiguous cases are excluded]; S-Pa: Null (5), RM-V (2); S-be: DEM (5), Null (1); RM-V (1), *-enye* (1); S: RM-V (4), *-enye* (4), Null (3), DEM (2); A: *-enye* (2), RM-V (1); O-Po: *-enye* (1); O: DEM (2); Obl: DEM (3); L: DEM (3), Null (1), RM-V (1); T: RM (9), Null (3).

[16] On the other hand, its anti-social image was continuously maintained by claims about Sheng's supposedly negative impact to formal education, especially children's learning of standard languages. However, most claims of this sort seem to lack sufficient scientific evidence. One of such typical claims is a tautological statement that Sheng as a non-standard variety gives bad influence to learning of standard languages (cf. Momanyi 2009: 134–136).

[17] English translation of the song as cited in the article.

[18] One of the interviewees was then an editor of the contemporary literature magazine called *Kwani?*, which is famous for focusing on the literal works composed in Sheng. He later became an independent writer and novelist.

[19] https://www.shujaazinc.com/goodbye-well-told-story-hello-shujaaz-inc-a-letter-from-our-ceo/ (accessed: 7 July 2020).

[20] The interview took place in the company's office located in a suburban business park in Karen in September 2019.

[21] One of the most well-known cases is the creation of different dialects, though the difference is mostly lexical, from one estate to another, which is reported in Kioko (2015).

[22] I am indebted to Mike Mburu, the marketing manager of the Kenyan contemporary art publisher *Kwani Trust*, for the most of information mentioned in this section.

[23] An interesting case of the unconsciousness to the standard may be seen in the happening broadcasted in July 2019 that a member of parliament was forced out from the parliament due to a debate she brought in a session when she claimed the word of Swahili for 'speaker' should be 'mzungumzishi' (which is rather an archaic or 'too prescriptive' form), not 'spika', the term that is used in the Swahili version of the constitution (in the article 106 in Part 3). While the issue is essentially related to an arrogant image associated with prestigious coastal varieties, the frivolous reaction from other MPs may also be seen as typical sentiment to an eccentric sensitivity for the standard in general public.

Acknowledgements

This work is mostly based on the fieldwork I carried out in Nairobi from August to September 2019, where I met and interviewed with various people including Paul Ekuru, Kevin Muraguri (Well Told Story), and Mike Mburu (Kwani Trust), to whom I am grateful for their kind understanding and cooperation to my research. An earlier version of this chapter was partially presented at the international workshop 'Sociolinguistic perspectives on variation in Swahili – new approaches to the study of language and its social context in East Africa' held at Johannes Gutenberg University Mainz from 30 November to 1 December 2019, where I had fruitful discussions with the participants especially Shuichiro Nakao, Nico Nassenstein and Chege Githiora, to whom I am indebted for their productive comments that brought me new insights discussed in this chapter. My thanks also go to Yuko Abe for inspiring discussions I had with her on sociolinguistic situations in Africa in general. However, any shortcomings are my own responsibility. Finally, this work is part of research outcome of the following projects: JSPS KAKENHI Grant Number JP16H06318, ILCAA's joint research project 'An Inter-disciplinary Approach to the Diversity and Dynamics of Swahili Varieties' and JSPS's Core-to-Core Program: B. Asia-Africa Science Platforms (2018–2020) 'Establishment of a Research Network for Exploring the Linguistic Diversity and Linguistic Dynamism in Africa (ReNeLDA)'. I hereby acknowledge their financial support.

References

Abdulaziz, M. H. and Osinde, K. (1997) 'Sheng and English: Development of mixed codes among the urban youth in Kenya', *International Journal of the Sociology of Language*, Vol. 1997, Issue 125, pp. 43–63.

Bailey, R. A. (1995) 'The Bantu *languages* of *South Africa*: Towards a sociohistorical perspective', in R. Mesthrie (ed.) *Language and Social History: Studies in South African Sociolinguistics*, Cape Town: David Philip, pp. 19–38.

Blommaert, J. (2010) *The Sociolinguistics of Globalization*, Cambridge:

Cambridge University Press.

Bokamba, E. G. (2015) 'Multilingualism as a sociolinguistic phenomenon: Evidence from Africa', in E. C. Zsiga, O. T. Boyer, and R. Kramer *(eds) Languages in Africa: Multilingualism, Language Policy, and Education*, Washington DC: Georgetown University Press, pp. 21–48.

Bosire, M. (2009) *Sheng: The Phonology, Morphology and Social Profile of an Urban Vernacular*, Ann Arbor: ProQuest (UMI Dissertation Publishing).

Brenzinger, M. (1992) *Language Death: Factual and Theoretical Explorations with Special Reference to East Africa*, Berlin and New York: Mouton de Gruyter.

Calvet, L.-J. (2006) *Towards an Ecology of World Languages*, Cambridge: Polity.

Castells, M. (1997) *The Information Age: Economy, Society and Culture, Volume 2: The Power of Identity*, Oxford: Blackwell Publishers.

Clark, M. K. and Koster, M. M. (2014) *Hip Hop and Social Change in Africa: Ni Wakati*, London: Lexington Books.

Comrie, B., Haspelmeth, M. and Bickel, B. (2015) *The Leipzig Glossing Rules*, Department of Linguistics of the Max Planck Institute for Evolutionary Anthropology and Department of Linguistics of the University of Leipzig (https://www.eva.mpg.de/lingua/pdf/Glossing-Rules.pdf) (accessed: 2 January 2021).

Crystal, D. (2000) *Language Death*, Cambridge: Cambridge University Press.

Dixon, R. M. (1997) *The Rise and Fall of Languages*, Cambridge: Cambridge University Press.

Eberhard, D. M., Simons, G. F. and Fennig, C. D. (eds) (2019) *Ethnologue: Languages of the World*, 22nd edition, Dallas: SIL International (http://www.ethnologue.com) (accessed: 2 January 2021).

Ferrari, A. (2004) 'Le Sheng: Expansion et vernacularization d'une variété urbaine hybride à Nairobi', in A. Akinlabi and O. Adesola (eds) *Proceedings of 4th World Congress of African Linguistics*, Cologne: Rüdiger Köppe, pp. 479–495.

García, O. and Wei, L. (2014) *Translanguaging: Language, Bilingualism and*

Education, London: Palgrave Macmillan.

Githiora, C. (2018) *Sheng: Rise of a Kenyan Swahili Vernacular*, Suffolk: James Currey.

Halliday, M. A. K. (1978) *Language as Social Semiotic: The Social Interpretation of Language and Meaning*, London: Edward Arnold.

Heine, B. (1979) 'Some linguistic characteristics of African-based pidgins', in I. F. Hancock (ed.) *Readings in Creole Studies*, Ghent: E-Story Scientia, pp. 89–98.

Hyman, L. M. (2003) 'Segmental phonology', in D. Nurse and G. Philippson (eds) *The Bantu Languages*, London: Routledge. pp. 42–58.

Illich, I. (1973) *Tools for Conviviality*, New York: Harper and Low.

Kamwangamalu, N. M. (2013) 'English in language policies and ideologies in Africa: Challenges and prospects for vernacularization', in R. Bayley, R. Cameron and C. Lucas (eds) *The Oxford Handbook of Sociolinguistics*, Oxford: Oxford University Press, pp. 545–562.

Kiessling, R. and Mous, M. (2004) 'Urban youth languages in Africa', *Anthropological Linguistics*, Vol. 46, No. 3, pp. 303–341.

Kioko, E. M. (2015) 'Regional varieties and "ethnic" registers of Sheng', in N. Nassenstein and A. Hollington (eds) *Youth Language Practices in Africa and Beyond*, Berlin: De Gruyter Mouton, pp. 119–148.

Kraus, P. A. and Grin, F. (2018) *The Politics of Multilingualism: Europeanisation, Globalisation and Linguistic Governance*, Amsterdam: John Benjamins.

Krauss, M. E. (1992) 'The World's languages in crisis', *Language*, Vol. 68, No. 1, pp. 4–10.

Labov, W. (1970) 'The study of language in its social context', *Studium Generale*, Vol. 23, pp. 30–87.

Lüpke, F. (2016) 'Uncovering small-scale multilingualism', *Critical Multilingual Studies*, Vol. 4, No. 2, pp. 35–74.

Macaulay, R. (2001) 'Vernacular', in R. Mesthrie and R. E. Asher (eds) *Concise Encyclopedia of Sociolinguistics*, Amsterdam and New York: Elsevier, pp. 420–422.

Manessy, G. (1994) *Le français en Afrique noire*, Paris: L'Harmattan.

Mansour, G. (1993) *Multilingualism and Nation Building*, Clevedon and

Philadelphia: Multilingual Matters.

Mazrui, A. A. and Mazrui, A. M. (1985) *Swahili, State and Society: The Political Economy of an African Language*, Nairobi: East African Educational Publishers.

Mbaabu, I. and Nzuga, K. (2003) *Sheng-English Dictionary: Deciphering East Africa's Underworld Language*, Dar es Salaam: TUKI.

Milroy, J. (2007) 'The ideology of the standard language', in C. Llamas, L. Mullany and Stockwell, P. (eds) *The Routledge Companion to Sociolinguistics*, London: Routledge, pp. 133–139.

Milroy, J. and Milroy, L. (1997) *Authority in Language: Investigating Standard English* (third edition), London: Routledge.

Momanyi, C. (2009) 'The effects of "Sheng" in the teaching of Kiswahili in Kenyan schools', *The Journal of Pan African Studies*, Vol. 2, No. 8, pp. 127–138.

Moseley, C. (ed.) (2010) *Atlas of the World's Languages in Danger, 3rd edition*, Paris: UNESCO Publishing.

Mufwene, S. S. (2017) 'Language vitality: The weak theoretical underpinnings of what can be an exciting research area', *Language*, Vol. 93, No. 4, e202–e223 (https://doi.org/10.1353/lan.2017.0065) (accessed: 2 January 2021).

Muraya, O. (2015) 'Half tribe: Full Luo, full Kikuyu', in B. Kahora (ed.) *Kwani? Vol. 08*, Nairobi: Kwani Trust, pp. 283–293.

Myers-Scotton, C. (1979) 'Nairobi and Kampala varieties of Swahili', in I. F. Hancock (ed.) *Readings in Creole Studies*, Ghent: E-Story Scientia, pp. 111–128.

Nakao, S. 2018. 'Dynamics of Arabic in Northeastern Africa: Convivial multilingualism', *The 9th "African Potentials" Project Meeting*, Kyoto University, Kyoto, 16 June 2018 (in Japanese).

Nassenstein, N. (2015) *Kisangani Swahili: Choices and Variation in a Multilingual Urban Space*, Munich: LINCOM.

Nassenstein, N. and Bose, P. B. (2016) *Kivu Swahili Texts and Grammar Notes*, Munchen: Lincom.

Nassenstein, N. and Hollington, A. (eds) (2015) *Youth Language Practices in Africa and Beyond*, Berlin: Mouton de Gruyter.

Nyamnjoh, F. B. 2017. 'Incompleteness: Frontier Africa and the currency of conviviality', *Journal of Asian and African Studies*, Vol.

52, Issue 3, pp. 253–270 (https://doi.org/10.1177%2F0021909615580867) (accessed: 2 January 2021).

Peck, R. R. (2018) 'Love, struggle, and compromises: The political seriousness of Nairobi underground hip hop', *African Studies Review*, Vol. 61, Issue 2, pp. 111–133 (https://doi.org/10.1017/asr.2017.143) (accessed: 2 January 2021).

Romaine, S. (2002) 'The impact of language policy on endangered languages', *International Journal on Multicultural Societies*, Vol. 4, No. 2, pp. 194–212.

Rüsch, M. (2016) 'It's all the same!? A comparison of two Luo-based youth languages', *22 Afrikanistentag*, Humboldt-Universität zu Berlin, Berlin, 17–18 June 2016.

Shinagawa, D. (2007) "Notes on the morphosyntactic bias of verbal constituents in Sheng texts', *Journal of Hermeneutic Study and Education of Textual Configuration (HERSETEC)*, Vol. 1, No. 1, pp. 153–171.

―――― (2012) 'Multilingual situations in Kenya after implementation of the 2010 constitution', in Y. Sunano (ed.) Rethinking multiligualism, Tokyo: Sangensya, pp. 530–563 (in Japanese).

―――― (2019) 'The syntactic distribution of relativizers and the development of *-enye* relative constructions in Sheng', *Swahili Forum*, Vol. 26, pp. 122–141.

Skutnabb-Kangas, T. (2002) 'Why should linguistic diversity be maintained and supported in Europe? Some arguments', in *Guide for the Development of Language Education Policies in Europe: From Linguistic Diversity to Plurilingual Education, Reference Study*, Strasbourg: Language Policy Division, Council of Europe (www.coe.int/T/E/Cultural_Co-operation/education/Languages/Language_Policy/Policy_development_activities/Studies/Skutnabb-KangasEN.pdf.) (accessed: 7 January 2021).

Spyropoulos, M. (1987) 'Sheng: Some preliminary investigation into a recently emerged Nairobi street language', *Journal of the Anthropological Society of Oxford*, Vol. 18, Issue 2, pp. 125–136.

UNESCO's website on 'Languages and Multilingualism'

(http://www.unesco.org/new/en/culture/themes/cultural-diversity/languages-and-multilingualism/) (accessed: 20 June 2020).

UN General Assembly (2007) Resolution adopted by the General Assembly on 16 May 2007 (Sixty-first session, Agenda item 114. A/RES/61/266)
(https://digitallibrary.un.org/record/601542?ln=en) (accessed: 7 January 2021).

Wainaina, B. (2003) 'Kalamashaka: Interview by Binyavanga Wainaina', in B. Wainaina (ed.) *Kwani? 01*, Nairobi: Kwani Trust, pp. 53–59.

Whiteley, W. H. (ed.) (2017 [1971]) *Linguistic Surveys of Africa: Language Use and Social Change: Problems of Multilingualism with Special Reference to Eastern Africa*, Oxon: Routledge.

Zsiga, E. C., Boyer, O. T. and Kramer, R. (2014) *Languages in Africa: Multilingualism, Language Policy, and Education*, Washington DC: George University Press.

Chapter 5

Flexibility and the Potential of 'African Multilingualism': A Case of Language Practice in Tanzania

Sayaka Kutsukake

1. Introduction

In Africa,[1] the multilingual situation exists as a 'norm' (Kamwangamalu 2016; Lüpke and Storch 2013; Sunano 2007; Wolff 2016; among others), and the notion of 'language' contrasts with that of European monolingual ideologies[2] (see Lüpke and Storch 2013). Some languages, such as English and French, are mainly linked to the development of modern European nation-states. They, as *national languages*, have commonly played the role of a facilitator of both unity and identity, as well as that of discontinuity and division within the modern nation-state (Blommaert and Vershueren 1998: 202). In this context, the notion that children grow up with one language is perpetuated and this language, which is the national language as well as the *mother tongue*, has been viewed as an essential part of individual personality and both social and cultural identity (Wolff 2016: 189). The strong emotional attachment of individuals to languages corresponds to the assumption that language is representative of the main identity maker through which individuals assign themselves to specific ethnicities.

Notably, however, 'one of the strangest ideas to come out of colonial linguistics was the "mother tongue" as the language of one's own ethnic group' (Lüpke and Storch 2013: 349) in the African context. This idea almost completely negated the richness of linguistic variation and language use regardless of administered ethnocentrism. Additionally, it created an image of speakers as mere recipients of a tradition, namely of one ethnic language that is passed on from mother to child, within the boundaries of the 'tribal' space (Lüpke and Storch 2013: 349). In this context, losing one's language was equivalent to losing a fundamental and essential tool to represent oneself.

However, in Africa, multilingualism – the use of several languages in a given group or community – has been the norm, and essentially, monolingual individuals are far from the norm. As Lüpke and Storch (2013) clarified, in Africa, multilingualism is fostered through several social factors, such as exogamy, child-fostering, economic interdependencies and mobility. It is obvious that the notion of language formed in such a context contrasts with that of European monolingual ideologies.

Nevertheless, many sociolinguistic studies on Africa (e.g., Altmayer and Wolff (eds) 2013; Kamwangamalu 2010; Wolff 2016) have not been successful in abandoning the conventional way of studying languages, as their main goal is to promote 'the status of African languages'. Therefore, their pluralistic view of multilingualism articulated through the 'language as a resource' view allows for the persistence of a particular 'Eurocentric mind-set in Western perceptions that moulds pervasive language ideologies' (Wolff 2016: 1). Although, as Wolff insists, people in Africa 'enjoy their vital inherited ethnolinguistic and cultural plurality as an enriching experience and make use of multilingualism as a resourceful tool for social and economic interaction' (Wolff 2016: 3), this restricted view means that descriptions of the African language situation continue to be incomprehensively complex.

Opinions that consider identity as a closed and stable set of inherited features, disregarding the possibility of change and transformation, have been widely criticised. Therefore, in recent studies in sociolinguistics, a more dynamic and fluid view of identity has come to be considered. More importantly, this view sees the process of using language to understand what human beings do *with* language and how they cross language boundaries to make sense of their socio-cultural worlds. The new paradigm emerged with different labels such as *translanguaging* (García and Li 2014), *translingual* (Canagarajah 2013), *transglossic practices* (Sultana et al. 2015), and *metrolingualism* (Pennycook and Otsuji 2015). These developing studies investigated certain situations in Africa, especially those in urban spaces or educational contexts, with a plurality of approaches that placed translanguaging[3] within an interdisciplinary framework.[4] However, these studies did not provide sufficient clarity as to the African context. Instead, they represented cases from Africa as random examples of translanguaging. On the other hand, an increasing number of critical studies on languages in Africa have recently appeared, revealing and clarifying the ecological situation of African languages and their multilingual norms, as well as challenging the problems of metadiscursive regimes to describe language in the European context (Juffermans 2015; Lüpke and Storch 2013; Kutsukake 2019; Makoni and Mashiri 2007; Mc Laughlin 2008; Sunano 2007; Yoneda 2012a, 2012b; among others). Although these studies share similar attitudes of challenging the conventionally constructed view of 'language', in line with developing theories in sociolinguistics, they have not been sufficiently integrated into these theories yet.

The language question in Africa can, thus, be read from a different perspective using translanguaging theory, and the theory itself can be enriched and developed from African perspectives. To provide evidence for validating this point, this study offers a specific example of actual language practice in rural areas of Tanzania, based on fieldwork conducted by the author from 2015 to 2016. The findings of this study complement those of previous studies dealing with languaging in Africa, thus demonstrating the possibility of integrating these findings, collectively, with theories of translanguaging. This study also aims to make a clear distinction between the African view of language and the one in the European context. The purpose is to draw on the notion of translanguaging in the context of multilingualism in Africa to examine and reveal ways in which people in Africa recruit and mobilise a range of resources from their linguistic repertoires in a flexible and convivial manner (Nyamnjoh 2017).

2. Conceptual Framework: Translanguaging and the African Multilingual Norm

2-1. Translanguaging

The term translanguaging comes from the Welsh *trawsieithu* (translated into English by Baker 2001) and was used to refer to a pedagogical practice; therefore, the term came to be used exclusively in educationists' studies earlier. However, it was later adapted to the sociolinguistic study, the concept of translanguaging encouraging theorising that goes beyond language. Recently, it has been developed as a specific theory of language, proposing an integrated approach to the understanding of language, multilingualism and multilingual practices in the context of the unprecedented mobility of this century (Li 2017: 18). According to García and Li (2014), translanguaging refers to the assumption that a linguistic repertoire can never be split into just one language or another. Consequently, bilingual or multilingual speakers select meaning-making features and freely combine them to reach the full potential of meaning making, cognitive engagement, creativity and criticality (García and Li 2014: 42). To examine the strategies that multilingual speakers use to switch between languages in interactions, 'code-switching' is a more established and widely known theory. However, it is language-oriented theory that highlights languages as discrete codes or systems and describes the speaker's movement between them (Baynham and Lee 2019: 25). Conversely, the essential foreground of translanguaging theory is the speaker being user-oriented and having a boundary-crossing dimension as seen in *multilingualism from below* (Pennycook and Otsuji 2015).[5]

The separation of language could only be practised with labelling, which is the ideological act of demarcating certain codes in relation to certain identities and interests (Canagarajah 2013: 6).[6] Therefore, the disinvention of 'language' was needed (see Makoni and Pennycook 2007). To rethink language not as *a thing* but as a dynamic activity, it was necessary to be creative and shift the focus from 'language' to 'languaging' (Baynham and Lee 2019: 15). This shift in terminology from noun to verb challenged the idea that language, as a system, exists independent of its speakers and their social lives

(Makoe 2018: 16). Thus, there has been a greater focus on the practices of language users because of the adoption of the term 'languaging', which deconstructs 'language' to detach it from ideologies, such as monolingualism and nationhood.

Another essential part of translanguaging is that the theory is not intended to 'protect individual languages'. As Li (2016, 2017) stated, in the post-multilingual era of challenges, simply having many different languages is no longer sufficient either for the individual or society. However, it is necessary to have a more complex interweaving of language, where boundaries between languages and the relationship between language and the nation-state are constantly being reassessed, broken or adjusted by speakers on the ground. In this sense, as translanguaging refers to the act of languaging beyond languages as systems, it is finally possible for us to see how people use 'language' beyond the norms of established European nation-state formations.

2-2. Language and the African Multilingual Norm

It is said that the African continent is home to approximately one-third of the world's living languages, numbering around 2,000 (Lewis et al. (eds) 2015; Wolff 2016). Many linguists are aware of the problems associated with defining languages and counting them. However, they often feel that they need to quote these numbers because of the dominant ideology that perceives languages in these terms. This study also shares a similar perspective as the multilingual situation in Africa is obvious. However, notably, African linguistic diversity in terms of enumerability is a way of constructing separate languages whose boundaries may not necessarily have any social or functional reality (Makoni and Mashiri 2007: 70). Although it is not necessary to eliminate the use of the term 'language/languages', as it is considerably omnipresent, it is crucial to pay attention to the use of the term by questioning the value attached to it.[7]

As previous studies have pointed out, 'language' is *created* by linguists and missionaries (Lüpke and Storch 2013: 3) or *invented*, particularly as part of Christian/colonial and nationalistic projects (Makoni and Pennycook 2007: 1) through documentation and *comes into existence* by being a 'named language' (see also Blommaert and

Rampton 2011; Yoneda 2012b). The metadiscursive regimes that have emerged to describe languages are part of a process that perpetuates the epistemic violence visited on the speakers of those languages as they came into existence (Makoni and Pennycook 2007: 21). However, in the African context, there is no clear notion of 'language' possessing a discrete identity (Lüpke and Storch 2013: 3). Speakers of many African languages often do not 'own' or 'have' a specific first language but rather control several linguistic varieties that they use as resources and means of defining the Self and the Other. In this way, they create as well as bridge boundaries (Lüpke and Storch 2013: 210). In conventional sociolinguistics, language contacts have been regarded as a factor causing competition between languages owing to language ideology, as speakers are often expected to own and attach themselves to one language. However, this is not the case in the African context and language contacts do not signify an evolution towards monolingualism. This is because multilingualism does not routinely conceptualise language in the plural but instead treats language as a verb, emphasising fluidity and creativity as well as the local resources and conditions for language practice (Juffermans 2015: 2). In community-oriented societies like Africa, multilingualism is a part of social practices in general but also, and more specifically, part of a set of cultural techniques (Lüpke and Storch 2013: 77).

2-3. Problems in Making the African Multilingual Norm a 'Problem'

Earlier studies have observed that language diversity is accused of causing delays in political and economic development (cf. Fishman 1966; Fishman et al. (eds) 1968; Pool 1972; Webb and Kembo-Sure 2000, among others), as '[s]ocial divisions and potential for conflict are often fuelled by language as a symbol of socio-cultural identity' (Webb and Kembo-Sure 2000: 11). The tremendous ethnolinguistic fragmentation in Africa has also been used to justify poor growth and lack of stability because the multilingual situation could present an obstacle to agreements concerning public goods (Easterly and Levine 1997; Keefer and Knack 2002). European-style nationalism based on the construction of one monolithic, overarching identity, which is grounded in the use of a shared language, is the only option needed to manage coexistence in the shared space of a nation-state. Owing to the significant influence of the European experience on our general understanding of the formation of the nation-state, there has been an expectation that African states will be rationalised in the same manner, specifically through education and by the establishment and penetration of a national language.

The 1992 publication entitled *Linguistic Imperialism* by Robert Phillipson made *the language question* in Africa (Djité 2008; Mazrui 1997; Kamwangamalu 2016) a burning issue. At the heart of the debate was the problem of defining the role of African languages in juxtaposition with ex-colonial languages, especially in the educational system (Kamwangamalu 2016: 2). Most studies have insisted that the languages inherited by colonial masters, such as the French, English and Portuguese, should be replaced by African languages to achieve 'decolonisation of the mind' (wa Thiong'o 1986). Additionally, since the 1990s, *multilingualism as value* was brought from Europe into Africa and affected its language policies (see Figueira 2013; Sunano 2007; Yoneda 2012a; among others). Subsequently, various policies aiming at promoting ethnic languages were proposed and implemented. However, the result was, as Kamwangamalu (2010) regretted, that 'they [we]re not matched with practical steps to use indigenous languages in education or to make them economically or politically useful to their users' (Kamwangamalu 2010: 4).

The lack of success of language planning policies in Africa is, as Makoni and Mashiri (2007) pointed out, 'not due to unwillingness or inability on the part of African governments to implement language policies but is due to a theoretical tendency to treat African languages as if they were real objects' (Makoni and Mashiri 2007: 63). Furthermore, as Li (2017) clarified, there has prevailed the uncritical view of sociolinguistic communities about 'multilingualism' being concerned with the protection of individual languages. As language and socio-cultural identity are thought to be intrinsically linked, maintaining one's language means maintaining one's identity (Li 2017: 18). Concerns regarding uncompromising *linguistic rights* (see Skutnabb-Kangas and Phillipson (eds) 1994) could be most relevant to the European context, where the strong emotional attachment of individuals to specific languages corresponds to the assumption that language represents the main identity-maker in terms of belonging to specific ethnicities or nations. The problem lay in this notion being applied to other societies in the world, including Africa, thus resulting in the controversial issue of the 'language situation in Africa', wherein there is an enormous diversity of languages to protect. The point is, as Li stated, conservationist discourses surrounding endangered languages do not typically pay any attention to the actual use of language in everyday life (Li 2017: 6). Thus, how people in Africa use language as part of their norm has been ignored and not given any consideration during discussions of their linguistic rights.

In an edition of the *Language Death*, Brenzinger and Dimmendaal (1992) dealt with situations of language endangerment in eastern Africa and stated that all instances of language death are the result of language shift (Brenzinger and Dimmendaal 1992: 3). Here, presumably, the dominant metaphors of language shift were applicable to Africa, although these metaphors were generated in situations outside of Africa. However, in Africa, many languages survive, although 'killer languages' (Batibo 2005) can penetrate a community. Moreover, in many cases, speakers acquire new languages without losing their respective ethnic languages (Lüpke and Storch 2013; McLaughlin 2008). It is obvious that the dominant metaphor of language shift is questionable in the African context as well. Therefore, without strategies to deconstruct the notion of language and the metadiscursive regimes of European thought to describe language, most discussions regarding multilingualism reproduce the same concept of language that underpins all mainstream linguistic thought. Consequently, multilingualism has come to mean, merely, a pluralisation of monolingualism. As Lüpke and Storch stated, it is ironic that multilingualism, coupled with the endangerment discourse, contributes to its ongoing disempowerment by not considering the distinct ecological situations of African languages (Lüpke and Storch 2013: 273–274).

The language situation in Africa has been described with immense confusion because of the pluralistic view of 'multilingualism as a value'. Recently, many studies have criticised the theoretical constructs regarding languages that have been brought into Africa, such as applied linguistics and sociolinguistics, and also the conflictual, essentialist model of multilingualism adopted by many advocates of endangered languages within and outside of academia (Kamei 2004; Kutsukake 2019; Li 2016, 2017; Makoni and Meinhof 2004; Smakman and Heinrich (eds) 2015; Sunano (ed.) 2012). However, the notion of language constructed in a formal European sense is still easily exported to Africa through various metaphors and results in dramatic misconceptions of the language situation in Africa. Therefore, we still need sociolinguistic research that will allow us to arrive at a differentiated analysis. It is in this context that translanguaging theory is expected to be at the forefront of putting 'multilingualism from below' into theorisations of multilingualism, enabling us to see how people fare in Africa. Therefore, in the following sections, this study investigates language practice in Tanzania through a translanguaging lens.[8]

3. Method

3-1. Context

In Tanzania, the language situation has been widely covered in discussions regarding language policy, especially in the post-colonial context. The country has often been considered to have 'succeeded' in its language policy, rooted in the declaration of Swahili as its national and official language, although there are approximately 120 languages spoken in the country. This situation is indeed quite rare for sub-Saharan African countries. The emphasis on Swahili was firmly supported by administrative measures in the context of language nationalism and the spread of primary education in the 1970s. Swahili even spread to rural areas traditionally dominated by local ethnic languages (Heine 1976; Polomé 1980). Tanzania is a country experienced in the process of constructing a certain public space with one language – Swahili – thus creating the opportunity to share its notion of language with that of the European context, at least to some extent.[9]

The language of instruction in schools has also been a major issue in Tanzania. For example, many studies have insisted that the language of instruction in secondary schools ought to be Swahili to enable students to achieve higher grades (see Brock-Utne 2007; Rubagumya 1991). However, these arguments have ignored the fact that it is the Tanzanian people themselves who have a strong desire for the use of English in education. Moreover, a new trend has recently emerged among some researchers expressing concern about the negative effect of Swahili in the initial years of education. This concern is based on the assumption that Swahili is not the students' 'mother tongue', and ethnic languages are therefore better understood (Roberts 2015; Rubagumya et al. 2011; Wedin 2010; among others). This new trend is drawing attention from the essentialist model of multilingualism. This concern, then, for the most suitable language to be the medium of instruction in schools in Tanzania, results in treating its people as passive subjects who are not subjective and are, instead, oppressed by colonial and neo-colonial legacies, without the option of resistance. This misconception occurs because the chief arguments around it are fundamentally based on the notion of an exclusive language, in a similar fashion to those of modern European nation-states. In making such alignments, the notion of language in Africa has not been translated into practical and beneficial outcomes.

The penetration of Swahili into rural areas and its influence on the ethnic languages spoken in those areas have also been burning issues in language studies in Tanzania. Research conducted from the 1980s onwards points to an apparent language 'shift' from ethnic languages to Swahili (Batibo 1992; Mekacha 1993; Yoneda 1996; among others). However, more recent studies have revealed that language shift in local communities has not occurred and is not occurring in the way that had been expected (Kutsukake and Yoneda 2019; Marten and Petzell 2016; Yoneda 2010; among others).

3-2. Data Collection

This study is based on research conducted from 2015 to 2016, pertaining to the recognition of language use and practices of the Njombe region in the southern part of Tanzania[10] where the Bena and Kinga languages, both Bantu languages, are widely spoken. According to Muzale and Rugemalira (2008: 79), Bena was found to be the language of the 13th largest and Kinga to be that of the 38th largest ethnic community in Tanzania, respectively. Several studies on the Bena language exist. For example, Morrison (2011) has written a reference grammar of Bena, and Bernander (2012) has pointed out the significant influence of Swahili on the language. On the other hand, the Kinga language has not been as extensively studied compared to Bena, and no significant research paper or study on the language could be found. The fieldwork was conducted in a village called Matiganjola in Njombe district, where Bena is the most influential ethnic language, and the Iwawa ward in Makete district, where Kinga is the most influential ethnic language. People in these communities consider themselves using their ethnic languages significantly. Most of the residents in the village in Njombe district make a living from agriculture, while most in the Iwawa ward are involved in a larger variety of occupations as it is located at the centre of Makete district.[11] In both areas, most residents believe in Christianity, especially in Protestantism, and many of them said that they had concluded their academic learning while in primary school. However, the younger generation has recently been, more often than not, continuing education up to secondary education.[12] Using snowball sampling, 60 subjects in Matiganjola and 62 in the Iwawa ward were interviewed. Four persons self-identified as belonging to other ethnicities than Bena in Matiganjola and nine other than Kinga in the Iwawa ward. Questions were designed to investigate their language use recognition and linguistic awareness of the language used. Further, 15 out of 60 subjects in Matiganjola and 9 out of 62 in the Iwawa ward, who identified as speakers of Bena and Kinga, respectively, were also asked to participate in an extra interview regarding their attitude to language. The author conducted the research in Swahili and was accompanied by a local facilitator in each area to help when interviewees felt more comfortable answering the questions in their ethnic languages. As part of the survey, participants were asked to list the languages they could speak in a given context, such as at home, at their work places and in markets, or when talking to people from a certain age group, such as children or the elderly.[13]

Simultaneously, this study is based on a collection of recorded conversations. Six monologues and three conversations in Matiganjola and five monologues and one conversation in the Iwawa ward were recorded and videographed. The participants were aged between 20 and 70 years.

3-3. Data and Analysis

3-3-1. Recognition on Language Use

Many people indicated that the use of their ethnic languages is declining because they were more likely to use Swahili in many situations. They explained that social change and high mobility enhanced the use of Swahili in their communities. There was a 54-year-old woman in Matiganjola village who claimed that she used to speak only Bena when talking to friends in the same age bracket, but she had begun using Swahili with them recently. In Matiganjola village, people identified themselves as speakers of an average of 2.38 languages,[14] and 45 of them said that they speak Swahili and Bena, and the others added a few more languages to their repertoire. Simultaneously, in the Iwawa ward, people identified themselves as speakers of an average of 2.60 languages; 35 of them said that they speak Swahili and Kinga, and the others, especially those who self-identified as belonging to an ethnic group other than Kinga, added 1 to 4 languages to their repertoire. In this study, only one 70-year-old woman in the Iwawa ward, who had no educational background, identified herself as a monolingual speaker of Kinga.

'Using only Swahili' is the most frequent answer when talking to preschool children and young people (32 and 33 out of 60 respectively in Matiganjola and 40 and 36 in the Iwawa ward). However, there are still some people who answered they use 'only Bena/Kinga' (4 and 6, respectively, in Matiganjola and 11 and 6, respectively, in the Iwawa ward). Using 'Bena/Kinga and Swahili' was the answer given by 24 and 20 people, respectively, in Matiganjola and 11 and 20, respectively, in the Iwawa ward. In rural Tanzania, there is seldom the need to use English in everyday life. However, a man in his 60s from Matiganjola village said he uses English occasionally.

Although people claimed that they were using different languages in the same community, this analysis of language use can be more understandable from the perspective of translanguaging, wherein people are languaging in their language repertoire rather than using languages as distinct systems. Perhaps younger generations have a larger repertoire in Swahili and the same applies to the elders with respect to Bena/Kinga. Despite their differences, language use is flexible enough to bridge the gap between generations and enable communication in the community as a whole.

3-3-2. Language Attitudes

Language attitudes were, on the whole, very similar in both areas, though some people in Iwawa ward were comparatively more aggressive when talking about the value of the Kinga language and the necessity to protect it.[15] In the interviews, all participants indicated a positive attitude towards Swahili and they all suggested that it is good that Swahili had spread to all parts of Tanzania. Simultaneously, English was considered a crucial language, especially in education.[16] Almost all participants responded negatively to the idea of using ethnic languages in school. They indicated that the use of an ethnic language for 'mother tongue education' could not make education better because, for most children, ethnic languages were no longer the most familiar language. Furthermore, many people were nervous about the attribution of official status to ethnic languages for various reasons, such as the fear that it could lead to ethnic conflicts, isolation and division in communities. However, people felt that the Bena and Kinga languages were also important to them. Moreover, many of them believed that the extinction of an ethnic language is an impossibility. They described the important role of ethnic languages in communicating with the older generation and the fact that they are an intrinsic part of tradition and culture. Most of them believed that their children would somehow acquire Bena/Kinga in the future, and some of them voiced their plans to teach the languages to their children, although not immediately.

Mostly, participants showed a positive attitude towards all languages, but they could also be negative about each language in specific contexts. This was because of the function of each language in a given community. Although they were more likely to show a positive attitude towards Swahili and English, they naturally believed that their ethnic language could be maintained because a language needs to preserve its functions in the community as a medium of paying respects to elders. As languages already have labels, people in

Africa are not completely free from seeing themselves through the lenses assigned to the languages in which they converse. However, their acceptance of the use of certain language names in their discourses did not necessarily signify that there was a competition between the languages to be exclusively engaged. It is obvious that they have a notion of language that is different from the one associated with the monolingual ideology, as they are not choosing one language over another but demonstrating their adaptability towards any other language to strengthen their potential.

3-3-3. Actual Language Practice

Example 1 is a part of a conversation between two young women in Matiganjola village who are in their 20s. The author asked them which language they were conversing in, and they answered that it was Bena.

Example 1 (*Italic* = Bena, <u>Underline</u> = Swahili, <u>**Underline+Bold**</u> = Swahili word with Bena prosody)
[1] A: *Yuve, muyáángu* <u>doto</u>, *i-*<u>píndi</u> *shíla Waa-ndi-wonelága ndému* <u>yako</u>. <u>Kwa</u> <u>víle</u>
ndáá-li ndí-li hela <u>ngufu</u>, **<u>nñini</u>**?
[You, my friend, my younger sister, nowadays you look down on me. Is it because I am powerless or what?]
[2] B: <u>Nawe</u> *wa-li* **<u>mkolóòfi</u>** *mbona*? *Wa-li* <u>mtundu</u> <u>mno</u>.
[You, why are you rude? You are so rude.]
[3] A: *Ka, ka.* <u>Mbona</u> *sindaa-li* <u>mtundu</u> *ha-m-na.* **<u>Kátika</u>** <u>ni-fanye</u> *ishí u-hu-ni-tova u-ndi-gíte déna hu-nyíle, kaa.*
[Oh-oh, I am not rude, I am not. After making me do this to fight against me, you run away.]

Although 'Bena language' spoken here has a generous sprinkling of Swahili words, speakers still consider themselves to be speaking their ethnic language, which they distinguish from 'Swahili'. From the translanguaging perspective, Bena is maintained as one of the most important language repertoires.

On the other hand, Example 2 is a part of a conversation between two young women in the Iwawa ward who are in their 20s. The author asked them which language they were conversing in, and they answered that it was Swahili.

Example 2 (*Italic* = Kinga, <u>Underline</u> = Swahili, **<u>Underline+Bold</u>** = Swahili word with Kinga prosody)
[1] C: … <u>Zaidi</u> <u>zaidi</u> <u>tena</u> *ndilikulyasa une* <u>tena</u> *kwitiyo.* <u>Maana kipindi kile</u> siku nyingine mtu akabomowa akabeba <u>Shilingi</u> 60,000 <u>akafanyiwa kule</u>… <u>nani</u>… **<u>kumwambo</u>** *uku ku* Veta *uku* …
[Moreover, I was also stealing. I mean, the other day s/he was beaten when s/he was bringing 60,000 TZS at the… I mean … that side of village …]
[2] D: *Lino uwe twi tuli na* <u>máisha</u> **<u>mákuumu</u>** <u>kabisa</u>!
[Now, we have a very difficult life!]
[3] C: <u>Ndio</u> <u>maana</u> <u>nakwambia</u> <u>sasa</u>! …
[Yes, that is what I am telling you! …]

As already mentioned, languages such as Bena, Kinga and Swahili have had labels for a long time; therefore, people talk about the world through convenient lenses. However, the gap between the description of these languages and the reality shows us that their language use is not restricted to the boundary defined by those labels.

The following examples, 3 and 4, are monologues recorded in Matiganjola village explaining how to cook ugali, a staple food usually made with corn flour. The participants were asked to try to speak in the Bena language.

Example 3 is an explanation by a woman in her 60s.

Example 3 (*Italic* = Bena, <u>Underline</u> = Swahili, **<u>Underline+Bold</u>** = Swahili word with Bena prosody)
'Ndi-kaláv' lúleenga, ndi-fyaagili luváánza, ndi-fyagili <u>nyumba</u>. <u>Ndi-chemsh</u>' *lúleenga, ndi-*<u>teng</u>' *i-*<u>sufulia</u>, *ndi-*<u>**dzemha**</u> *ndi-teleh' ndi-sang'* <u>ugali</u>, <u>na-chukua</u> <u>maji</u>. **<u>Na-nááwa</u>** <u>na-kula</u>'.
[I fetch water, and I sweep first, I sweep the house. I boil water, I put a pan, I boil and stir Ugali, and I take water. I wash (my hands) and eat.]

Although this woman was in her 60s and expected to have more of her repertoire in Bena, she ended up giving her explanation mostly in Swahili. Subsequently, another woman in her 70s, who watched the recording, came to the author and explained that the speaker in Example 3 was nervous about being recorded by the author, who is a foreigner, so she consequently mixed up the two languages. The woman then said she would like to be recorded saying she would do 'much better' than the speaker in Example 3. The following is a part of her conversation.

Example 4 (*Italic* = Bena, <u>Underline</u> = Swahili, **<u>Underline+Bold</u>** = Swahili word with Bena prosody)
'<u>Yaani</u> *li-li lya hu-lamúha, unééne pe ndí-vesa ndi-láámha, ndi-fyáágili* <u>nyumba</u>, *ndi-kodz' móóto, ndi-púfy' lúleenga lwa hu-púguha míího.* ... <u>Halafu</u> <u>tena</u> *háángi ndi-sáánga, ndi-sáánga ndi-kaúla ndi-víha pa-***<u>méésa</u>**.'
[I wake up, and when I wake up, I sweep the house, make a fire, and warm up some water to wash my face. ... Then, I stir again, I stir (and), I dish it up and put the plate on the table.]

Although this woman was arguably much better prepared to speak more exclusively in Bena, she did include a certain number of Swahili words in her explanation, proving there is no such thing as a 'pure form'. This language practice, which emerged in the 'Bena ethnic community', shows that Swahili has become part of 'their language' repertoire. Although conventional studies have often considered this kind of language use as an 'error' caused by a lack of competence, translanguaging perspectives completely deny such conceptions. Moreover, these examples finally make it possible to understand how people in Africa flexibly form a new type of language use to enable meaning making for the entire community in this changing world.

4. Findings and Discussion: Flexibility and the Potential of 'African Multilingualism'

As we have seen above, the translanguaging theory can be employed to explain language practice in Tanzania. The country has, as described, one of the most 'successful' one-language policies, a result of its nation-state building exercise. However, the reality on the ground shows a different notion of language and linguistic practice. Therefore, the translanguaging theory could be useful to understand various contexts in Africa in terms of explaining how people talk about the world and each other.

It is really inspiring how people in Africa maintain an understanding of their language practice from their perspective and shy away from monolingual orientation, although the notion of language must have been affected by the policy-oriented, top-down approach to multilingualism. As this series of volumes recognises, one of the defining characteristics of 'African Potentials' is heterogeneity and bricolage. The value system in African society is not static and fixed; rather, it is a fluid combination of practices and beliefs conjoined due to the necessities of life. This is also true for the practice of language (cf. Nakao 2018). This remarkable flexibility has come to be seen as a loss of linguistic conventionalism by mainstream sociolinguistics, but this proposition is not true. Rather, it is a strategy that helps manage cultural and linguistic diversity in precarious situations. This study claims that this flexibility and adaptability in languaging can be seen as an agentive social strategy of conviviality in the African people. Conviviality is a recognition of and provision for the fact or reality of being incomplete, and it is maintained by a sense of community affirmation through network-based relationships (Nyamnjoh 2017). If one adopts the view that language ecologies are situated in and agentively maintained by such social strategies, it becomes clear that languages must change continuously to accommodate constantly changing realities (Lüpke and Storch 2013: 339). This is how people in Africa manage their multilingual norm along with their multilingual practice.

On the other hand, the translanguaging framework emerged in the context of the challenges of post-multilingualism (Li 2016, 2017). It contributed to changing the conventional paradigm of language that sees people in Africa exerting convivial agency rather than being held back as passive victims. Multilingualism in Africa was there as a norm even before the theoretical models of 'multilingualism' were introduced to the continent. Thus, it is better to note that 'African Multilingualism' is not only distinguished from the idea of *multilingual* practice that 'typically conceives of the relationship between languages in an additive manner' (Canagarajah 2013: 7). It is also not equal to *translanguaging* as described in the context of the challenges of post-multilingualism. Rather, it would be better to provide examples to add different perspectives to translanguaging theory for it to be more comprehensive. Moreover, translanguaging can be deepened and maximised by being reflected through such flexible and convivial ways of being. This is way of making the most of one's resources for achieving inclusiveness 'with negotiated collective interests through provision for the incompleteness of others as a source of potency' (Nyamnjoh 2017: 262).

Although people in Africa had to recognise the widespread European notion of language, especially due to the colonial language policies that persisted because of colonialism in a postcolonial state, it has not really taken root with them. Rather, speakers can flexibly adopt the concept and thereby become more liberated. What we should learn from them, as Lüpke and Storch also stated, are the following: how they construct knowledge about their own societies and how they do this by sometimes borrowing images that the European formalised view has of them, and by drawing on modes of interpretation available within their societies (Lüpke and Storch 2013: 196).

Translanguaging as a convivial language practice of African Multilingualism tolerates the incompleteness of both the Other and the Self. Knowing the method of languaging to expect in certain places or contexts, thus complementing the social needs and meeting the collective interests of society, helps to keep multilingual repertoires alive and allows the speakers to be tolerant towards and flexible with others. This way of being can, thus, make the boundary defining 'ours' and 'theirs' precarious, thereby allowing speakers to gain more fluidity.

Endnotes

[1] 'Africa' means sub-Saharan Africa in this study. The author of this study is aware that there are also certain countries in Africa that have more

heterogeneous linguistic landscapes. This study indeed lacks concrete data and discussions to claim that even those countries share the same or similar notions of language, which this study shows the 'African notion of language' to be. However, if, as this study concludes, the African notion of language and its flexible multilingual practices are due to the convivial way of being of the people in Africa, it is less evidential to exclude those countries because they seem to have heterogeneous linguistic landscapes. Therefore, this study retains the term 'Africa', awaiting discussions to clarify this point in future research.

[2] Although this study recognises that terms such as 'European' or 'Western' are not necessarily representative of tangible realities, it uses the terms to highlight the contrasts. In this study, the term 'European' is used to represent the specific context of the fact that some historically hegemonic European countries, especially in Western Europe, had experienced in the 18th and 19th century, as part of their state-building and modernisation processes, a corresponding turn towards the one state, one nation, one language norm.

[3] In this study, the term 'translanguaging' is used as an umbrella term for the new paradigm of studies dealing with daily language practices *from below*.

[4] For example, Makoe (2018) reported on an example of a racially desegregated primary school in South Africa, and Mensah (2018) captured communicative repertoires in advertising space in Lesotho in *Translanguaging as Everyday Practice* edited by Gerardo Mazzaferro. Only the works by Makalela used a translanguaging framework to provide a reorientation of multilingual education with regards to the African value system and its multilingual space (Makalela 2015a, 2015b, 2017).

[5] Multilingualism from below is about how people get along with their multiple linguistic resources in their daily lives rather than the local implementation and appropriation of a top-down language policy (Pennycook and Otsuji 2015: 13). It is about the non-hegemonic world of daily language use and does not assume that equality is in any way necessary to recognise multilingualism (Pennycook and Otsuji 2015: 12).

[6] Irvine (2008) noted that linguistic research in Africa, in the precolonial and into the colonial period, was conducted predominantly by missionaries. The persistence of rival orthographies between missionaries, especially rival standardisations of other aspects of language, created some artificial boundaries. Simultaneously, equally artificial boundaries were created by a

standardisation process that grouped quite different varieties together in the interest of efficiency or of political unification (Irvine 2008: 336). See more details in the following section.

[7] There are also discussions on the usage of terms such as 'ethnic language', 'indigenous language', 'minority language', etc. For example, it is argued that the concept of 'indigenous language' has been invented using a post-colonial prism through which pre-colonial Africa is seen (Makoni and Mashiri 2007: 72). This study uses the term 'ethnic language' to conveniently pinpoint specific languages because it is also true that they are known by these labels. However, this study is based on the idea that the imagery of language boundaries does not discretely exist; therefore, the use of the term does not aim to reproduce the fiction.

[8] This study recognises that there are voices critical of the idea of translanguaging. For example, Wolff (2018) warned that translanguaging theory can be insulting for many linguists and sociolinguists and create unnecessary meta-theoretical divides within sociolinguistics. However, this study believes that the translanguaging theory points out the problematic issues contained in ideas such as '(named) language' and tries to deconstruct it rather than to merely discard all the conventional metaphors as Wolff (2018) criticised. Such criticism could be valid as translanguaging as a theory is still developing. Nevertheless, this study supports that bringing African perspectives to the mainstream of the discussion can contribute to the theory as can sound new hypotheses, solid new theory building and/or advances in methodology of research.

[9] For most postcolonial African countries, decisions concerning language during the colonial period were highly influenced by the type of 'language resource' available at the time of independence. In Tanzania, the fact that the Germans institutionally entrenched Swahili, which has now emerged as a strong lingua franca, by using it in schools and the administration, accorded the language prestige and helped it spread further (Smith 1978; Abdulaziz 1980).

[10] The research originally focused on four linguistic communities – Bena, Kinga, Ngoni and Yao – in the southern part of Tanzania. A total of 359 subjects participated in the interviews, and 70 of these subjects participated in an extra interview. Although each linguistic community had certain tendencies, it is difficult to present all the results in this study owing to the space constraint. Therefore, only results from the rural Bena and Kinga

communities have been shown. However, similarities in the participant's notion of language, as demonstrated in the following section, are common to all four languages.

[11] Although it is a district capital, it takes more than five hours from the regional capital of the Njombe region through poor traffic network to get anywhere. Therefore, the Iwawa ward can be considered to be a rural one.

[12] In the Iwawa ward, many elders, especially women, had no academic background to report.

[13] See more details and all the results of the research in Kutsukake (2018).

[14] As Juffermans admonished, '[t]o ask someone how many languages he or she speaks is to presuppose qualities of countability and enumerability on his or her language repertoire' (Juffermans 2015: 1). Although the question in this research was 'please list all languages you can speak' and did not aim to clarify the number, it was still based on the prediction of the enumerability of languages. The author admits that the research contains the ideology that this study is trying to expose. However, some results are valid by virtue of demonstrating that the notion of the language of people in Tanzania is different from what the author had expected.

[15] In 2016, a project to translate the Bible into the Kinga language by the SIL was ongoing following a request from residents; therefore, the discourse on language conservation was probably heated at the time.

[16] An old woman aged 60, who never went to school, in the Iwawa ward, said, 'We want to change ourselves with new languages. Even I, being a very old woman, want to learn English!'

Acknowledgements

This work was financially supported by JSPS KAKENHI Grant Number JP15J02518; JP20J00887; JP16H06318. I wish to thank Nobuko Yoneda, Daisuke Shinagawa, Patrick Heinrich and Nico Nassenstein for their constructive feedback on an earlier version of the manuscript. I extend my sincere gratitude to people of Matiganjola and the Iwawa ward. I take responsibility for any mistakes in this chapter.

References

Abdulaziz, M. H. (1980) 'The ecology of Tanzanian national language policy', in E. C. Polomé and C. P. Hill (eds) *Language in Tanzania*, Oxford: Oxford University Press, pp. 139–175.

Altmayer, C. and Wolff, H. E. (eds) (2013) *Africa: Challenges of Multilingualism*, Frankfurt: Peter Lang.

Baker, C. (2001) *Foundations of Bilingual Education and Bilingualism*, Bristol: Multilingual Matters.

Batibo, H. (1992) 'The fate of ethnic community languages in Tanzania', in M. Brenzinger (ed.) *Language Death: Factual and Theoretical Explorations with Special Reference to East Africa*, Berlin: Mouton de Gruyter, pp. 85–98.

────── (2005) *Language Decline and Death in Africa: Causes, Consequences, and Challenges,* Clevedon: Multilingual Matters.

Baynham, M. and Lee, T. K. (2019) *Translation and Translanguaging*, London: Routledge.

Bernander, R. (2012) 'Contact induced change in Bena (G63) – A study of "swahilization" in a Tanzanian vernacular language', MA (magister) thesis, University of Gothenburg. (https://gupea.ub.gu.se/bitstream/2077/30635/1/gupea_2077_30635_1.pdf) (accessed: 8 January 2021).

Blommaert, J. and Rampton, B. (2011) 'Language and superdiversity', *Diversities*, Vol. 13, No. 2, pp. 1–22.

Blommaert, J. and Vershueren, J. (1998) 'The role of language in European nationalist ideologies', in B. B. Schieffelin, K. A. Woolard and P. V. Kroskrity (eds) *Language Ideologies: Practice and Theory*, Oxford: Oxford University Press, pp. 189–210.

Brenzinger, M. and Dimmendaal, G. J. (1992) 'Social context of language death', in Brenzinger, M. (ed.) *Language Death: Factual and Theoretical Exploration with Special Reference to East Africa*, Berlin: Mouton de Gruyter, pp. 3–5.

Brock-Utne, B. (2007) 'Learning through a familiar language versus learning through a foreign language: A look into some secondary school classrooms in Tanzania', *International Journal of Educational Development*, Vol. 27, No. 5, pp. 487–498.

Canagarajah, S. (2013) *Translingual Practice: Global Englishes and*

Cosmopolitan Relations, New York: Routledge.

Djité, P. G. (2008) *The Sociolinguistics of Development in Africa*, Clevedon: Multilingual Matters.

Easterly, W. and Levine, R. (1997) 'Africa's growth tragedy: Policies and ethnic divisions', *Quarterly Journal of Economics*, Vol. 112, No. 4, pp. 1203–1250.

Figueira, C. (2013) *Languages at War: External Language Spread Policies in Lusophone Africa: Mozambique and Guinea-Bissau at the Turn of the 21st Century*, Frankfurt: Peter Lang GmBH.

Fishman, J. A. (1966) 'Some contrasts between linguistically homogeneous and linguistically heterogeneous polities', *Sociological Inquiry*, Vol. 36, No. 2, pp. 146–158.

Fishman, J. A., Ferguson, C. A. and Gupta, J. D. (eds) (1968) *Language Problems of Developing Nations*, New York: Wiley.

García, O. and Li, W. (2014) *Translanguaging: Language, Bilingualism and Education*, New York: Palgrave MacMillan.

Heine, B. (1976) 'Knowledge and use of second language in Musoma region: A quantitative survey', *Kiswahili*, Vol. 46, No. 1, pp. 49–59.

Irvine, J. T. (2008) 'Subjected words: African linguistics and the colonial encounter', *Language & Communication*, Vol. 28, pp. 323–343.

Juffermans, K. (2015) *Local Languaging, Literacy and Multilingualism in a West African Society*, Clevedon: Multilingual Matters.

Kamei, N. (2004) 'Language and happiness: Three basic requirements for linguistic rights', *Advanced Social Research*, Vol. 1, pp. 131–157 (in Japanese).

Kamwangamalu, N. M. (2010) 'Vernacularization, globalization, and language economics in non-English-speaking countries in Africa', *Language Problems & Language Planning*, Vol. 34, No. 1, pp. 1–23.

―――― (2016) *Language Policy and Economics: The Language Question in Africa*, London: Palgrave Macmillan.

Keefer, P. and Knack, S. (2002) 'Polarization, politics and property rights: Links between inequality and growth', *Public Choice*, Vol. 111, No. 1-2, pp. 127–154.

Kutsukake, S. (2018) 'Reconsideration of the language problem in multilingual Tanzania: From the perspective of the gap between globalisation and multilingualism', PhD thesis, Osaka University (in Japanese).

―――― (2019) 'Impacts of Western perspectives on "multilingualism"', *Journal of Multicultural Innovation*, Vol. 6, pp. 181–200 (in Japanese).

Kutsukake, S. and Yoneda, N. (2019) 'Contact-induced language divergence and convergence in Tanzania: Forming new varieties as language maintenance', *Swahili Forum*, Vol. 26, pp. 181–204.

Lewis, M. P., Simons, G. F. and Fennig, C. D. (eds) (2015) *Ethnologue*, Dallas: SIL International Publications.

Li, W. (2016) 'New Chinglish and the post-multilingualism challenge: Translanguaging EFL in China', *Journal of English as a Lingua Franca*, Vol. 5, No. 1, pp. 1–25.

―――― (2017) 'Translanguaging as a practical theory of language', *Applied Linguistics*, Vol. 39, No. 2, pp. 1–23.

Lüpke, F. and Storch, A. (2013) *Repertoires and Choices in African Languages*, Berlin: Mouton de Gruyter.

Makalela, L. (2015a) 'Moving out of linguistic boxes: The effects of translanguaging for multilingual classrooms', *Language and Education*, Vol. 29, No. 3, pp. 200–217.

―――― (2015b) 'Translanguaging as a vehicle for epistemic access: Cases for reading comprehension and multilingual interactions', *Per Linguam*, Vol. 31, No. 1, pp. 15–29.

―――― (2017) 'Bilingualism in South Africa: Reconnecting with ubuntu translanguaging', in O. García, A. M. Y. Lin and S. May (eds) *Bilingual and Multilingual Education*, Cham: Springer, pp. 297–309.

Makoe, P. (2018) 'Translanguaging in a monoglot context: Children mobilising and (re) positioning their multilingual repertoires as resources for learning', in G. Mazzaferro (ed.) *Translanguaging as Everyday Practice*, Cham: Springer, pp. 13–30.

Makoni, S. and Mashiri, P. (2007) 'Critical historiography: Does language planning in Africa need a construct of language as part of its theoretical apparatus?', in S. Makoni and A. Pennycook (eds) *Disinventing and Reconstituting languages*, Clevedon: Multilingual Matters, pp. 62–89.

Makoni, S. and Meinhof, U. (2004) 'Western perspectives in applied linguistics in Africa', *AILA Review*, Vol. 17, No. 1, pp. 77–104.

Makoni, S. and Pennycook, A. (2007) 'Disinventing and reconstituting languages', in S. Makoni and A. Pennycook (eds) *Disinventing and Reconstituting languages*, Clevedon: Multilingual Matters, pp. 1–41.

Marten, L. and Petzell, M. (2016) 'Linguistic variation and the dynamics of language documentation: Editing in "pure" Kagulu', in M. Seyfeddinipur (ed.) *African Language Documentation: New Data, Methods and Approaches (Special Publication Language Documentation & Conservation 10)*, Manoa: University of Hawai'i Press. pp. 105–129.

Mazrui, A. (1997) 'The World Bank, the language question and the future of African education', *Race & Class*, Vol. 38, No. 3, pp. 35–48.

Mc Laughlin, F. (2008) 'The ascent of Wolof as an urban vernacular and national lingua franca in Senegal', in C. Vigouroux and S. Mufwene (eds), *Globalization and Language Vitality: Perspectives from Africa*, London: Continuum, pp. 142–170.

Mekacha, R. D. K. (1993) *The Sociolinguistic Impact of Kiswahili on Ethnic Community Languages in Tanzania: A Case Study of Ekinata*, Bayreuth: Bayreuth University Press.

Mensah, H. A. (2018) 'Communicative repertoires in advertising space in Lesotho: The translanguaging and commodification nexus', in G. Mazzaferro (ed.) *Translanguaging as Everyday Practice*, Cham: Springer, pp. 175–194.

Morrison, M. E. (2011) *A Reference Grammar of Bena*, PhD thesis, Rice University.

Muzale, H. R. T. and Rugemalira, J. M. (2008) 'Researching and documenting the languages of Tanzania', *Language Documentation & Conservation*, Vol. 2, No. 1, pp. 68–108.

Nakao, S. (2018) 'Dynamics of Arabic in Northeastern Africa: Convivial multilingualism', *The 9th "African Potentials" Project Meeting*, Kyoto University, Kyoto, 16 June 2018 (in Japanese).

Nyamnjoh, F. B. (2017) 'Incompleteness: Frontier Africa and the currency of conviviality', *Journal of Asian and African Studies*, Vol. 52, No. 3, pp. 253–270.

Pennycook, A. and Otsuji, E. (2015) *Metrolingualism. Language in the City*, London and New York: Routledge.

Phillipson, R. (1992) *Linguistic Imperialism*, Oxford: Oxford University

Press.

Polomé, E. C. (1980) 'Tanzania: A socio-linguistic perspective', in E. C. Polomé and C. P. Hill (eds) *Language in Tanzania*, Oxford: Oxford University Press, pp. 103–138.

Pool, J. (1972) 'National development and language diversity', in J. A. Fishman (ed.) *Advances in the Sociology of Language, Volume II*, Hague: Mouton, pp. 213–230.

Roberts, D. (2015) 'Cracks in support for two Tanzanian rural primary schools with high performance on national exam', *International Journal of Educational Development*, Vol. 43, pp. 32–40.

Rubagumya, C. M. (1991) 'Language promotion for educational purposes: The example of Tanzania', *International Review of Education*, Vol. 37, No. 1, pp. 67–85.

Rubagumya, C. M., Afitska, O., Clegg, J. and Kiliku, P. (2011) 'A three-tier citizenship: Can the state in Tanzania guarantee linguistic human rights?', *International Journal of Educational Development*, Vol. 31, pp. 78–85.

Skutnabb-Kangas, T. and Phillipson, R. (eds) (1994) *Linguistic Human Rights*, Berlin and New York: Mouton de Gruyter.

Smakman, D. and Heinrich, P. (eds) (2015) *Globalising Sociolinguistics: Challenging and Expanding Theory*, London: Routledge.

Smith, S. A. (1978) 'Language planning and language policy in Tanzania during the German colonial period', *Kiswahili*, Vol. 48, pp. 73–80.

Sultana, S., Dovchin, S. and Pennycook, A. (2015) 'Transglossic language practices of young adults in Bangladesh and Mongolia', *International Journal of Multilingualism*, Vol. 12, No. 1, pp. 93–108.

Sunano, Y. (2007) *Post-Colonial States and Their Languages: Language and Society of Francophone Senegal*, Tokyo: Sangensha (in Japanese).

────── (ed.) (2012) *Multilingualism Reconsidered: Comparative Studies on Multilingualism*, Tokyo: Sangensha (in Japanese).

wa Thiong'o, N. (1986) *Decolonising the Mind: The Politics of Language in African Literature*, London: J. Currey.

Webb, V. and Kembo-Sure (2000) *African Voices: An Introduction to the Languages and Linguistics of Africa*, Oxford: Oxford University Press.

Wedin, Åsa (2010) 'Classroom interaction: Potential or problem? The case of Karagwe', *International Journal of Educational Development*,

Vol. 30, No. 2, pp. 145–150.

Wolff, H. E. (2016) *Language and Development in Africa: Perceptions, Ideologies and Challenges*, Cambridge: Cambridge University Press.

―――― (2018) 'Multilingualism, translanguaging, and linguistic superdiversity: An Africanist's perspective on "language"', *Nordic Journal of African Studies*, Vol. 27, No. 2, pp. 1–21.

Yoneda, N. (1996) 'The impact of the diffusion of Kiswahili on ethnic languages in Tanzania: A case study of Samatengo', in S. Hino (ed.) *African Urban Studies IV*, Tokyo: Research Institute for the Study of Languages and Cultures of Asia and Africa, pp. 29–73.

―――― (2010) 'Swahilization of ethnic languages in Tanzania: The case of Matengo', *African Study Monographs*, Vol. 31, No. 3, pp. 139–148.

―――― (2012a) 'Multilingualism from Europe and multilingual situation in Africa', in Y. Sunano (ed.) *Multilingualism Reconsidered: Comparative Studies on Multilingualism*, Tokyo: Sangensha, pp. 118–141 (in Japanese).

―――― (2012b) 'Reconsideration on literacy in Africa', *Language and Society*, Vol. 14, pp. 43–66 (in Japanese).

Chapter 6

Kiswahili Language and Its Potentiality for African Development

Shani Omari Mchepange and Mussa M. Hans

1. Introduction

Kiswahili is one of the Bantu languages originated in the coast of East Africa many centuries ago. Unlike other well-known lingua franca elsewhere in Africa, 'Kiswahili successfully went through standardisation process which enabled it to have fairly stable and reliable orthography, lexicography and grammar' (Mkude 2005: 1). The language has developed extensively and it is not only a language of wider communication in the East African region but also is one of the African languages that are being taught in various universities across the world. Various entities played important roles in its development since during the colonial period to present. This includes heads of states, politicians, education institutions, media practitioners, writers, publishers and policymakers, just to mention a few. 'Though educational policies in Tanganyika, Kenya and Uganda converged for a time in the 1920s, in general, quite various policies were pursued in relation to Kiswahili language' (Whiteley 1969: 57). For instance, since 1960s East African state leaders have developed Kiswahili in many aspects. For example, Julius Nyerere the former President of Tanzania adopted Kiswahili as a national language in 1962 and made it the official language of the state in 1967 and English as a second official language (Rubagumya 1990) and Jomo Kenyatta of Kenya and Milton Obote of Uganda opted for English as the official language (Muaka 2019). But recently, Kiswahili has been made a national and official language in Kenya alongside English (Republic of Kenya 2010) and in Uganda Kiswahili is given the status of a second official language (EAKC 2019: 99). In general, today Kiswahili has been adopted as national and/or official language by almost all East African countries. In other East African countries such as Burundi, Kiswahili was recognised as one of the official languages by the Constitution of Burundi in 2005 (EAKC 2019) alongside Kirundi, English and French. In Rwanda, Kiswahili is an official language together with French, English and Kinyarwanda (Mlaga 2018) and in the Democratic Republic of Congo, Kiswahili is a national language alongside Kikongo, Kiluba and Kilingala while French is an official language.

Apart from Western and Eastern universities, Kiswahili has been taught in various African universities since 1960s. For instance, the University of Ghana started in 1964 and the Sebha University, Libya, started in 1984. Other Libyan universities that teach Kiswahili are Al-Feteh University and Nasser University (Chebet-Choge 2012; Amidu 1996 in Dzahene-Quarshie 2013). Recently, some non-Eastern African universities and schools have started teaching Kiswahili courses. African universities which have introduced Kiswahili are the University of KwaZulu-Natal since 2012 (Chipila 2020) and the University of Zimbabwe since 2013 (Dzomba 2019). In South Africa, Kiswahili was introduced as an optional subject in schools in 2020. The plan is under way to have introduced Kiswahili in local schools in Namibia by 2021 (Tjitemisa 2020).

Kiswahili has been thriving across Africa in terms of its status. In July 2004, the African Union (AU) endorsed Kiswahili as one of its official languages alongside English, Portuguese, Arabic and French. In 2016 the East African Legislative Assembly (EALC) resolved that Kiswahili shall be one of the official languages of the East African Community (EAKC 2019: 1). In August 2019 the Southern African Development Community (SADC) adopted it as one of its official languages. And for many years Kiswahili has been used as an important language in printing and publication. In addition, many broadcasting stations throughout the world include Kiswahili programmes in their schedules. These include BBC (British Broadcasting Corporation), DW (Deustch Welle), RFI (Radio France Internationale) and VOA (Voice of America). Kiswahili is also used on social media platforms and websites.

The aim of this chapter is to uncover a potentiality of Kiswahili for African development in its various spheres such as education, trade and economy, politics and diplomacy, and culture. This study is motivated by the aforementioned recent achievements of the Kiswahili language encountered so far. This chapter is among other works that investigated the role of Kiswahili in Africa, be it in East and Central Africa, in the Great Lakes region or at continental level (see Kiimbila 1971; Fishman 1972; Massamba 1989; Mulokozi 2003; Kishe 2003; Dzahene-Quarshie 2013; Kanana 2013; Mutembei 2014; EAKC 2019; Muaka 2019, just to mention a few). This chapter hinges its analysis on Fishman's work, 'National Languages and Languages of Wider Communication in the Developing Countries', that argues that 'a common indigenous language in the modern nation states is a powerful factor of unity. Cutting across tribal ethnic ties, it promotes a feeling of a single community. Additionally, it makes possible the expression and development of ideas, economic targets and cultural identity' (Fishman 1972: 198; Wiseman and Simuforosa 2014: 892).

The data of this study were collected by interviewing some Kiswahili professionals within the East African region, namely Tanzania, Rwanda, Kenya and Uganda. The aim was to get their views regarding the potentiality of Kiswahili in fostering development and unity in Africa. Also, due to the nature of the study a number of existing literatures on Kiswahili in Africa was also consulted. This chapter is divided into five sections: The first section is an introduction where brief information on the status of Kiswahili and the purpose of this chapter is provided. The methodological part of the chapter is also presented in this section. Section two is the core part of the chapter; it immerses itself in examining the role of Kiswahili for African development. This is followed by recommendations on improving the language and making development attainable. The fourth section is the conclusion.

2. Kiswahili Potentiality for African Development

The African continent hosts more than 2,000 languages and Kiswahili ranks among the first ten of the languages of the world. The number of Kiswahili speakers continues to increase. Kiswahili is one of the widely spoken indigenous languages in Africa. It is estimated that about 150 million people in Africa speak Kiswahili (Dzahene-Quarshie 2013). These speakers are found in Tanzania, Kenya, Uganda, Burundi, the Democratic Republic of Congo, Comoros, Rwanda and beyond. They speak Kiswahili to varying degrees of proficiency. The following section is going to discuss how Kiswahili can serve as a language for African development.

2-1. *Kiswahili for African Development in Trade and Economy*

Kiswahili, as a language of trade and of wider communication, started to be used during the times of Arab slave trade in East Africa. Massamba (1989) postulates that historically, with the establishment of trade and relation along the coast, Kiswahili became gradually more important as a language of wider communication. The Arab slave traders realised the importance of Kiswahili and contributed to its spread along the East African coast and to the interior (Massamba 1989). During the German domination in East Africa, from 1884 until the First World War, Kiswahili brought about a closer contact with the Germany. Kiswahili became the language of government and commerce which every European in the country had to learn (Damman 1956: 9). This is to say that in East Africa and elsewhere in Africa, 'there is a direct link between African languages and the economy' (Muaka 2019: 133). Regarding the East African community (whose partner states are Tanzania, Burundi, Kenya, Rwanda, South Sudan and Uganda) and Great Lakes Region EAKC (2019: 87–88) has the view that Kiswahili is an important communication tool necessary for business communication. It has a facilitative role in business and trade which are the key drivers of the four pillars of regional integration and sustainable development in the EAC: Customs Union, Common Market, Political Confederation and Monetary Union. Indeed, we argue that Kiswahili plays and will play a significant role for development of the economy and facilitating cross-border trade in the East African regions, the Great Lakes Regions and beyond. Kiswahili is also important in order to develop business relations based on mutual respect as well as for effective communication. This is due to the fact that developing trust with clients and partners requires appropriate language.

The language can also be used in other African regional economic organisations in some contexts. These regional organisations include the Common Market for Eastern and Southern Africa (COMESA)[1], the Economic Community of West African States (ECOWAS)[2], the Southern African Customs Union (SACU)[3] and the Southern African Development Community (SADC)[4]. For instance, the SADC Industrialisation Strategy and Roadmap 2015– 2063 highlights the importance of technological and economic transformation of the SADC region through industrialisation, market integration, modernisation, skills development, science and technology, financial strengthening and deeper regional integration (SADC 2015). As one of the main goals of these organisations is to promote economic cooperation, development and integration among member states, we argue that this can partly be attained by the use of Kiswahili as a tool of communication and unification. Apart from oral communication in doing business (for those who are able to communicate) among citizens from these regional blocs, Kiswahili can be used in the manuals of their products alongside other international languages spoken in the respective regions, that is, English, French, Arabic and Portuguese or other language, depending on where a product originated. The export products from African countries to other parts of the world such as United States of America, Europe and Asia can also incorporate the Kiswahili language in their manuals of products such as automobiles, electronics and pharmaceuticals. As a 'language is the basis for communication which in turn is necessary for collaboration and cooperation, hence, it can be used as language of business and trade' (EAKC 2019: 33, 57).

Therefore, establishment of these regional economic organisations will prove useful not only for economic development among member states as they create markets for their products within Africa but also beneficial for Kiswahili spread and growth. As Kiswahili is one of the official working languages of the African Union and the SADC and some of the member states of these organisations have adopted Kiswahili as their national or official language or teach it as a subject in their education institutions, this will not be a problem. In addition, as some of the SADC countries are landlocked, adoption of Kiswahili as a formal language in the region is a good opportunity for the use and spread of the language. The language will be used in business as Kenya and Tanzania's seaports serve most of the Eastern, Central and Southern African landlocked countries including Burundi, Ethiopia, Rwanda, Sudan, Southern Sudan, Uganda, Zambia and Zimbabwe. Thus, having some Kiswahili knowledge may speed up their business, trade and mutual understanding as well as developing trust with clients and partners.

Additionally, Kiswahili professionals from East African countries and beyond will be hired in those countries which recently introduced Kiswahili in schools as well as in broadcasting media. Language specialists like translators and interpreters will be given permanent or temporary employment opportunities, thus reducing unemployment in African countries. An initiative taken by some countries such as South Africa to introduce Kiswahili as one of optional languages is commendable. As Muaka (2019) points out:

> While not all African languages are taught as foreign languages, the widely spoken languages such as Swahili, Yoruba, Hausa, Zulu, Wolof, Amharic, Somali, and to some extent Kinyarwanda and Lingala are in demand. These languages are taught both in the diaspora and the regions where they are spoken. These languages are a key source of money to both governments and the targeted communities (Muaka 2019: 142).

Likewise, to emphasise teaching Kiswahili as a language will create employment to native and non-native Kiswahili teachers and professionals. Another advantage is that teaching and learning Kiswahili in more African countries will prepare their citizens to work elsewhere within and outside the continent. Also, as there will be a need for teaching and learning materials such as textbooks, literary books, audios and videos, this will be a good opportunity for writers and publishers.

2-2. Kiswahili and Development of Education in Africa

The decision of promoting Kiswahili as an official and national language in various East African partner states and the desire and determination to use it in the official domain, means that we cannot ignore its importance in education. It should be noticed that, in countries where Kiswahili is one of their official and/or national languages, Kiswahili is further advanced compared to other countries, Thus, Kiswahili has to be promoted as a medium of instruction at various levels of education from primary to tertiary level. For instance, in Tanzania, after independence, Kiswahili was introduced as a medium of instruction in all public primary schools (Massamba 1989). Although proponents of using English and French *in East Africa* can disagree, arguing that Kiswahili is incapable of handling scientific and modern technology (cf. Massamba 1989; Kiimbila 1971 emphasis is ours), we argue that a language cannot be developed if it is not used in various domains including in the education sector. The importance of Kiswahili as the language of daily communication cannot be ignored by scholars and policy makers and, therefore, it should be reflected in the educational policy. Even during the colonial period in Tanganyika, people from outside the continent recognised the importance of the Kiswahili language. For example, in the 1850s Ludwig Krapf as quoted by Whiteley (1969: 2) advances the importance of Kiswahili to his readers as follows:

> Now if we reflect that the Kisuaheli is spoken, at least understood from the Equator down to the Portuguese settlements at Mozambique, consequently, that … it offers the key to the language of the Interior with which it is intimately related, we cannot help attaching great importance to this language. The scientific traveller who intends to collect information on the coast or to make researches in the interior can hardly proceed without the knowledge of this language.

The quotation highlights the importance of Kiswahili in education, particularly in conducting research, during the colonial period. We should ask ourselves one important question regarding this quotation: 'If the language was of that importance during the colonial period when we had no standard Kiswahili language, what should we do now at a time in which we have standard Kiswahili with a lot of literatures?' Something has to be done, particularly in educational system, to adopt Kiswahili as a medium of instruction to develop our education and economy.

Research shows that most developed countries in the world use their own languages in education, science and technology. Various scholars and admirers of indigenous African languages have highlighted their importance for development in education. For instance, Mutembei (2014) argues that the use of Western languages in African education systems ruins creativity and the ability to innovate of their people.

The use and adoption of Kiswahili in African schools (starting with East African schools) will make Kiswahili terminology increase and grow to cater for different needs and disciplines, including terminology in science and technology, trade, business, etc. as the number of speakers will grow as well as its vocabulary and use. In addition, being widely spoken on the continent, an increasing interest in the adoption of Kiswahili as one of the official working languages in regional organisations such as the SADC and AU and its continued introduction in schools and universities will spark more research in Kiswahili studies. This is because Kiswahili has been a popular research area in many African countries as well as at universities across the world. This is good for the development of the African continent in terms of knowledge and academia. Introduction of the Kiswahili language in schools in other African countries will awaken East African governments to revise and critically evaluate their education policies so as to give Kiswahili a due importance as a medium of instruction in schools. This will make them cast aside dependence on foreign languages (Dahir 2018). Adoption of Kiswahili in more African schools is a sign that Africans recognise it as a language for African development.

2-3. Kiswahili and African Development in Politics

In Tanganyika during the colonial period, Kiswahili was used as a means of communication under both German and British district administration. The colonialists considered Kiswahili not only as a 'neutral' indigenous language but also the language of power (Massamba 1989). During the struggle for independence Kiswahili played an important role in uniting people. In 1962, the then Tanganyika government designated Kiswahili as the national language. President Julius Nyerere became the first African head of state to address the parliament in an indigenous African language (Kiswahili) but initially English was the language of the House (Massamba 1989; Mutembei 2014). Kenya declared Kiswahili as the national and official language in 2010, and it is one of the official languages of Parliament (EAKC 2019) alongside English. Kiswahili is the most widely spoken language in the East African Community. Thus, its continued spread and increasing use in the region demonstrate that the language has a significant role to play.

EAC Vision 2050 and SADC Industrialisation Strategy and Roadmap 2015–2063 aligned to the African Union Agenda 2063. With Kiswahili as a common language of wider communication in Africa, it is expected that it will serve as 'an important agent of change and transformation' on the continent (EAKC 2019: 14). In committing regional integration and unity, promoting peace and security, fighting for liberation, solving inter-state and intra-state conflicts and consolidation of democracy and good governance, common language is important. In its study that sought to establish how Kiswahili use can contribute to both national and regional integration and sustainable development, EAKC (2019: 19) opines that 'as a language of wider communication in the EAC, as a working language of SADC and the AU, Kiswahili is quickly becoming a language of international relations in Africa'. The choice to add Swahili in the official languages of the AU was to recognise the power of this language in bringing Africans together (Mutembei 2014).

In Tanzania during the years of the struggle for independence, Kiswahili was used by nationalists/politicians as a language of liberation (Massamba 1989). It is reported that some of freedom fighters from Angola, Namibia, South Africa and Zimbabwe in the 1960s, who later became heads of states, learned some Swahili. For instance, Magufuli's speech at the 39th SADC Heads of states summit held in August 2019 in Dar es Salaam, revealed that Tanzania's first president and father of the nation, Mwalimu Julius Nyerere, played a big role in liberating various countries on this continent, as many African freedom fighters were trained in Tanzania and Kiswahili was their major language of communication (see also wa Kuhenga 2019; Karangwa 2006). In supporting Nyerere and other former African presidents' idea of having one common language in Africa, in October 2018 Julius Malema, South African politician and leader of the Economic Freedom Fighters (EFF), called for adoption of Kiswahili as African's common language. It is evidenced that 'many countries are taking a keen interest in Kiswahili because it is one of the major lingua francas of Africa; optimists have it that it will eventually be the major lingua franca of Africa' (Massamba 1989: 77; Khumalo 2018). Regarding South Africa, Dahir (2018) and Khumalo (2018) write that the introduction of Kiswahili, Africa's most internationally recognised language, as one of the optional language subjects in South African classrooms, hopes to promote greater social cohesion among Africans, as well as offer more opportunities to Swahili speakers from East African countries. An increase in the number of Kiswahili speakers could be very useful in the long run and help to combat the increase in xenophobia across South Africa, and it will bring a sense of togetherness and African-ness (Khumalo 2018; Dahir 2018).

Dahir (2018) further notes that the act of political leaders such as Joaquim Chissano, Mozambique's then-president and the chairman of the African Union in 2004, delivering his speech in Kiswahili rather than the AU's official languages (English, Portuguese, Arabic and French), and the SADC chairperson and Tanzanian President, John Joseph Pombe Magufuli, to address his speech in Kiswahili in 39th Ordinary Summit of SADC Heads of State and Government was significant for Kiswahili development in Africa and the world at large. The adoption of Kiswahili to be among the five official languages in AU alongside with English, Portuguese, Arabic and French, and SADC's declaration of Kiswahili as the fourth official working language alongside English, French and Portuguese are remarkable decisions. Kiswahili being an official language of the African Union and SADC, official language in some of the SADC countries and the lingua franca in most of East Africa and parts of Central and Southern Africa has a great potential to foster the regional and continental integration agenda. The chairperson of the Pan South African Language Board David Maahlamela said:

> This milestone achievement towards recognition and elevation of

indigenous African languages across the SADC region forms part of the greater effort in ensuring development, usage and intellectualization of our heritage languages. The inclusion of Kiswahili will help prevent the marginalization of African languages (Mutethya 2019: 1).

The decision will also stimulate Kiswahili to be taught in more African countries of the regional bloc and beyond and accelerate its spread, which is good for their political and economic integration. As Scotton (1978: 70) says, 'an indigenous regional lingua franca, does not only foster pride but builds bridges between its people, leading to mutual understanding and greater political and economic unity'. Indeed, Africa people have to acknowledge what fathers of Pan Africanism, Kwame Nkrumah and Julius Nyerere, advocated for African linguistic unity as a pertinent tool for the promotion of African unity (Dzahene-Quarshie 2013). In addition, 'Swahili could have contributed to the restoration of peace in the African Great Lakes region,[5] where all parties to the conflict speak the common language' (Kishe 2003; Kambale 2004). Thus, Kiswahili could be used as a language of unification among member states.

2-4. Kiswahili and Social-Cultural Development in Africa

So far Kiswahili has been used to some extent in none East African countries in a number of areas such as education, religion and arts. It is considered that Kiswahili is an easy language to learn. Kiswahili, being Bantu and agglutinating language, shares many similar features in terms of word formation and grammatical structure with other Bantu languages (Khumalo 2018). Regarding the teaching of Kiswahili in South African schools, Julius Malema, a South African politician, and South African Education Minister, Angie Motshekga, advocate for Swahili to become a lingua franca in Africa. The two said that the move was meant to promote unity and social cohesion with fellow Africans (Khumalo 2018; Dahir 2018). Apart from social cohesion, Kiswahili can be also used in arts and literature. For instance, it has been reported that there are some Kiswahili religious songs used in some Zimbabwean churches such as Zimbabwe Assemblies of God Africa (ZAOGA) (Dzomba 2019). This practice may create a sense of unity when the devotees of those churches visit Kiswahili speaking countries and attend a mass conducted in Kiswahili or those from Kiswahili speaking countries visit respective churches in Zimbabwe. This may create an inspiration for one to learn or teach the language, hence the language continues to spread.

Collaborations among African singers or musicians have also made a significant contribution to African social development. Apart from collaborations among East African singers, other collaborations are between East African singers and those from Southern, Northern, Central and Western Africa. Some of these collaborations are between Mukudzeyi Mukombe (Jah Prayzah) from Zimbabwe and Nasibu Abdul Juma (Diamond Platnumz) from Tanzania in their song *Watora Mari* (Jah Prayzah ft. Diamond Platnumz 2016), Nasibu Abdul Juma with a Nigerian singer, David Adedeji Adeleke (Davido), in their track *Number One Remix* (Diamond Platnumz ft. Davido 2014) and Charles Njagua Kanyi (Jaguar), a Kenyan musician, collaborated with Mafikizolo group from South African in the song *Going Nowhere* (Jaguar ft. Mafikizolo 2016). Other collaborations are witnessed among movie artists, etc. As these collaborated song lyrics contain some Kiswahili, they help the language spread and inspire the respective musicians or their fans to learn some Kiswahili. These collaborations among African singers publicise them and make them feel more integrated, which is good for African unity. 'Kiswahili demonstrates the potential not only for Africa's integration, but indeed the ability to maintain social and development and mutual understanding and respect' (Mutembei 2014: 330). In this phenomenon, culture is transmitted very largely through the Kiswahili language.

3. Recommendations

It has been revealed in this and previous studies that Kiswahili has a crucial role to play in fostering economic, social and political integration. The following are important things that need to be done to improve the mission:

Those Africans who still have negative attitudes towards and perceptions of Kiswahili have to change their minds and support the progress accorded to Kiswahili and hope for a bright future. This call is also for non-Eastern African heads of states to embrace and support Kiswahili. Apart from being taught in schools, leaders of African countries have to make effort to learn Kiswahili. For instance, Dzomba (2019: 9) points out that the act of President Robert Mugabe to conclude his farewell speech on 19 November 2017 with the Kiswahili words 'Asante sana' (Thank you very much) surprised many people within and outside Zimbabwe. The use of Kiswahili among Zimbabwean leaders shows the possibility of the language to spread quickly within the country, as it interested some Zimbabweans. We also insist that heads of African states when addressing the masses can insert few simple Swahili words such as a greeting and farewell; this can create a sense of political unity among African states and motivate and inspire their citizens to learn the language.

Kiswahili can be assigned value by making it a medium of instruction in secondary schools and tertiary level education in some East African countries. Though the opponents of Kiswahili consider it as incapable of conveying scientific and new knowledge which of course is not always true, we suggest that the examination papers can be written in any language that a student is capable of, either English/French or Kiswahili and that a student be given a chance to answer in the language of his/her choice. It does not make sense for countries to declare Kiswahili as their national language while it is not given the importance to be used as a medium of instruction in their education systems. Muaka (2019: 136) argues that African 'languages are as good as any other linguistic product on the market. What African languages lack are policymakers and stakeholders who can advocate for them both at the policy level and at the functional level'. In this 21st century, politicians, language planners and policymakers have to be more serious and not swerving in their language policy.

Countries that introduce Kiswahili in their schools and universities should dispatch as many teachers as possible to Kiswahili-speaking countries to attend trainee programmes so as to facilitate teaching Kiswahili in their countries. It is expected that, when coming back to their countries, they will not only serve their nations but also minimise the cost of paying Kiswahili experts from other countries. As well, there should be provision of trained and qualified Kiswahili teachers and teaching materials (books, programmed learning materials, audio and video tapes, etc.) to the countries in need. Textbooks for teaching Kiswahili grammar and literature, teachers' guides and multilingual dictionaries and small dictionaries from other African languages to Kiswahili and vice versa have to be prepared. Some simple literature such as children's books from other languages can also be translated into Kiswahili.

To enhance Kiswahili and to promote linkages and networking with other universities or schools teaching Kiswahili in Africa, conferences, colloquiums or symposiums organised by various associations of Kiswahili such as the East African Universities Swahili teachers Association (CHAKAMA) and the Global Association for the Promotion of Swahili (CHAUKIDU) have to be also convened in the countries whose Kiswahili programme is nascent. For instance, they can be held in the schools or universities that offer Kiswahili courses in Zimbabwe, Namibia, South Africa, etc. This will encourage the learners and teachers of Kiswahili in those countries. It will also provide a good opportunity to listen to their problems regarding teaching and learning Kiswahili in those countries and plan for the future.

International companies should also include Kiswahili translations in instructions to users of their products such as pharmaceutical, agricultural and ICT products. This will make Kiswahili vocabulary increasingly grow in various fields such as science and technology, health, agriculture and many more. This may motivate more people worldwide to learn the language or political leaders and language policymakers to plan more for its development.

4. Conclusion

This chapter devoted itself in examining the potentiality of Kiswahili in African development in its various domains. It has been discussed that Kiswahili, as a language of wider communication in the EAC and as a working language of the SADC and the AU, has a pivotal role to play for African development. Economically, it has been revealed that Kiswahili can accelerate trade and create employment among its nationals. Politically, it is emphasised that

Kiswahili has potential in fostering regional and continental integration, greater social cohesion among Africans and African-ness. In terms of culture and education, Kiswahili as an indigenous African language can not only promote development of ideas, creativity and innovation of Africans but also a feeling of a single community and expression of cultural identity.

Endnotes

[1] COMESA is the largest regional economic organisation in Africa, with 19 member states namely Burundi, Comoros, D.R. Congo, Djibouti, Egypt, Eritrea, Ethiopia, Kenya, Libya, Madagascar, Malawi, Mauritius, Rwanda, Seychelles, Sudan, Eswatini, Uganda, Zambia and Zimbabwe.

[2] ECOWAS is formed by 15 members namely Benin, Burkina Faso, Cabo Verde, Cote d'Ivoire, The Gambia, Ghana, Guinea, Guinea-Bissau, Liberia, Mali, Niger, Nigeria, Senegal, Sierra Leone and Togo.

[3] SACU members include Botswana, Lesotho, Namibia, South Africa and Swaziland.

[4] SADC member states are Angola, Botswana, Comoros, Democratic Republic of Congo, Eswatini, Lesotho, Madagascar, Malawi, Mauritius, Mozambique, Namibia, Seychelles, South Africa, Tanzania, Zambia and Zimbabwe.

[5] The African Great Lakes region comprises Burundi, the Democratic Republic of the Congo, Kenya, Malawi, Rwanda, Tanzania and Uganda.

Acknowledgements

This work was supported by JSPS KAKENHI Grant Number JP16H06318.

References

Amidu, A. A. (1996) 'Kiswahili, a continental language: Is it possible? part II', *Nordic Journal of African Studies,* Vol. 5, No. 1, pp. 84–106.

Chipila, R. A. (2020) (personal communication) on 29 January 2020. University of Dar es Salaam.

Chebet-Choge, S. (2012) 'Fifty years of Kiswahili in regional and international development', *Journal of Pan-African Studies*, Vol. 4, No. 10, pp.172–203.

Dahir, A. (2018) 'South African schools will start teaching Kiswahili to students from 2020', *Quartz Africa*, 18 September 2018 (https://qz.com/africa/1393922/south-africa-to-teach-kiswahili-in-schools/) (accessed: 20 March 2019).

Damman, E. (1956) 'German contributions to Swahili studies in recent decades', *Journal of the East African Swahili Committee*, Vol. 26, pp. 9–17.

Diamond Platnumz ft. Davido (2014) 'My number one remix', *A Boy from Tandale*, Dar es Salaam: Sheddy Clever.

Dzahene-Quarshie, J. (2013) 'Ghana's contribution to the promotion of Kiswahili: Challenges and prospects for African unity', *The Journal of Pan African Studies*, Vol. 6, No. 6, pp. 69–85.

Dzomba, E. (2019) 'Historia na maendeleo ya Kiswahili nchini Zimbabwe', *Kioo cha Lugha*, Vol. 17, pp. 1–14.

EAKC (East African Kiswahili Commission) (2019) *Capacity Assessment of the Development and Use of Kiswahili in the EAC*, Zanzibar: East African Kiswahili Commission.

Fishman, J. A. (1972) 'National languages and languages of wider communication in the developing countries', in A. S. Dil (ed.) *Language in Sociocultural Changes: Essays by Joshua A. Fishman*, Stanford: Stanford University Press, pp. 191–223.

Jaguar ft. Mafikizolo (2016) *Going Nowhere*, Nairobi: Switch Studios.

Jah Prayzah ft. Diamond Platnumz (2016) *Watora Mari*, Dar es Salaam: Wasafi Records.

Kambale, K. (2004) 'Culture: Congolese welcome Swahili as official African language', *IPS (Inter Press Service)*, 9 August 2004 (http://www.ipsnews.net/2004/08/culture-congolese-welcome-swahili-as-official-african-language/) (accessed: 2 January 2020).

Kanana, F. E. (2013) 'Examining African languages as tools for national development: The case of Kiswahili', *Journal of Pan African Studies*, Vol. 6, No. 6, pp. 41–68.

Karangwa, J. D. (2006) 'Kiswahili katika karne ya 20: Chombo cha ukombozi, utaifa na ukandamizaji', *Kioo cha Lugha*, Vol. 4, pp. 62–72.

Khumalo, T. (2018) 'South Africa embraces Swahili', *DW (Deutsche Welle)*, 3 October 2018 (https://www.dw.com/en/south-africa-embraces-swahili/a-45742261) (accessed: 2 January 2020).

Kiimbila, J. K. (1971) 'Matumizi ya Kiswahili nchini, shuleni na vyuoni', in G. A. Mhina, J. K. Kiimbila and M. M. R. Alidina (eds) *Kichocheo cha Uchunguzi wa Kiswahili*, Dar es Salaam: Tanzania Publishing House, pp. 60–69.

Kishe, A. M. (2003) 'Kiswahili as vehicle of unity and development in the great lakes region', *Language Culture and Curriculum*, Vol. 16, No. 2, pp. 218–230.

Massamba, D. P. B. (1989) 'An assessment of the development and modernization of the Kiswahili language in Tanzania', in F. Coulmas (ed.) *Language Adaptation*, Cambridge: Cambridge University Press, pp. 60–78.

Mkude, D. (2005) *The Passive Construction in Swahili*, Tokyo: Research Institute for Languages and Cultures of Asia and Africa.

Mlaga, W. (2018) 'Historia ya Kiswahili nchini Rwanda: Kielelezo cha nafasi ya utashi wa kisiasa katika ustawi wa lugha ya Kiswahili', *Kioo cha Lugha*, Vol. 16, pp. 1–20.

Muaka, L. (2019). 'Linguistic commodification and Africa's linguistic identities: Creating a nexus!', in E. M. Lisaza and L. Muaka (eds) *African Languages and Literatures in the 21st Century*, Macmillan: Palgrave, pp. 127–148.

Mulokozi, M. M. (2003) 'Kiswahili as a national and international language', *Kiswahili*, Vol. 66, pp. 66–80.

Mutembei, A. (2014) 'African languages as a gateway to sustainable development, democracy and freedom: The example of Swahili', *Alternation, Special Edition*, Vol. 13, pp. 326–351.

Mutethya, E. (2019) 'SADC adopts Kiswahili as 4th working language' *China Daily*, 22 August 2019 (https://www.chinadaily.com.cn/a/201908/22/WS5d5ded0ba310cf3e35567377.html) (accessed: 3 January 2020).

Republic of Kenya (2010) *The Constitution of Kenya*, Nairobi: Government Printers.

Rubagumya, C. M. (1990) *Language in Education in Africa: A Tanzanian*

Perspective, Clevedon: Multilingual Matters.

SADC (Southern African Development Community) (2015) *Industrialization Strategy and Roadmap 2015–2063*, Harare: SADC.

Scotton C. M. (1978) 'Learning lingua francas and socioeconomic integration: Evidence from Africa', in Cooper, R (ed.) *Language Spread, Diffusion and Social Change*, Bloomington: Indiana University Press, pp. 63–93.

Tjitemisa, K. (2020) 'KiSwahili coming in 2021', *New Era*, 7 January 2020, pp 1–2.

wa Kuhenga, M. (2019) 'Kiswahili as Africa's symbol of cultural independence', *Daily News*, 23 August 2019.

Whiteley, W. (1969) *Swahili: The Rise of a National Language*, London: Methuen.

Wiseman, M. and Simuforosa, M. (2014) 'The United Nations decade of education for sustainable development (2005–2014): Language policies in Africa revisited', *Scholars Journal of Arts, Humanities and Social Sciences*, Vol. 2, No. 6A, pp. 888–894.

Part II

Literature

Chapter 7

Swahili from the Perspectives of 'Language' and 'Literature'

Keiko Takemura

1. Swahili in Tanzania: Its Circumstances as a 'Spoken Language'

The United Republic of Tanzania (Tanzania), located in East Africa, is a nation established after the merger of the former continental Tanganyika and the islands of Zanzibar when both became independent from the British territory, the former in 1961 and the latter in 1963. It is a country with more than 120 ethnic groups. When Tanganyika became independent in 1961, it chose Swahili, unique to the African continent, as its national language. Tanzania followed, making it its official language in 1967. Among the languages used in the African continent, Swahili is quite a special case.

Currently, except for English classes, language used for teaching all subjects at public elementary schools is Swahili. It is also the most frequently used language in newspapers, radio/television broadcasting and by public institutions, etc. Please refer to the chapter of Kutsukake (this volume) and Mchepange and Hans (this volume) for more information on this area.

We can say the following regarding the 'native speaker' (or a 'first language speaker') and the degree of acceptance of Swahili in Tanzania:

- The 'native speakers' of Swahili reside on the coast and islands of Tanzania.
- More than 120 ethnic groups living in Tanzania should theoretically have different mother tongues.
- However, Swahili can be used for practically all purposes in Tanzania.

In addition to this, people who do not speak Swahili as their mother tongue often say that Swahili is no longer just the language for the people of the Swahili region but that it is the language of everyone living in Tanzania and claim that it is an indispensable language in their daily lives. With this, Swahili has created a language environment in Tanzania unlike in other countries on the African continent.

However, the linguistic status of Swahili is not definite. In secondary education and beyond, English is the medium of instruction. A few years ago, a Bill was approved by the Diet to switch the language for teaching at elementary schools to English. As globalisation is progressing in the 21st century, the recognition that African languages cannot compete in the world is spreading among Tanzanians. Many people are aware that they cannot get good jobs unless they have a high English proficiency level. How Tanzania will steer its language policy in the future is thus an essential theme in looking at multilingual societies.

Based on my experience of the problematic situation surrounding Swahili in Tanzania of the last 34 years, it appears that, although Swahili is used much more frequently than English, its status is not high. For instance, my experience was that, although employees of luxury hotels are expected to have a high proficiency in English but, in spite of this, they would switch to Swahili after realising that I understood it. In the urban areas of Tanzania, I would often hear conversations in Swahili and, when communicating with women who had little school education in the rural areas of the islands in Zanzibar, Swahili was the only option. By default, children who are supposed to receive public education also speak Swahili and not English. In other words, Swahili is the most frequently used spoken language (Figure 1).

Figure 1. A chemistry class in the first grade of a secondary school in the northern region of Unguja

Students could hardly understand the teacher's explanation in English, thus the teacher re-explained everything in Swahili (Photo taken by the author in 1998)

2. Current Status of 'Written Language' in Tanzania: An Opportunity to Experience Literature

As of 2020, books in English and Swahili have been available for purchase at bookstores in the city centre and suburban shopping malls of Dar es Salaam, the former capital on the Swahili coast, as well as in the current capital, Zanzibar City on the island of Unguja (Figure 2). Swahili literature, textbooks and dictionaries are also published. One can find enough materials to be used for the Swahili language majors at universities in Japan. On the other hand, available English books tend to be superficial introductions of Tanzania aimed at tourists, alongside the so-called 'foreign books', such as the literary works 'selling' worldwide. Nevertheless, many textbooks to be used for the secondary education and above are written in English. Thus, Swahili and English are competing as the 'written language' of Tanzania.[1]

Figure 2. Dictionary of idioms, etc. (Photo taken by the author in 2016)

On the other hand, what is the treatment of Swahili literary works in public education? In elementary school (seven-year system), *Hadithi ya Watoto* (a story for children) is used as a short reading material during Swahili classes, equivalent to the *kokugo* ('national language') classes in Japan. Such 'stories' are initially created for textbooks, and many of them use the themes of right and wrong to teach morals or everyday situations to teach the norms of good behaviour. In addition, the so-called oral literature, including proverbs, riddles and folk tales, is also used as texts.

In the regular secondary school course (four-year system), students read fictional narratives and learn oral literature during the first two years of Swahili classes. In the latter two years, literary theory finally appears as a unit. Secondary schools' students also read short plays and short stories. In the upper secondary school (two-year system), literature is included in the linguistics classes. Works such as authentic Swahili novels, plays and poetry appear in textbooks. Sometimes, translations of English and French literary works are included. Some examples are Shakespeare's *The Merchant of Venice* translated by Nyerere, the first president, and 'So Long a Letter' by Mariama Bâ, a well-known female writer in Senegal.

At universities, in departments of Literature or Education, students studying Swahili (taught as Tanzanian National Language subject) study Swahili, English and French literary pieces, learn theories of translation, literature and critique methods. Students also read works translated into Swahili, such as the masterpiece *Things Fall Apart* (Fortunatus 1967) (originally in English) by a Nigerian writer

Chinua Achebe, who is known as the father of African literature, and George Orwell's *Animal Farm* (Ndulute 1973).

However, it can be said that most students can encounter literary works only while they are enrolled in the educational institutions. Literary works are thus materials treated in class. When they do not go to educational institutions, most people do not have access to books, let alone literary pieces. The cheapest books that Tanzanians can buy at bookstores are around 3,000 Tanzanian shillings.[2] With this much, a family of ten members can buy enough fish to prepare a side dish for dinner or about two kilograms of corn flour used for staple dishes. Few wonder whether to buy food for dinner or a book.

Also, among the people the author met, only university faculty members and managers of major banks had bookshelves at home. In most of the homes of people with no cash income, only their religion's scriptures can be seen. In some areas of Tanzania, even school textbooks are shared among students. At present, it is not possible for children to take textbooks home for preparation and review, so it is common for children to have no books to read at home.

In Tanzania, it is difficult to read books daily, but how do people increase their contact with literature? People in most parts of the African continent have handed down literature for many years. The same phenomenon has occurred in the Swahili language regions of Tanzania. Oral works of literature are used in various situations there. For example, in Zanzibar's elementary and secondary schools, a play called *ngonjera* is performed, which is like an epic dialogue (Figure 3). This situation is possible because it is quite common to recite epics in Swahili. Similarly, at village weddings, selected children can be seen reciting the epic *Celebrating the Bride and Groom* and receiving 'tips'. Combined with various epics, lyric poetry and song culture spun out from the influence of Islamic culture, the tradition of creating and reciting poetry remains. This situation is also a literary practice, and the author believes it is necessary to preserve it.

Figure 3. A scene from a *ngonjera* drama at Chaani Elementary School in Chaani village, Unguja (Photo taken by the author in 1997)

3. Does Reading Take Root?

One member of a 'reading family' whom I know is Said Ahmed Mohamed Khamis (pen name: Said Ahmed Mohamed). He is a linguist as well as a world-renowned Swahili writer. The reason why Said wanted to become a writer was his jealousy of his aunts who told all kinds of old tales in his childhood. When they delivered stories, they changed the voices, at times subtly changing the expressions they used to make their stories funny. Said was especially jealous of how they learned long stories by heart as if they had books in their head. He too hoped to become able to tell a story that would entertain, surprise and impress people. It was inevitable, after receiving graduate school education, that he chose the work of spinning words, especially the form of descriptive literature rather than oral tradition. It is no exaggeration to say that Said is the most energetic producer of Swahili writers in existence (Figure 4).

Figure 4. Said Ahmed Mohamed's recent full-length novel
(Photo taken by the author)

In the past, I had an interview with Said (Takemura 1995). When asked, 'Why do you write your work in Swahili?', he answered, 'I have written the works for everyone who can read the Swahili language because I want to write the story in Swahili.' 'I never use any language other than Swahili when writing my works.' He added, 'I write my works in a language unique to Africa that people have thought it to be a "undeveloped language" in the world. I also strongly want to prove that Swahili is enough language to write works of literature.'.Elena Bertoncini, a well-known scholar of Swahili literature, recognises Said as a 'social' writer (Bertoncini-Zúbková et al. 2009). Said's works, which deal with various social issues, Said's anger, and doubts, convey them straight to the readers. However, his Swahili expressions in his works are so complicated that even a native speaker would describe it as 'esoteric'. He passionately believes, 'I can write Swahili's works as Shakespeare could express the works in English, Balzac in French, and Tolstoy in Russian.' Said tried to prove by his writing activities that Swahili is not an 'undeveloped language'.

Here, the author wants to introduce a work by Said which is the play, *He is too much! (Amezidi)*' (Mohamed 1995). This 91-page work consists of a prologue called 'Songs of the Elderly,' a total of ten scenes in the main story and an epilogue called 'Songs of Children Who Have Not Been Seen' and features two characters, Ame and Zidi. The story proceeds as the above two characters perform a play within a play or impersonate another person depending on the scene. The author summarises the outline of each scene below.

Scene 1:

Ame and Zidi are in a cave. The story goes on without the reader knowing what is reality or a dream. As Ame snores and sleeps, Zidi, who has two cassava, comes to wake him up and says that 'dawn' has come. However, Ame does not care about it. Zidi says, 'Just getting up is not the same as awakening and recognising,' but Ame does not think the difference is essential. Eventually, they remember being hungry but realise that Zidi's two cassavas are the last food of the year. It has not rained for a whole year, the crops have died and the grasslands have disappeared, and it is a desert as far as the eye can see. Ame asks, 'Did you ask the United Nations for help? Or did you ask the Western World, EC, for help?' When Zidi asks, 'Why do I have to ask?' Ame replies, 'He is asking too much. If you ask, they will do something about it.' Unable to beat hunger, the two finally decide to strip the cassava and eat, but they do not even have a knife in the cave. Zidi says he does not have a knife because he does not import it from the United States. He ridiculed himself, saying, 'It is a shame to think. It hurts my head. First, Africans think things that Americans, British and French cannot think of!' In the end, the two stripped the cassava with their nails, but as there was no match, they could not light a fire to bake it. While they bite the raw cassava, the curtain goes down.

Scene 2:

Ame and Zidi are in the cave. They are in their common dream. They insist that the cave is a palace. They ponder the furnishings and dishes prepared by the servants in the castle. Velvet sofas imported from Paris, large ebony tables, fine rugs imported from Iran, extensive bookshelves, silver vases, glass cupboard with jewellery are lined up in it. Moreover, there are TV sets and video decks, a picture painted by a famous painter, a rocking chair and a milk-coloured phone on the phone stand. Looking at the phone, they remember that they have been absent from work for days but did not call their boss. Then, each calls the office and promises to bring a medical certificate for the number of days they have been absent. They conclude that Doctor Vuai, who is like their 'sibling', will write their medical certificate. Because they think, 'in this world, siblings, friends and people from the same village should help each other'. Both continue to talk about the palace's furnishings, arguing that Benz and BMW are also parked outside. While doing that, they become hungry again, let the fantasy servant prepare a meal and the curtain goes down while they enjoy a luxurious dinner in their imagination.

Scene 3:

Ame and Zidi are in their imagination. Zidi sits on an invisible sofa in the cave. Zidi's lover Mari (Ame is wearing female clothing) arrives there. Zidi is pleased with Mari's visit and tries to show off some furnishings, but Mari says it does not exist. Furthermore, someone laughs offstage. Zidi seems uncomprehending, 'Who is laughing?', but Mari says, 'It is your laughing voice.' Zidi laughs, asking (to the audience), 'Why doesn't everyone understand our wealth?' Ame comes in instead of Mari and asks why Zidi is laughing. When Zidi says, 'What we see doesn't look like Mari. She doesn't know we're wealthy.' Ame comforts, 'She'll notice it soon.' Furthermore, they sing 'a song to praise the black colour'. The curtain goes down, while they sing the song that they have abundant resources and plenty of money, and that white people should invent and work, and they should only buy what is necessary.

Scene 4:

Ame and Zidi are in their imagination. Ame and Zidi are in a cave, but Ame is a student and Zidi is a teacher. The cave is like a classroom in a school. The teacher's desk, students' desks and about 70 students other than Ame do not appear on the stage. When asked by student Ame, 'I'm forced to recite Archimedes' principle repeatedly. Is this useful for me?', Teacher Zidi cannot answer. Furthermore, when the student asks, 'Why can't I build a submarine even if I learn Archimedes' principle?' or the other student asks, 'What is a submarine?', Teacher Zidi cannot find the answer. But the students themselves answer, 'You don't have to build it. Because we are rich, so we don't need to think or invent it by ourselves. We should just wait for the white people to think and invent it. It's okay. White people have been using us for a long time, so we should use white people.' In the meantime, the radio news says that the drought has killed thousands of people in the village. There is a strange odour coming from outside the classroom, and the students complain that it is a corpse, but Teacher Zidi says that the people outside had 'the rest of death'. The curtain goes down when the students shout to the teacher, 'He's too much!'

Scene 5:

Ame and Zidi are in their common dream. The cave is an office. Ame is the boss and Zidi is a subordinate. The boss gives his subordinate a thick list to read. The subordinate notices something and starts laughing, and the boss also laughs when he sees his subordinate laughing. However, the boss immediately blames his subordinate for the laughter. His subordinate explains he is crying and not laughing. The boss then adds that he too cried rather than laughed. After a brief silence, the boss asks his subordinate to repair the broken water heater, refrigerator and phone. The subordinate replies, 'Not yet.' The boss gets angry, 'What are the young college graduated technicians recently hired doing?' 'They only know the theory, they can't repair it in reality,' explains his subordinate. He adds, 'Isn't the theory more important for the boss?' The boss orders, 'That's right. Call technicians from foreign countries and order replacement parts from foreign countries!' And he gets back to the list mentioned above. The list was created by the boss and his subordinate to hide their embezzlement. They are planning to blame other employees in the office. The boss gathers all the employees and threatens that 'the one who is embezzling the country's money is in this.' The boss tells everyone to accept a salary cut, and the curtain goes down.

Scene 6:

Ame and Zidi are in their imagination. In the cave, Ame and Zidi are arguing about whether to go 'outside' or 'back'. Zidi wonders if Ame will stick to going out. Zidi asks, 'Why are you so persistent?' Ame answers, 'to protect myself'. Zidi is an officer from the Inspection Department (Marsa) of the National Taxation Bureau and comes to the cave (a palace and an office) to audit it. Zidi, who pretended to be aware of everything, suddenly adopts a Marsa-like attitude and begins to investigate the office. Ame begins to tremble. Upon investigation, fraud becomes apparent. Zidi tells Ame, 'You're in jail.' When Ame screams, 'I have no choice but to do it ...,' Zidi offers further fraud. Zidi says, 'If I have my share, I'll do something more.' Moreover, he says, 'Because we are siblings, we protect each other, love each other and help each other. When we eat, we share it with our siblings. This is free and an autonomy. We could not do this in the colonial era!' The curtain goes down when they toast with whiskey and burn documents to cover up their fraud.

Scene 7:

Ame and Zidi are in their common dream. Ame, dressed as Mari, appears in the cave again. Mari wears a skirt above her knees, a blouse showing her navel and long boots that extend to her knees. Mari has heavy make-up on her face, has shaved her eyebrows and lined her lips with sticky lipstick. She comes into the cave with a Monroe walk. Zidi and Mari engage in incoherent conversations by swearing and comforting each other, but suddenly Zidi takes an attitude that looks through Mari's heart, 'In your heart, "a tree" that symbolises the beauty of European rashes has grown in order to be able to become a rash'. Mari also looks into Zidi's heart and shouts, 'There is "a tree" in your heart. There is a stupid "tree" that ruins the world.' They swear at each other that they are not old-fashioned humans with dark skin, but realise that they end up at the same destination. Mari finds herself in a world of darkness and dust, 'in a hole' that looks comfortable but is full of suffering. Mari wants to go deeper, but Zidi argues that he must leave. Eventually, the curtain goes down after breaking up with 'each person has his or her own way'.

Scene 8:

Ame and Zidi are in the cave of their imagination. A strange odour drifts around, and a horde of mosquitos attack Ame and Zidi. Although they are afraid of getting malaria, they have no medicine. Zidi says he should invent quinine. Ame says he should buy it instead of inventing it by himself. The old drug is no longer effective because malaria parasites have become resistant to the medicine. Zidi suggests inventing the medicine themselves. Ame says it is better to sleep. Then he calls out to the audience, 'We all love sleeping, right?' Moreover, 'We've been here for 100 years. I don't know if we are opening our eyes with sleeping or if we are sleeping with our eyes opening. Anyway, the darkness is wonderful because we can sleep soundly.' They sing the song of such a content. Suddenly, Ame begins to suffer from abdominal pain. He is so hungry that he feels pain. Then Zidi also complains of abdominal pain. Then, beef meat falls from the sky. They pull it from each other to make it their own. Eventually, they get tired of the fight and decide to share it. 'EC' is written on the meat, which indicates that it is an aid product. However, the meat gives off a strange odour. The curtain goes down when they bite the raw meat (being without a flame or match to light a fire on which to cook it) while they think it is rotten.

Scene 9:

Ame and Zidi are in the cave of their imagination and the real world. Zidi shouts to Ame, 'I remembered our "birthday" celebration party!' They discuss that they must give a bigger feast than last year. Zidi says that they must spend a fortune on the party and invite friends from the African continent and friends from Western countries who always care about and help them. But Ame suddenly asks Zidi, 'Where do you get that big buck?' Zidi replies that they should get it again at the 'special place' they got last year. During such a conversation, Zidi suddenly holds his stomach and collapses on the stage. He says he has cholera because he ate raw meat yesterday and tells Ame that he has had diarrhoea many times since last night. Zidi wants water, but there is no water supply in the palace (cave). Water pipes in the neighbourhood have been shut down for years, even though they pay for the water. Furthermore, Ame says that all the people around him have died. Zidi also expressed his feelings that they had been deceiving themselves, saying, 'I can't escape from the truth anymore.' Eventually, Zidi dies, saying, 'Dying is rest. The world is full of rest. We have been searching for that rest and hurried to get the rest early.'

Scene 10:

It is an event in the cave of imagination and the real world. Ame is crouching alone. The mosquito's wings are noisy. When Ame asks, 'Where are you, Zidi?', Zidi's voice replies from the other world. Ame argues with Zidi, 'Here is Africa, not the other world.' The thunder roars, and the laughing voice of mockery comes from nowhere. Ame asks the audience, 'Can you hear that voice ridiculing yourself? Can you hear the self-deprecating voice that springs from the depths of your heart?' Driven by illusions, Ame laments that no matter how big he says or how good his speech is, he cannot stop people from dying. Eventually, Ame suffers from abdominal pain and flutters on the ground. At the end of the suffering, Ame speaks to the audience. 'We are destined to die because of our stupidity. The more the village is wiped out, the more people die. The pain gets worse and the fun gets more and more. If there is happiness that is full of pain, there is also pain that is full of happiness. Would you like to experience this delightful pain with us? If you don't do anything, you can enjoy this delightful death.' And Ame dies.

Throughout the story, the readers (audience) see Ame and Zidi in a certain country of the continent of Africa that has emerged from the colonial state and became an independent country, soaked in the joy of its independence, not making efforts on its own, just relying on aid. It is the depravation of Ame and Zidi who lead a lazy life. Said depicts the deception and corruption of African society one after another, such as the deception in the educational field seen in Scene 4, and the embezzlement concealment work named 'African sibling bond' seen in Scene 5 and Scene 6. In every situation, they mock that they are wealthy but in reality, they are hungry and almost dead. In Scene 8, raw meat, which is an EC aid, falls from the sky, and they eat it as it is. They get cholera because of the meat. Zidi dies in Scene 9, and Ame dies in Scene 10. The highlight is the scene where Ame dies at the end, telling the readers (audience), 'It is the destiny that we have to die because of our stupidity.' Problems such as political corruption, turmoil and poverty after African countries' independence would be a bad legacy of rule by the former suzerains. However, instead, Said argues that African people who refuse to 'wake up' and do not look directly at the truth cause such a tragedy. The author insists this is a very bitter book of self-criticism.

Now then, who can 'read' this Said's 'Swahili-speaking' work? If in a Tanzanian area, or a little more broadly Swahili-speaking area, how many people would be able to understand and read his works properly? Unfortunately, it is questionable how well people who rarely read and write can read Said's works. Despite Said's own beliefs and his feelings for Swahili native speakers, it seems that only a handful of elites can read and criticise his works in the end. Once his work was used as a unit in a national language textbook for secondary education and above. In the case of a feature-length novel, however, the entire work was not adopted in the textbook. As mentioned earlier, it was not easy to read his works because the students could not bring the text home.

I, however, do not consider the above situation to be pessimistic. When I was visiting Zanzibar for research in 2015, I received a report that the mayors of the villages of Zanzibar had launched a library construction project. The village mayors reported that they were doing their best with the slogan, 'Let's build a library! Give children a reading habit!' Also, the Ministry of Education of Tanzania is energetically trying to publish an enlightenment book series for children and holds 'Book Week' events. As mentioned earlier, in Tanzania, bookstores started to sell such a series of books. I consider it necessary to verify the results of these efforts, and at the same time, it is necessary to look at the spread of novels on the internet instead of physical books as digitalisation progresses. Instead of buying and reading books, it is possible to send and read private novels on SNS by making full use of digital devices such as smartphones and tablets. People must meet the following conditions to access these devices: (i) they can afford them to some extent, (ii) they can read and write, and (iii) they have the skills to master the device. I insist that we must examine people's trends toward 'physical books' and the trends of 'reading' in the ever-accelerating internet society.

I add that I hope to contribute to the spread of reading habits in Tanzania and plan the following. I have been translating Japanese picture books with my university students in the 'Swahili Translation Practicum' class at the Major-Language of Swahili, School of Foreign Studies, Osaka University (Figure 5). My students and I have already translated more than 30 books into Swahili, including Japanese folk tales, works written by Japanese picture book writers and overseas picture books translated into Japanese. I understand that many things need to be solved, such as copyright issues. I will clarify that this translation work is not done to make profits or solve all potential problems. Then we hope to donate the above translated books to libraries located in Swahili-speaking areas, including Tanzania, and pass them on to children for reading.

Figure 5. Together with students, the author translated picture books read in Japan into Swahili (Photo taken by the author)

Endnotes

[1] However, the enrolment rate in secondary school is about 20 per cent of the schoolgoing-age population. Nearly 80 per cent of the Tanzanian people cannot read books written in English, or even if they can, they can hardly understand them.

[2] As of early September 2020, the foreign exchange rate is as follows:

one US dollar = 2,319 Tanzanian shillings. The amount of monthly income of each civil servant is about 200,000 to 300,000 shillings.

Acknowledgements

This work was supported by JSPS KAKENHI Grant Number JP16H06318.

References

Bertoncini-Zúbková, E., Gromov, M. D., Khamis, S. A. M. and Wamitila, K. W. (2009) *Outline of Swahili Literature: Prose Fiction and Drama (Second edition, extensively revised and enlarged)*, Leiden: Brill.

Fortunatus, K. (1967) *Shamba la Wanyama*, Nairobi: East African Publishing House.

Mohamed, S. A. (1995) *Amezidi*, Nairobi: East African Educational Publishers.

Ndulute, C. (1973) *Shujaa Okonkwo*, Nairobi: East African Publishing House.

Takemura, K. (1995) 'Interview with Said Ahmed Mohamed, writer in Swahili language', *Education and Research on Literature of the World at Osaka University of Foreign Studies,* Minoh: Osaka University of Foreign Studies, pp.107–136 (in Japanese).

Chapter 8

Cultural Transformation and the Reconstruction of Tradition in Yoruba Popular Music

Katsuhiko Shiota

1. Introduction

Yoruba popular music is a modern cultural phenomenon born out of the process of modernisation and urbanisation, which has resulted in the reception and mixing of traditional and foreign elements of culture.

The first issue of the academic journal, *Popular Music*, published in 1981, explained that popular music is peculiar to societies where industrialisation has led to a division of labour, and where there is a clear separation between producers and consumers. It is created by professional artists, sold by large distribution organisations and played through mass media (Popular Music 1981).

Yorubaland in southwestern Nigeria underwent a transformation from its traditional society to a modern one with the introduction of modern industry from the late 19th to the early 20th century during British colonial rule. Lagos, which was the centre of colonial rule in Yorubaland, was one of the first regions to experience urbanisation in West African coast. At the beginning of the 20th century, with the emergence of the record industry, local musicians began to record their performances and commercialise them.

Rapid urbanisation brings together people of various ethnic, linguistic and cultural backgrounds and disconnects them from their previous contexts. There, people gradually lose their traditional sense of belonging, while at the same time find themselves commonly confronted with new social and economic problems. In addition, the identity of the self is also reaffirmed, not in terms of the traditional tribal sense of belonging but in terms of the social strata of occupation, class and nationality. It is at this point that popular music begins to make its presence felt. This is because popular music 'plays an important role in mediating, shaping and expressing the reaffirmation of one's sense of social belonging' (Manuel 1988: 46).

This chapter investigates the process of unification of the Yoruba nations and their inhabitants, which were independent before colonisation, through the collapse of the Oyo Empire, or the centre of Yorubaland, and colonisation by the British into a unified Yoruba nation. At the same time, the evolution of Yoruba popular music throughout history reflects the process of Yoruba national unification by incorporating and reinterpreting traditional and foreign elements.

Regarding the creation and development of popular music, Coplan points out that the process of creating music that mixes various elements with ethnic musical resources in the city and serves as a common language for audiences with different backgrounds is similar to the process of pidgin language generation (Coplan 1978: 110, 1979–80: 51). In this chapter, I will examine the diverse and complex Yoruba traditional music as a resource for popular music production.

2. Historical Background

2-1. A Brief History of Yorubaland

The ethnic group now known as the Yoruba were originally divided into several independent states with different cultures, dialects and political organisations, with a common descendent, Odùduwà, the founder of the Ilé-Ifẹ̀ kingdom. However, it was not until the second half of the 19th century that the term 'Yoruba' was used to refer to them as a whole. Until then, the Yoruba had no common sense of belonging and were not unified as a nation, nominally or practically. The independent states that existed until the 19th century included the Èkìtì, Ìjẹ̀sà, Ègbádò, Ìjẹbu and Ọ̀yọ́ and were at war with each other. The British, who colonised the area in the late 19th century, planned to unite these states as one Yoruba nation, and Christian missionaries, whose interests coincided with those of the colonial government, began to standardise the language. Eventually, the entire territory of the Yoruba nations came to be known as 'Yorubaland' (Johnson 1921).

Prior to this unification, Òyó was the most powerful region in Yorubaland. Founded in the 14th century by Òrànyàn, Òyó has since been the centre of the Yoruba states. Located in northern Yorubaland, Òyó not only prospered economically through trade with Hausa, Nupe and other northern Muslim countries, but also developed culturally through the gradual penetration of advanced Arab and Islamic cultures. Òyó also formed tributary system with neighbouring states, further strengthening its power base as the Òyó Empire.

Òyó reached its peak in the 17th and 18th centuries but was subsequently weakened by blunders and shifts in geopolitical power relations. From the second half of the 18th century onwards, there was a series of defections of tributary states in the south. In the 19th century, Òyó was subjected to the jihad of the Hausa-Fulani from the north; although the capital moved south, the population did not cease to disperse and the empire collapsed in the mid-19th century. Thereafter, a state of warfare in the Yoruba states would continue until the end of the 19th century (Crowder and Abdullahi 1979).

On the other hand, compared to the inland area where Sahara trade flourished, the southern coast was largely neglected until the 15th century. In the 16th century, however, the situation changed dramatically. Europeans began to visit the coast in search of slaves and gold. The slave trade, in particular, brought tremendous economic benefits to the Africans on the coast and raised the economic and military status of the southern states, which led to the weakening of Òyó (ibid.).

The slave trade was abolished in the 19th century, but British involvement in the land continued. The British established a consulate in 1851 in Lagos, the heart of the coastal region, and became sovereign in 1861. Once the colonisation of Lagos was complete, the colonial government was tasked with ending the state of war in Yorubaland in order to secure trade routes to the interior. The war ended in 1892 with the parties accepting the mediation of the colonial government, resulting in almost all of Yorubaland coming under the protection of the British the following year in 1993 (ibid.).

2-2. The 'Yoruba' as an Ethnic Identity

It is important to note here that it was only in 1892 that the Yoruba were unified by external pressures. That is to say, as far as history is concerned, the people of Yorubaland had never previously acted under any kind of unified identity. Firstly, the name 'Yoruba' itself is said to be derived from the Hausa word *Yarriba*, which refers to the inhabitants of Ọ̀yọ́, and in any case, was not a generic term for the inhabitants of Yorubaland (Johnson 1921).

Many records suggest that 'Yoruba' was not an accepted concept for a unified people in the 19th century. For example, Koelle's *Polyglotta Africana*, compiled in 1854 from data collected from freed slaves in Freetown, includes a collection of Yoruba dialects of *Aku* languages (Koelle 1854 [1963]). Within this collection, Yoruba is treated as one of the 12 languages that make up the Aku language group (Shiota 2010: 170). In the preface of the book, Koelle also criticises the missionary's attempt to refer to these languages as together under the name of Yoruba, saying:

> For the last few years they (= missionaries) have very erroneously made use of the name 'Yórūba' in reference to the whole nation, supposing that the Yórūban is the most powerful Aku tribe. But this appellation is liable to far greater objections than that of 'Aku', and ought to be forthwith abandoned; for it is, in the first place, unhistorical, having never been used of the whole Aku nation by anybody except for the last few years conventionally by the Missionaries; secondly, it involves a twofold use of the word 'Yórūba', which leads to a confusion of notions, for in one instance the same word has to be understood of a whole, in another, only of part; and, thirdly, the same being thus incorrect, can never be received by the different tribes as a name for their whole nation. If e.g., you call an Idṣẹbuan or a Yā́gban a Yórūban, he will always tell you, 'Don't call me by that name, I am not a Yórūban;' just, e.g., as the Wúrtembergians or Bavarians would never suffer themselves to be called Prussians (Koelle

1854: 5).

Rejection of the name Yoruba could refer to imposition of the name itself. In addition, the title of the Yoruba language newspaper, *IWE IROHIN*, published in 1860, has a proviso: 'FUN AWON ARA EGBA ATI YORUBA (For Ẹ̀gbá and Yoruba People)'. This supports the idea that Yoruba was not perceived as a superordinate concept of a local country like Ẹ̀gbá, but as a country on a par with it (Peel 2000).

The war-torn inhabitants of Yorubaland in the 19th century chose peace instead of accepting colonial rule. They would inexorably realise that their previous sense of tribal belonging would not be powerful enough to secure their place in the new Nigerian colony. Their first task at the start of the 20th century was to build a Yoruba national consciousness.

3. Yoruba Traditional Music and Its Cultural Transformation

As mentioned in the previous section, the Yoruba did not become a unified ethnic group until the second half of the 19th century. Previously, all states in Yorubaland had their own language and culture. But the most economically prosperous of them all, the Ọ̀yọ́ empire, influenced by the Muslim countries, which were the advanced powers of the Sahel before the 18th century, had developed a highly prestigious court culture and had become the cultural centre of Yorubaland. Ọ̀yọ́ introduced its own court culture to the surrounding tributary countries, where the Ọ̀yọ́ culture was mixed with local culture and became the unique culture of the region (Omojola 2012). This chapter introduces the Yoruba traditional music that has become a cultural resource for the creation of popular music and refers to how the music was transmitted and transformed.

3-1. Traditional Religions and Musical Instruments

The historic music of Yorubaland must have been diverse and regional in character, given the diversity of cultures. Here, however, we will focus on music associated with religious events. This is because much of the traditional music that has been handed down to the present day, and which is still being recorded and studied, is related to religious events. It is also true that the religious events that are the most important to the Yoruba occur when their creativity is most expressed.

The traditional religion of the Yoruba is polytheistic, and the gods are called *òrìṣà*. There are said to be more than 400 *òrìṣà*s in the whole of Yorubaland, with the supreme god Olódùmarè at the centre. The *òrìṣà*s are considered to be intermediaries between Olódùmarè and humans. Each *òrìṣà* has its own followers and is worshipped with its own shrine and rituals, but no such form of worship exists in Olódùmarè. Although it is said that there are more than 400 *òrìṣàs*, in fact there is a great deal of regional variation, with each *òrìṣà* being worshipped by different names depending on the region. For example, the creator god Ọbàtálá is known by a number of aliases, such as Idẹta, Akirè, Ijùgbè, Ìràwé and Ọjà (Euba 1988).

Most musical instruments traditionally used among the Yoruba are percussion instruments (membranophone instruments, i.e., drums). Stringed instruments (three-stringed lute and one-stringed fiddle) are also found in some cases, but these belong to the northern Hausa-Fulani culture and are considered exotic instruments (Omojola 2012). The thumb piano (lamellaphone) is different from the usual percussion instruments and is considered to be a type of percussion instrument that produces sound by plucking a metal key attached to a resonant box with the thumb. In Yorubaland, the keys are generally thicker, and the resonator box is larger and plays the bass.

Traditional music in Yorubaland is believed to have been created and developed as a ritual ceremony of the *òrìṣà*. Euba presents the following legend of the birth of drums as the story of Adétóyèṣe Láoyè I, the king of Ẹdẹ, an authority on traditional music (Euba 1988).

> ...when Ọbàtálá lived on earth he had four wives and whenever he wished to dance, his wives supplied music by clapping their hands. In course of time, Ọbàtálá got bored with hand clapping and decided to

make four drums for his wives to play. The drums were named after the wives, Ìyánlá, Ìyá Àgan, Kẹ̀kẹ̀ and Afééré and they are the drums which form the *igbìn* ensemble that is used up till today by the devotees of Ọbàtálá (Euba 1988: 5–6).

According to this legend, Ọbàtálá is the creator of the *igbìn* drum. Each *òrìṣà* has a specific drum associated with it, which is always used in the rituals. Each drum is based on a set of several drums that are similar in shape but different in size and are referred to as a drum family (King 1961; Euba 1990 and others).

Other drums associated with the famous *òrìṣà*, besides Ọbàtálá, include Ṣàngó (god of thunder) and *bàtá* drums, Ògún (god of iron and war) and *ògìdàn* drums, and Ifá (god of divination) and *ìpèṣì* drums (King 1961). *Bàtá*, the Shango drum, constitutes a four-member drum family consisting of *ìyá ìlù*, *émélé-abo*, *émélé-akọ* and *kúdi* (Daramọla and Jeje 1967).

Another important feature of the Yoruba drums is that most function as a surrogate language. Every syllable of Yoruba and its dialects has either a high, medium or low pitch, or variants of them, in an ascending or descending pitch. These intervals can be played and arranged by the drum to mimic the tone pitch of the language. This technique is found in many parts of Africa, but the richness of the Yoruba language has allowed it to become more complex than many other African languages, which have two different pitches, high and low. In the *oríkì* (praise song), performed as part of a ritual ceremony, the drummer who leads the ensemble takes on the parts of the surrogate language and 'sings' the lyrics of praise to the gods incessantly (Euba 1988).

3-2. Patterns of Cultural Assimilation in the History of Dùndún

This section will focus on the *dùndún*, which is now regarded as the dominant traditional instrument of the Yoruba. Although *dùndún* is regarded as the leading instrument of the Yoruba tradition, it is in fact a relatively new introduction and was not the most traditional instrument. Traditional Yoruba music itself has been transformed into its present form by the acceptance and reformation of foreign elements.

We have mentioned that the Yoruba drum functions as a surrogate language, but the actual method of expression varies from drum to drum. The *bàtá* drum, for example, is double-sided with leather on both sides of its body. Its asymmetrical shape, with a large diameter on one side, allows the player to play low pitches on the large membrane and high pitches on the small membrane. In practice, sophisticated playing techniques such as finger pressure on the membrane surface, adjusting the force of the blow and adjusting the position of the percussion surface allow the performer to play and differentiate between more detailed scales, but this requires a high level of skill. Still, it is difficult for the performer to fully realise the expression of the language and for the audience to understand the content of the performance (Omojola 2012). Although the *bàtá* is said to be one of the oldest existing drums in Yorubaland and is considered one of the most representative of their culture, it is still not structurally perfect with regard to the surrogate language function, and other drums compensated for the structural inconveniences with skilled playing techniques.

Dùndún almost completely solved the problem of the drum's surrogate language function. *Dùndún* is an hourglass-shaped drum with leather stretched over both ends and tied with leather straps at both ends. The two membranes are exactly the same size, but only one side is used for playing. The leather straps that hold the membrane together are tightly stretched to withstand high tension and to efficiently transmit subtle changes in tension to the membrane. The player holds the drum tucked under an armpit and strikes the forward-facing membrane surface with a stick. When the arm is tightened, the tension is transmitted to the leather strap and the membrane is strained, producing a high-pitched sound. If the arm is loosened, the strap is loosened and the membrane becomes less taut, producing a low tone. If the straps are tightened sharply during the sound of strikes, a rising tone is produced, and if they are loosened, a falling tone is produced. This structure made it possible to fully express the complex pitch differences of the Yoruba language without strain.

Dùndún, like other drums such as *bàtá*, has several members that make up a drum family. The composition of the family is of several types, but one drum family, for example, consists of five different components: *ìyá ìlù*, *aguda*, *kànàngó*, *ìṣáájú* and *gúdúgúdú* (King 1961).

Dùndún is considered to be newer than other drums. Many theories try to explain its origin. According to Euba, it was introduced to Ọ̀yọ́ by the Borgu (Ibàrìbá) people living near the Niger River and from there it spread to various parts of Yorubaland. He also posits that it was introduced from Mecca to Ilé-Ifẹ̀, the birthplace of the Yoruba (Euba 1990). Either way, the picture of propagation could be that it was brought to Ọ̀yọ́ from somewhere outside Yorubaland and from there it spread to various parts of the country.

Hause, who examined the spread of the African instrument from its etymology, hypothesised that the *dùndún*-shaped drum originated in Asia and was brought to Africa by the Arabs, and that it was Hausa who brought the drum to Yoruba. As evidence of this, she cites a Hausa word for this type of drum, *kàlàngū*, which became *kànàngó*, a member of the *dùndún* family in Yoruba language. She also pointed out that the Hausa word *gàngā*, which refers to a tubular drum (the pitch of which cannot be changed), is also the origin of the word *gángan*, a member of the Yoruba *dùndún* family, and argued that the borrowing of drum-related vocabulary from Hausa to Yoruba corroborates the transmission of drums (Hause 1948).

It is not clear how the *dùndún* was brought to Yorubaland. However, in Hausaland, drums are also used in solo performances, small orchestral ensembles and song accompaniment. There is no constraint that the drums form a family and are played as an ensemble instrument like in Yoruba culture. It is likely that the *kàlàngū*, brought to Ọ̀yọ́ by the Saharan trade, was derived in the process of improving its form to suit Yoruba music performance, with new derivations of various sizes in imitation of the *bàtá* and other drum families.

Another reason why the *dùndún* is considered a foreign instrument is that this drum does not have an exclusive relationship with a particular *òrìṣà*. As already mentioned, the Yoruba drum was used to worship a particular *òrìṣà*, and is administered and played by the group performing that ritual, and is not played in any other place or for any other purpose. *Dùndún*, however, does not have a specific *òrìṣà* with whom it has such an exclusive relationship. This is why we must assume that this drum has a different history from ordinary drums.

King, who conducted a survey in the 1950s, reported that in Èkìtì, the drums played in the rituals shifted from the traditional drums, which were exclusively associated with the respective *òrìṣà*, to *dùndún* (King 1961). Due to its easiness of playing and richness in expression, *dùndún*, despite being a culture of foreign origin, has spread across Yorubaland and replaced the old-style drums. In the 1950s, the process of acculturation was still considered to be underway.

In this way, *dùndún* changed the form of Yoruba's traditional music, but *dùndún* itself developed differently in the culturally periphery areas, which are remote from Ọ̀yọ́, than in the centre during the process of its diffusion from Ọ̀yọ́ to the countryside. Euba divides the geographic distribution of *dùndún* in Yorubaland into more strongly traditionalised areas and less tenuous traditionalised areas (Euba 1990).

Euba cites Ọ̀yọ́, Òṣogbo and Ìbàdàn as the more strongly traditionalised areas, or as the heart of *dùndún* culture, and enumerates their characteristics as follows: *Dùndún* is an active element in cultural life, which is used in the creation of poetry and is played as a complete drum family. There is a guild of *dùndún* players, *dùndún* is used for both religious and non-religious events and *dùndún* is not used to accompany songs.

Also, peripheral areas of *dùndún* culture with weak traditionalisation include Lagos, Ìkòròdú, Ìjẹ̀bu-Òde and Ilẹ́ṣà, which are characterised by the following. The composition of the drum family is reduced, for example, *gúdúgúdú* is omitted, *dùndún* is played as an accompaniment to the songs, and performers are called in from outside. Furthermore, the *dùndún* is restricted exclusively to non-religious events, and local traditional drums are used for court and religious events. Euba describes *dùndún* as being 'simplified' and 'popularised' in areas where traditionalisation is weak (Euba 1990:

30).

3-3. Patterns of Cultural Transformation in the Popularisation of the Courtly Arts

We discussed the process of reinterpretation of *dùndún*, a new foreign musical instrument, to optimise its performance of traditional music in Ọ̀yọ́ and observed the process of its simplification and popularisation as it spread to the surrounding areas in the previous section. Here, we will discuss the pattern of reception and transformation of musical culture in Yorubaland and examine the process of popularisation of the courtly art that originated in Ọ̀yọ́ and its eventual popularisation as an itinerant performance.

One of the most prevalent performing arts in Yorubaland today is *egúngún*, a masked dance. Performed by masked dancers who imitate resurrected ancestor spirits and the performance of *bàtá* drum, *egúngún* is an ancestor worship ritual. Originally, *egúngún* was not open to the public, as it was protected by many taboos, and was a highly religious ceremony. *Egúngún* developed as a courtly art under the patronage of King Ogbolu in the first half of the 17th century during the heyday of Ọ̀yọ́. Performances were initially restricted to the court, but with the king's permission, *egúngún* was allowed to be performed outside the court, and its content changed from highly religious to more entertaining and popular, with dancers performing acrobatic dances and *bàtá* drum ensembles. The performers of *egúngún*, later called *alárìnjó* (travelling performers), began to tour from Ọ̀yọ́ to the provinces, spreading *egúngún* throughout Yorubaland. *Egúngún*, which was introduced to various regions under the names *eégún ọ̀jẹ̀* or *eégún apidán* (both meaning 'masked dance and magical spectacle'), mixed with local cultural and musical elements and gradually became indigenous (Omojola 2012).

Although some of *alárìnjó* underwent further transformations, the popularised *egúngún* are still performed in various parts of Yorubaland today. They expanded their repertoire to include musical theatre inspired by myths, folk tales, folk songs and so forth, and transformed themselves into a modern mass theatre troupe, and in the 1940s, prominent dramatists such as Hubert Ogunde and

Duro Ladipo appeared on the scene and contributed to the modernisation of Yoruba theatre (ibid.).

In conclusion, the traditional musical culture of Yoruba has always had a distinctly regional flavour. Among them, Ọyọ́ rose to prominence due to its economic prosperity from trade with the Muslim countries of the north, and it became the centre of the region and a hub for transmitting culture to the region. For example, *dùndún*, which was brought from the north and accepted in Ọyọ́, is an example of the musical culture that was optimised to Yoruba traditional music in Ọyọ́ and then disseminated to other parts of the country. Moreover, a pattern of cultural transformation can be seen in which courtly art developed independently within Ọyọ́ was opened to the public with permission of the king and popularised and then diffused to the provinces, where it became indigenous, as in the case of *egúngún*.

The next section examines how the Ọyọ́-originated musical culture, which spread around the periphery, was once separated from its traditional context, simplified and repurposed into new creations as a musical resource of society.

4. Urbanisation and the Establishment of Popular Music

4-1. Commercial Recording of Nigerian Music

In 1922, the earliest commercial recording of Nigerian music was made in England. This memorable first recording was made by Rev. J. J. Ransome-Kuti, who is a native of Abeokuta, a city in southwestern Nigeria. All but one of the 43 recorded materials are hymns in Yoruba. Most of the songs recorded here are still widely sung in churches although some see the solo piano-accompanied hymns as a kind of novelty recorded for Europeans, and Ransome-Kuti's work is highly regarded in Nigeria (Delano c. 1942).

The first commercial recordings in Nigeria were made in Lagos in 1929 and 1930 by the German company Odeon (Waterman 1990). The music recorded at this time satisfied the conditions of popular music as defined by musicologists as being urban, professionally evocative, mass appealing and hybridised from a variety of elements. This suggests that the popularisation of music in Lagos had already been completed before the advent of recording technology and the record industry.

The following section introduces the diversity of popular music that has developed there and examines the background to its creation and focuses on Lagos, the birthplace of popular music in Nigeria.

4-2. Brief History of Lagos and Its Inhabitants

Although some of the information overlaps with the section on the history of Yorubaland, a brief history of Lagos is given below. Lagos was originally an island that was not particularly noteworthy as already mentioned. The cultural centre in Yorubaland was the inland area where powerful countries like Ọ̀yọ́ were located, whereas the coastal area where Lagos was located was remote. Yoruba-speaking fishermen called Àwórì first moved in from the neighbouring continent and islands in the 15th century. Lagos gradually emerged as a keystone in the surrounding economic zone with the beginning of the slave trade in the 16th century, and by the 18th century, its population grew with the influx of Ìjẹ̀bu merchants of Yoruba descent, Edo people of the Benin Kingdom, and refugees from the Dahomey Kingdom (Waterman 1990).

The economic effect of the slave trade was remarkable, and it turned the attention of the interior countries, which had previously been interested only in the Saharan trade in the north, to the southern coastal areas. Changing the power balance in Yorubaland, the southern countries with trade routes to the coast gradually gained strength.

The demand for slaves in Latin America continued to be great although the slave trade was successively banned by Britain and France in the late 18th and early 19th centuries (1791 France, 1807 England), and smuggling trade continued to flourish. Lagos was the perfect land to evade the Royal Navy's crackdown, with its intricate coves, and the trade ban generated rather a lot of revenue.

Lagos became a direct British colony and subsequently the capital of the Southern Protectorate of Nigeria in 1861. By 1914, Lagos had a population of over 70,000, when the southern and northern protectorates were merged to form the Colony of Nigeria.

Because the Lagos Kingdom was so far from the Yoruba interior countries with mainstream culture that the inhabitants themselves recognised their own historical and cultural uniqueness and developed an Ọmọ-Èkó identity (Baker 1974), the native-born Lagosians and their communities were known as Ọmọ-Èkó and, like the rest of Yorubaland, were ruled by a king.

With its multicultural origins, can be glimpsed in its traditional music and instruments, the cultural complexity of the Ọmọ-Èkó society. The royal songs, *igbè* and *karajagba*, are said to have originated with the Awori fishermen, whereas the *gbẹ̀du*, a drum, is said to have been brought by a diplomat of the Benin Kingdom. The dance called *hunwe* and its music, used in religious rituals, were brought by early Dahomey immigrants, and the *dùrù*, a keyboard instrument, was brought by Ìjẹ̀bu merchants (Waterman 1990).

4-3. Immigration and the Emergence of an Elite Class

The presence of immigrants who were involved in the creation of popular music in Lagos is discussed in this section. In the 19th century, there were two types of freed slaves who immigrated to Lagos. After achieving economic success in the New Continent and brought with them their unique culture such as architecture, costumes and cuisine, the Aguda (*Àgùdà*) who were freed slaves from Brazil and Cuba settled in Lagos. Many of the Agudas were Catholics, asserting their own uniqueness and superiority over the locals and their sense of privilege, but they were also familiar with the traditional religion of the Yoruba. Aguda brought Latin American music and Western instruments, such as the guitar, tambourine, flute and concertina, and played samba, fado and polka in the Brazilian immigrant settlement. They were important because they entrenched a style of mixed culture and provided an urban style to the local music scene despite the fact that the Agudas made up only a small percentage of the population of Lagos. Similar groups with a mixed culture included immigrants from the United States and the British West Indies (mainly Jamaica and Trinidad and Tobago) (Waterman 1990).

Other freed slave immigrants are called Sàró. Sàró means 'Sierra Leone' in Yoruba. They were freed on their way to the New World as slaves, mostly of Yoruba descent, although they came from different regions and received a British education in Freetown before returning to Lagos. Sàró were baptised as Protestants and took English surnames. Sàró entered the civil service, became missionaries, doctors or lawyers and entered other professions, and constituted a petit-bourgeois hierarchy in Lagos by the late 19th century. They were often involved in political movements, but they also often acted pompously towards the locals and were derided as *òyìnbó dúdú*, 'black Europeans'. Moreover, they are said to have had a romantic fascination with the orthodox Yoruba culture (ibid.).

Some Sàrós had an affinity for Western tastes, and many enjoyed English-style teatime and classical music. They had no tribal sense of belonging as freed slaves, and they gradually came to play a central role in the creation of a 'pan-Yoruba' culture. They also brought Western rationalist techniques, institutions and ideas to Africa and were willing to partly integrate them with African ways of doing things.

Before the 20th century, the African elite began to be dissatisfied with the racist system and the European-biased trade policies of the colony, mainly composed of Sàró and other immigrants. They were also teased by Europeans for their half-hearted mastery of Western culture and branded by traditional Yoruba as a bad mixture of Yoruba and Western culture (ibid.). The social stresses they were experiencing formed a unique ideology that sought to affirmatively perceive the hybridised culture which was being built already, their 'Yoruba' consciousness as an ethnic group that went beyond their traditional tribal sense of belonging and the new standard Yoruba language that symbolised their identity and, as a result, became a force for the creation of a mixed and contemporary African culture.

The 20th century saw the development of political co-relationships despite the tensions between immigrants and indigenous peoples. For example, political movements in Lagos diverged into nationalist and collaborationist groups after the First World War, but the nationalist leader, Herbert Macaulay, was a descendant of Sàró (Oyewole and Lucas 2000). Although he was well versed in British bourgeois culture, he also drew attention to the eloquence of Yoruba music and put it to good use. His Nigerian National

Democratic Party (NNDP) had a 108-member group of *dùndún* players. The publicity of the songs and drums was no less than that of newspapers and other printed materials. Macaulay even took out newspaper advertisements protesting against the colonial government's preferential treatment of the drummer's guild of a collaborationist party, which suggests that control of the drum language was important in the political struggle (Waterman 1990). This can be regarded as an example of the use of traditional music in a contemporary context.

4-4. Popular Music in Lagos in the Early 20th Century

There were four main types of music popular in Lagos in the early 20th century according to Waterman: *sákárà*, *aṣíkò*, brass band/dance band and palmwine (Waterman 1990). We will discuss the four types of music in detail below, mainly with reference to Waterman's description.

a) *Sákárà*

Sákárà, originated in the Islamised northern Yorubaland and the adjacent Nupe areas and then spread to the south, was a popular music among Muslims. It was performed in Lagos between 1914 and 1925. The lyrics are mainly praise songs, characterised by religious morality and philosophical meaningfulness. The word *sákárà* appears to be derived from the Arabic word *zikr* (ذِكْر, a Sufi ritual) and refers to both the drums used in the performance, the genre of music and the style of dance. Initially, a three stringed guitar *móló* was used besides the drums and, later, it was replaced by a one-stringed fiddle *gòjé*. Listening to the recorded *sákárà*, the rhythm is often between 80 and 100 beats per minute, which is the same tempo as the traditional Yoruba dance beat. *Sákárà* is a mixture of traditional Yoruba and Arab music with call-and-response based singing, polyrhythm and praise songs. It was mainly Muslims who respected and practised Yoruba tradition in a highly Westernised city like Lagos in the 1920s. Despite being created by a complex of cultures, *Sákárà* was favoured by such Muslims and was perceived as really traditional Yoruba style music.

b) *Aṣíkò*

Aṣíkò was the music of choice for Christians and was played at Christian social occasions such as weddings and mission schools and church gatherings. *Aṣíkò* was widespread in the coastal cities of West Africa in the early 20th century and the music flowed into Nigeria as an exotic music genre, and by the 1920s, it had spread to inland cities such as Ìbàdàn and Abẹ́òkúta. *Aṣíkò* was played at a faster tempo than traditional Yoruba music, and the influence of Brazilian music was evident throughout, with men and women dancing across from each other and using a square frame drum as a symbol. Also, it is said that originally, the local Christian boys formed bands, each competing to represent the local community, and it seems to have had the same communal musical character as the Brazilian samba and the Trinidadian carnival bands.

Following a call-and-response format, *Aṣíkò* songs were sung in Yoruba or pidgin English, and the content of the songs included Christianity, interest in Western culture and other topics of current events. For example, the first airplane landing in Lagos in 1928, ruthless rent collection and violence, and a shooting incident triggered by a lawyer's betrayal have been recorded. There were also vulgar songs that seemed to be a mockery of those on the periphery of social norms.

Aṣíkò became popular as a music that blended all the cultural fragments found in the city, such as hymns, Yoruba proverbs, urban slang and Latin American rhythms, both indigenous and exotic, old and new. It also influenced the expansion of Christianity to the urban working class.

c) Brass band/Dance band

British troops were stationed in ports across West Africa, and military bands were formed around the mid-19th century. There was the Hausa-staffed Police Band, the bands of the West African Frontier Force and the West Indian Regiment, and the Salvation Army Band in Lagos. The military band began to play popular music in the 1920s, and the Calabar Brass Band (CBB), also known as the Lagos Mozart Orchestra, was the most popular brass band. CBB was a band led by immigrants from Calabar in Eastern Nigeria, and their performance was based on four/four time of a tuba with syncopation of drums, and here again, we can see the mixture of Western and African elements. While *sákárà* and *aṣíkò* mixed up various elements and were incorporated into the local musical context, brass band, on the other hand, maintained the style of Western military music while incorporating elements of Africa and Latin America. Therefore, the brass band should be considered African-style Western music, and there is a clear difference between the two, whereas *sákárà* and *aṣíkò* can be considered modern African music.

There was a boom in entertainment among the African elite in the 1930s, and the popular brass band was transformed into a dance band that played in exclusive clubs. These dance bands were already popular in Accra, Ghana, and musicians in Lagos who heard their performance at touring concerts and on records were directly and indirectly influenced by them, which led to the formation and development of highlife music in Lagos (Bender 2007).

d) Palmwine

Guitars were becoming more affordable in Lagos by the First World War. In British culture, the guitar was not considered a serious instrument, but rather an instrument played by amateurs at parties, where the African elite were adherents. After the First World War, 'palmwine music' became popular along the West African coastline including Lagos, along with the increase in the number of immigrant workers. Roberts describes it as 'personal music played by one or two musicians for their own expression and pleasure' (Roberts 1972: 241), although the genre of palmwine music encompasses a lot of music and classification remains ambiguous.

The spreading of vinyl records gave people a chance to hear guitar music from all over the world in the 1920s, including Cuban, American country and Hawaiian music. Guitarists in Lagos also became influenced by world music, but it was the Kru guitarists who contributed most to the establishment of guitar playing in West Africa. Kru were originally from Liberia, but their seafaring skills were so valued that they began working with Europeans as sailors in the 18th century. Kru had ample opportunity to experience the cultures of various parts of Europe, Latin America and Africa, and they also had a habit of playing music for entertainment. They developed various methods of guitar tuning and picking, which they passed on throughout West Africa. These made up the palmwine. Palmwine is a free and open musical genre, and although some musicians say there is no set style, it has gradually developed a local character, and its style has become more formulaic.

Because many of its performers were immigrants and the recordings were made in various languages, palmwine was also a music that had no ethnic barriers. The Ghanaian hit song, '*Yaa Amponsah*', originally recorded by the Kumasi Trio in 1928, became so popular in Lagos that a cover version was also released. The Jolly Orchestra was one of the leading cosmopolitan bands in Lagos at the time. The band's members varied from Yoruba, Sàró, Kru, Ashanti and others. In their song '*Olówó l'obìnrin mọ̀*' ('It is the rich man that women know'), the band sings 'If-a money go a woman go', and the song is about unstable relationships in the city. This motif did not exist in songs of the traditional African society, protected by ties of blood and community. This song shows how palmwine is characterised as an urban music of new era expressing the sentiments of lonely urban dwellers. The hit song '*Àtàrí Àjànàkú*' ('Head of elephant') also incorporates a traditional Yoruba proverb in its provocative, streetwise lyrics that show off their musical abilities. The lyrics also incorporate not only deep elements of the Yoruba language but also English and relatively concise Yoruba language, making the song more accessible to non-native Yoruba audiences. This sample shows that attempts to merge African traditions with new musical forms were being made by young people and immigrants. It is also interesting because it documents the very experimentation of expression in the new age African cities.

Lagos at the beginning of the 20th century was in a position to draw on a great variety of cultures as a social resource as mentioned above: traditional Lagos culture, Yoruba-Ọ̀yọ́ culture, Yoruba vernacular culture, Western culture, Latin American culture,

Christianity and Islamic culture, and so forth. The popular music that blossomed in this context should be understood as one of the cultures that local people with their previous tribal identities, foreign immigrants with global perspectives and migrants from all over Nigeria who were attracted by economic prosperity, constructed as they were forced to shift their sense of belonging to the new Lagos citizens and even to the Yoruba ethnic group.

5. Conclusion

This chapter has provided an overview of how Yoruba musical culture has been propagated and transformed, both in terms of traditional and popular music, and finally, we would like to summarise both of them as phenomena on the same horizon.

Yoruba traditional music originally developed under the aegis of religion and kingship, and its performance was limited to exclusive occasions. The same goes for traditional instruments, which had an exclusive relationship with a particular faith and their instrumentation was also complicated. *Dùndún*, which was an exotic instrument, was also modified to fit this traditional music and was integrated into the traditional context. Moreover, traditional music diffused from Ọ̀yọ́, the main stage of its development, to various parts of Yorubaland, where it began to show local transformations in different parts of the country. The musical culture became popularised by moving away from its core, and except for the distinctive parts, the rest of the culture became simplified as seen in the diffusion of *egúngún* and *dùndún*.

This transformation of musical culture has been spurred by urbanisation. An example that illustrates this movement is the rise of popular music in Lagos, documented in the early 20th century. Urbanisation in Lagos led to a diminution of ties to the community and bloodlines, and a rise in social and economic freedom for individuals. The musicians mixed global musical elements with simplified and materialised Yoruba traditional music to create a new era of music as if to reflect the growing ethnic consciousness in reaction to colonialism and the creation of a new Yoruba ethnic consciousness by an elite class with little traditional background, which was different from the traditional tribal sense of belonging.

Popular music that emerged during the colonial period became more 'ethnic' as the ethnic image of Yoruba became more firmly established. Tracking the subsequent development of popular music is a subject for future study, but we would like to conclude this chapter by introducing the birth of *Jùjú* as one example.

Jùjú was born as a development of palmwine and *aṣíkò* described in this chapter, and Tunde King, who started recording in the 1930s, is considered to be the founder of this music. Initially, it was performed by a small band consisting of stringed instruments such as guitar and banjo and percussion such as tambourine and *ṣẹ̀kẹ̀rẹ̀*, a calabash drum netted with strings of cowries, with the guitarist often doubling as a singer (Waterman 1990).

Jùjú began to show changes at the end of the 1940s, after the Second World War. It is worth noting that the *gángan*, one of the *dùndún* family's talking drums, was adopted. It was largely due to the development of microphones that *gángan*, the smaller, better looking, broader, and more expressive member of the family was introduced to *Jùjú* along with the Afro-Cuban percussions, conga and bongo. Electrical amplification made it possible to record songs and guitars and drums in a balanced way. Traditional instruments are taken out of their original contexts and incorporated into ensembles with foreign instruments through the power of modern technology. The music created in this way is integrated into traditional social events such as weddings, naming ceremonies and other events, thus returning to the Yoruba tradition once again. However, this is not a simple return to the past. As the Yoruba of their time choose and discard their own traditional resources, it is a new way of passing on traditions that reflects the will of the new era.

In his essay, *Dentou ni tsuite* ('A note on tradition'), Hideo Kobayashi states that tradition is not a habitual act that can be continued in a casual manner but can be maximised by the efforts and awareness of those living in the era (Kobayashi 1941). In the first half of the 20th century, a time of social upheaval from colonisation to independence, the fact that the Yoruba popular music was undergoing such a splendid reconstruction of tradition is a suggestive case for the possibilities of African culture in the future.

Acknowledgements

This work was supported by JSPS KAKENHI Grant Number JP16H06318.

References

Baker, P. H. (1974) *Urbanization and Political Change: The Politics of Lagos, 1917–1967*, Berkeley: University of California Press.

Bender, W. (2007) *Der nigerianische Highlife*, Wuppental: Peter Hammer Verlag.

Coplan, D. (1978) 'Go to my town, Cape Coast! The social history of Ghanaian highlife', in B. Nettl (ed.) *Eight Urban Musical Cultures*, Champaign: University of Illinois Press.

———— (1979–80) 'Marabi culture: Continuity and transformation in African music in Johannesburg, 1920–1940', *African Urban Studies*, Issue 6, pp. 49–76.

Crowder, M. and Abdullahi, G. (1979) *Nigeria: An Introduction to Its History*, London: Longman.

Daramọla, O. and Jeje, A. (1967) *Àwọn àṣà àti òrìṣà Ilẹ̀ Yorùbá*, Ìbàdàn: Oníbọn-Òjé Press & Industries (NIG.) LTD.

Delano, I. O. (c. 1942) *The Singing Minister of Nigeria: The Life of the Rev. Canon J. J. Ransome-Kuti*, London: United Society for Christian Literature.

Euba, A. (1988) *Essays on Music in Africa*, Bayreuth: Iwalewa Haus, Bayreuth University.

———— (1990) *Yoruba Drumming: The Dùndún Tradition*, Bayreuth: Bayreuth University.

Hause, H. E. (1948) *Terms for Musical Instruments in the Sudanic Languages: A Lexicographical Inquiry (Journal of the American Oriental Society, Supplement Vol. 7)*, Baltimore: American Oriental Society.

Johnson, S. (1921) *The History of the Yorubas*, Lagos: Church

Missionary Society.

King, A. (1961) *Yoruba Sacred Music from Ekiti*, Ibadan: Ibadan University Press.

Kobayashi, H. (1941) 'Dentou ni tsuite.' (A note on tradition). Tokyo: Asahi Shinbun (reissued in 2001 in *Kobayashi Hideo Zenshuu, Vol. 7*, Tokyo: Shinchosha, pp. 260-261).

Koelle, S. W. (1854) *Polyglotta Africana; or a Comparative Vocabulary of Nearly Three Hundred Words and Phrases in More Than One Hundred Distinct African Languages*, London: Church Missionary House (reprinted in 1963 with an index of D. Dalby, Graz: Akademische Druck - U. Verlagsanstalt).

Manuel, P. (1988) *Popular Music of the Non-Western World: An Introductory Survey*, Oxford: Oxford University Press.

Omojola, B. (2012) *Yoruba Music in the Twentieth Century: Identity, Agency, and Performance Practice*, Rochester: University of Rochester Press.

Oyewole, A. and Lucas, J. (2000) *Historical Dictionary of Nigeria, Second edition*, Lanham and London: The Scarecrow Press Inc.

Peel, J. D. Y. (2000) *Religious Encounter and the Making of the Yoruba*, Bloomington: Indiana University Press.

Popular Music (1981) *Popular Music, Vol. 1*, Cambridge: Cambridge University Press.

Roberts, J. S. (1972) *Black Music of Two Worlds*, New York: Praeger.

Shiota, K. (2010) 'The process of standardization and some aspects of modern Yoruba', *LiCCOSEC (Lingua-Culture Contextual Studies in Ethnic Conflicts of the World)*, Vol. 13 (Annual Report 2009), pp. 169–181.

Waterman, C. A. (1990) *Jùjú: A Social History and Ethnography of an African Popular Music*, Chicago: The University of Chicago Press.

Chapter 9

Literature for African Children: Creation and Publication of Children's Books in French-Speaking West African Countries

Haruse Murata

1. Introduction

To date, literary works written in French by authors from sub-Saharan Africa[1] have been published more frequently in France than in their authors' home countries (Ducournau 2017), where publishing and distribution systems are not yet fully developed. Moreover, a writer wishing to publish his/her book in France must be recognised by a French editor or critic, and French publishers assume that their readers are Westerners because, for readers in the writers' home countries, it is difficult to get hold of expensive books published overseas. Many authors cannot speak directly to African readers through their literary work, even when describing African society or history.

This study focuses on children's books and particularly children's literature[2] which have increasingly been published in French-speaking West African countries.[3] Following their independence from mainland France, only a few such books were published every year in the region, and for many years children who were able and wanted to read books only had access to new or old books imported from France. Of course, African children rarely appeared in such books, and neither their society nor culture were depicted. However, it is believed that the effort to create and publish children's books in the region since the 1990s has been changing this scenario, with the number of children's books produced by local writers and artists and published locally beginning to increase in the Ivory Coast and rising significantly in Benin and other countries in the 2000s.

Although this phenomenon is limited to children's books, and their number is still much lower than that of imported books distributed in the region, more locally published children's books are being delivered to African readers. This chapter covers the case of Benin, exploring the magnitude of ongoing and complex activities of diverse people required to achieve these results. More specifically, we will consider a co-edition led by a Beninese children's book publisher that allowed the publication of many children's books, while referring to our interviews from Benin, Senegal and Ivory Coast between 2014 and 2019. Subsequently, we will show that this co-edition allows African children to be more conscious of themselves and to know how to establish a relationship of give-and-take with others.

In the second section, we will show the twisted relationship between the writers, who express themselves in French, and the readers in African countries, results from the situation in which literature works are published more often in France than on the African continent and look back at the publishing history behind it by focusing on West Africa. Then we will examine the co-edition established by Beatrice Lalinon Gbado,[4] founder of Beninese children's book publisher *Editions Ruisseaux d'Afrique* [African Streams Editions][5] to overcome the difficulties in the publication and distribution of children's books by small publishers in African countries.

As an aspect of the 'African Potentials', Itaru Ohta noted the 'new knowledge and systems' that people are 'continuing to develop to make their lives better, referring to the knowledge taken from the outside world and to the systems they have used in response to changes in the ecological and social environment surrounding them' (Ohta 2016: xii). The co-edition Lalinon Gbado promoted with editors from neighbouring countries is exactly an embodiment of this 'African Potentials'. She combined her European knowledge of publishing with her relationship with African publishers to create and publish children's books in their own countries. This is a system initiated by the complementary combinations of different elements which publishers could apply to solve regional challenges.

In the third section, we will explore the concepts behind such collaborative publishing. Writers publishing their children's literature in French in West African countries have expressed their opinion that children should have access to books depicting their own society and culture. With regard to this matter, we will then analyse the claims of various authors and, especially Lalinon Gbado's, examining what she aimed to realise by developing her co-edition.

Children's books (and notably children's literature) published in the area comprise one genre of African literature written in French, whose history originates from the *Negritude* movement established in the 1930s by Black intellectuals from the French colonies. Today's authors, publishing children's literature works in French and aiming to raise awareness of their society and history among young readers, can be said to carry the intention of those who created the stream of African literature in this language. However, these writers are not recommending that children only look at their own society; thus, in this section, we will also focus on Lalinon Gbado's words, '*être soi*' [to be oneself], and consider how her co-edition aims to affect children.

In the fourth section, we will examine children's literary works published by *Editions Ruisseaux d'Afrique*. Through this co-edition, Beninese writers and illustrators address daily subjects in their texts and speak directly to African children, who can read about social problems, traditional values and the invisible existence surrounding them from the perspectives of the writer.

In this chapter, we will provide additional information on the research about publishing in the West African region by Foucault et al. (eds) (2010), Kloeckner (2003) and Pinhas (2005, 2008), and that of *Africultures* No. 57 (October–December in 2003), which we obtained from our interviews with local editors, authors and illustrators. Moreover, we will give further consideration to the co-edition led by *Editions Ruisseaux d'Afrique* through our interviews with Véronique Tadjo, a contemporary writer from Ivory Coast and with Lalinon Gbado, referring to Hugues's (2008) detail of the co-edition as well as to the interviews with Lalinon Gbado by Tervonen (2003) and Atchadé and Djogbénou (2016). We will also criticise some children's literature works, which has hardly been done by previous research and by the electronic periodical *Takan Tikou* edited by the *Centre national de la littérature pour la jeunesse, service du Département*

Littérature et art de la Bibliothèque nationale de France [National Centre of children's literature, Department of Literature and Art of the National Library of France] that every year reports about children's book publishing and its trend in the region.

2. Creation and Publication of Children's Literature in French-Speaking West African Countries

2-1. The Controversial Situation of African Literature Written in French

In French-speaking West African countries, publishing has been unable to achieve stable development even after their independence. Among the 364,000 books published worldwide in 1960, only 5,000 were published throughout the African continent, which accounted for just 1.4 per cent of total global publishing (Pinhas 2005: 74). This proportion remained the same in the 1990s, and most of the 14,000 books published in 1994 throughout the African continent were from countries such as Egypt, Nigeria and South Africa (Pinhas 2005: 74).[6]

In the case of literary works written in French by writers from sub-Saharan Africa, if 2,456 were edited in African or Western countries in 1960–1990 and 5,960 in 1991–2010, about half of them were published in France (Ducournau 2017: 93). These writers had several reasons to choose to publish their texts through French publishers. Domestic publishers were stagnant and their books were rarely distributed outside of the country; in addition, they wanted to reach a wider audience, and, for some of them, it was impossible to publish in their home countries due to censorship rules (Ducournau 2017).

However, African literature researcher, Claire Ducournau, observed that, if writers aim to be published in France, they must be recognised by French editors, honoured and reviewed in literary magazines and have established a career as writers (Ducournau 2017: 252), meaning that the success of an African writer depends on French editors, critics and journalists. Moreover, once a publication is accepted, the editor gives the author directions for the book's form, genre and size (Ducournau 2017: 253). For the editor, the book is a product for Western readers.

According to Ducournau, 'a series of material and symbolic mechanisms from the developed countries have had rampant and long-term influences on the production and commercialisation of most African literature works' (Ducournau 2017: 252).

Tadjo was deeply concerned about this situation, positing that the writers who seek recognition in France could become 'mere observers' of the African continent's chaotic reality for example, conflict, famine, corruption and infectious diseases, and would 'use Africa only as a source of ideas' (Tadjo 2003: 114), attempting to write works that engage the imaginations of Western readers.

What is seen here is the twisted relationship between African writers and readers: although a book may be written by an African author, individuals living in Africa would often be unable to read it due to several obstacles. Firstly, the number of people studying and reading French is limited; in Ivory Coast, for example, only about ten per cent of the population is able to read fluently and wish to read books (interview at *Direction du livre et de la lecture* [Book and Reading Bureau], Ivory Coast, on 9 October 2019). Secondly, books published in France are too expensive when compared to the purchasing power of the general population, and they are difficult to obtain. In Benin, Ivory Coast and Senegal where we visited, even if there are public libraries in each capital, it seems difficult for them to be equipped with new books every year. Finally, and more crucially, the overwhelming majority of books in bookstores and libraries are written by Western writers, particularly the French. Beninese writer and illustrator Hortense Mayaba recalled this reading experience: 'In my childhood, I read many European stories in the library but many things like 'snow' or 'fir trees' didn't fit our reality, so I felt some kind of frustration' (private message, 9 October 2018).

At the same time, literary works by African writers seem to be only written for African readers as many of them deal with Africa's historical facts and contemporary events. For example, Emmanuel Dongala's *Johnny chien méchant* [*Johnny Mad Dog*] (2002) depicts the Republic of the Congo's civil war, which Dongala himself experienced, and one of its main characters is a child soldier. In this story, African readers might find to be asked a question: how should we raise our children in Africa?

Nevertheless, the reality is that writers are caught in a twisted situation where they can neither speak directly to African readers through their work nor witness their reaction.

2-2. Publishers in French-Speaking West African Countries

If most African writers can now publish their texts in Africa, could it be possible to change this situation? To examine this possibility, we will briefly examine the history of publishing by focusing on French-speaking West African countries.

In this region, two types of publishers emerged after the countries' independence: those founded and led by the government and, after the 1990s, several small privately managed ones.

One representative example of these government-led publishers is *Centre d'Edition et de Diffusion Africaines* [African Edition and Diffusion Centre] (CEDA), established in 1961 in Ivory Coast (Ducournau 2017: 98; Keïta 2008: 206); however, 75 per cent of the company's initial capital was fronted by French publishers such as *Hatier* (Ducournau 2017: 98–99; Keïta 2008: 206; Pinhas 2005: 78).

Senegal's poet and first president, Léopold Sédar Senghor, also launched *Nouvelles Editions Africaines* [New African Editions] (NEA) in 1972. In 1974 Senegal, Ivory Coast and Togo took 20 per cent of NEA's capital to open a branch in each country. In this case, the rest of the funds (40 per cent) were borne by French publishers such as *Hachette* (Ducournau 2017: 98–99; Keïta 2008: 209; Pinhas 2005: 78).

Through these publishers, though funded by French publishers, African writers were able to publish their manuscripts without the need for recognition in France, and the result was significant. NEA, for example, published representative literary works of some of the first African female authors writing in French, such as Aminata Sow Fall and Mariama Bâ, and made them known to the world.

These publishers were eventually privatised due to financial difficulties. The CEDA was privatised in 1991, and from then onwards its largest shareholders were French publishers, including *Hatier* (Pinhas 2005: 78).

NEA was dissolved in 1988. Its Ivory Coast branch resumed in 1992 as *Nouvelles Editions Ivoiriennes* [New Ivorian Editions] (NEI) and was funded by the Ivorian government (20 per cent), domestic shareholders (50 per cent), and *Edicef*, a French publisher belonging to the *Hachette Group* (30 per cent) (Pinhas 2005: 78). However, the 2000s political crisis in Ivory Coast negatively impacted their businesses, and CEDA and NEI merged in 2006 to form NEI-CEDA (Keïta 2008: 216). The publisher now belongs to *Hachette Livre*, born from the merger of major French publishers *Hachette*, *Didier* and *Hatier*.

While government-led publishers have been privatised and now belong to leading French operations, a number of small, independent publishers that are not funded by foreign investment have also been established in French-speaking West African countries since the 'market opening' of the 1990s in the sub-Saharan African region (Hugues 2008: 245). However, such publishers only have a small domestic book market, and public purchasing power is low in these countries. Moreover, 'they sorely lack, in general, institutional and financial support' (Pinhas 2005: 77); consequently, the number of titles they publish each year is limited, and they find difficulties in developing distribution systems independently (Pinhas 2005: 74).

One of the keys to resolving this shortage of funds is the publication of school textbooks, which account for 75 to 90 per cent of the entire book market in French-speaking African countries (Kloeckner 2003: 71) and are the most profitable publishing products although most been published by French, Quebecer and Belgian publishers (Pinhas 2005: 74), whose overwhelming financial power allows their participation and acceptance in international bids for textbooks (Pinhas 2005: 79). This is impossible for small domestic publishers, who are underfunded and uncompetitive and thus unable to benefit from the enormous textbook market to stabilise their management.

In Ivory Coast, CEDA and NEI, who were funded by French publishers, monopolised textbook publishing for many years. Thus, while these companies increased their publication of children's books in the 1990s (Pinhas 2005: 74, 76), this was thanks to the financial headroom provided by textbook publishing. There was, however, another factor in this increase. Tadjo, mentioned above, who wanted African children to read books, has been publishing her children's literature works since the late 1980s through CEDA and NEI (interview on 20 November 2017), and they have been widely accepted in the country. N'Guessan Kouadio Céléstin, director of the NEI-CEDA's production division, said that 'in Ivory Coast, Tadjo is a hero of children's literature. She inspired other children's literature writers' (interview on 7 October 2019). Her children's literature, particularly the books she herself illustrated, inspired the emergence of other writers in this genre, such as Fatou Keïta and Annick Assemian, and created a trend for the production and publication of children's books in Ivory Coast; in the 1990s NEI and CEDA published one-third of children's books in French in sub-Saharan Africa (Pinhas 2005: 78).

Incidentally, since 2002 the Ivorian government has opened the textbook market to other domestic publishers as explained by Henri N'Koumo, *Directeur du livre, des arts plastiques et visuels* [Director of the Contemporary and Visual Arts and Books Bureau], in an interview on 9 October 2019. Thanks to this measure, some domestic textbook publishers, such as *Les Classiques Ivoiriens* [The Ivorian Classics] and *Editions Eburnie* [Eburnie Editions] were established and have been able to realise self-sustained management, which means that they receive subsidies neither from the government nor international organisations or funds from foreign publishers. Dramane Boaré, president of *Les Classiques Ivoirians*, stated that textbook publishing is essential to the independent management of publishers (interview on 4 October 2019); according to him, the profit generated from publishing textbooks for pre-school, primary or secondary education courses allows stable management and publication of other genres. The two publishers abovementioned are now leaders in the publication of children's literature in Ivory Coast.

The improvement in publishers' funding situations, in addition to the writers' motivation, has thus made it possible to publish literary works representing the lives, culture and adventures of African children.

2-3. Editions Ruisseaux d'Afrique in Benin and Lalinon Gbado's Co-Edition

In this way, from the 1990s the number of children's books published in French-speaking West African countries increased.

In 1989 the first edition of the French magazine *Takam Tikou* listed 193 children's books written in French and taking Africa as their subject that had been published in France and sub-Sahara African countries between 1975 and 1988 (*Association des amis de la Joie par les livres* 1989). Among them, 161 were published in Africa and for 92 books, the author was estimated to be African by his/her name.

By 2004 the number of children's literary works produced by African writers and/or illustrators in French and published in sub-Saharan Africa was 415 (Pinhas 2005: 75).

It ought to be noted that the textbook market being open to all domestic publishing companies in Ivory Coast was peculiar. Since small publishers were suffering from a shortage of funds in many countries without such opportunities, how did the publishing of children's books develop at the beginning of the 2000s? The key was co-editions, which allowed 300 children's books to become available in Benin by 2016. About 200 of them were published by *Editions Ruisseaux d'Afrique* after 2003, including approximately 100 picture books (Atchadé and Djogbénou 2016), and the beginning of the 2000s is exactly when *Editions Ruisseaux d'Afrique* began its co-editions with African publishers.

Why and how did Lalinon Gbado develop the concept of co-edition? As a writer, editor and psychology specialist engaged in child counselling, she believed that 'for the mental development of a child, it is important for them to know their origin, but in Benin, there were no books which showed Beninese children this' (interview on 12 October 2019). Thus, in 1989 she founded her own publishing company, *Editions Ruisseax d'Afrique* though initially it had no means of publishing and could not distribute many books. She described how the idea of the co-edition was devised in such a situation:

> Around the beginning of the 2000s, I participated in an editor's seminar held in France. I brought there a dummy of a book and showed it to the editors from other African countries. Then, an editor of *Cérès*, a Tunisian publisher, and of *Ganndal*, a Guinean publisher, agreed to publish it together. They said that they had been wanting to do such a thing. The editor of *Ganndal* also said that he knew an Ivorian editor who would join us. It was *Editions Eburnie*. Our co-edition started in this

way (interview on 12 October 2019).

Except for *Cérès*, it was small publishing companies from French-speaking West African countries who gathered to establish this co-edition, which was a system created through a combination of knowledge and technology learned from Europe, the experience of African publishing companies and a cooperative relationship between them.

However, it ought to be noted that this co-edition venture did not always allow publishing companies' self-sustained management: it was an activity supported by developed countries and international organisations that aimed for financial independence after a lengthy effort. Lalinon Gbado explained in an interview: 'When *Editions Ruisseaux d'Afrique* prints 3,000 to 5,000 copies of a children's book, it takes about three to five years to sell them out. But, if we publish a book by a co-edition, the cost each company bears is reduced, and distribution and sale can also be divided up by all the participating companies' (Tervonen 2003: 102). As Lalinon Gbado suggested, even if the participating companies suffered from scarce funds and experience, they could publish and distribute more children's books by making the most of their African Potentials or the co-edition system.

The co-edition led by *Editions Ruisseaux d'Afrique* was also supported by a reliable relationship between Lalinon Gbado and some Beninese writers and illustrators who had already produced books for local children before its foundation. Between them, they founded *Association des Auteurs et Illustrateurs de Livres pour Enfants* [Association of Writers and Illustrators of Children's Books] (AILE) in 1995 (interview with Hector Sonon on 13 October and with Mayaba on 10 October 2018). From the 1990s to the early 2000s members of the AILE and Lalinon Gbado participated in workshops on the skills required for picture book production, which were organised as part of the programmes for the promotion of reading supported by the French Ministry of Culture. The workshop lecturers were famous picture book writers and illustrators, such as Marie Wabbes from Belgium, Tadjo from Ivory Coast and Dominique Mwankoumi from the Democratic Republic of the

Congo. These workshops offered opportunities for the Beninese artists to strengthen their ties and nurture their talents. After its foundation, *Editions Ruisseaux d'Afrique* published many of these artists' works.

When *Organisation Internationale de La Francophonie* [International Organisation of La Francophonie] cut its funding for the co-edition in 2004, the cost became difficult to sustain. Nevertheless, Lalinon Gbado told us about her intention to continue publishing children's books:

> Because I believe there is no other thing we should do. Neither the government nor the institutions who want to promote culture subsidise us. We are convinced that this is what the government is responsible for. So, we wait for things to evolve as they should. We hope that the government and the institutions who finance cultural activities will understand one day that ... it is important to give more space to books in society (interview on 12 October 2018).

Since Lalinon Gbado shares the view of the people who have long contributed to the production of children's literature in the region, we suppose that she has a strong intention to do so. We will consider this point in the next section.

3. Views behind the Production of Children's Literature

3-1. Children's Literature in the History of African Literature in French

Children's literature produced in French-speaking West African countries belongs to the long and wide stream of African literature in French, the origin of which is found in the *Negritude* movement born during the 1930s in France and initiated by black students from the French colonies.

Martinican poet Aimé Césaire was the first writer to use the word '*Negritude*' in his article in *L'Etudiant Noir* [*The Black Student*] in 1935. He explained the meaning of this notion in 1959 as 'the awareness of being Black, simple recognition of the fact, which implies acceptance, having responsibility for his Black destiny, his history and his culture' (Kesteloot 1963: 113).

Negritude was a statement of black students, who refused to be assimilated into French culture and considered themselves black and Africans treated as inferior human beings (Nakamura 2013: 113). Most black intellectuals at the time were educated and had learned French in their colonial homelands, becoming familiar with French values and history and being assimilated into French culture. However, the more they longed for assimilation, the deeper they were caught in the framework of thinking that assumed the inferiority of black people. The black intellectuals of the Negritude movement wanted to reject this framework and get a foothold to express who they were (Sunano 2004: 258); if European thinking and its history had refused the values and ways of thinking of black people, they needed to create their own words and expressions to describe themselves. They also needed to know themselves. These black intellectuals undertook these quests in the form of poems and novels.

3-2. Literature Describing African Children

African countries are now independent, and Negritude is not a central notion in the criticism of African literature in French. However, as we have seen, African writers have not yet been able to sufficiently propose their own expression about Africa and African people to local readers; therefore, they still seem to be stagnating on the quest of 'who we are' that was present during the birth of African literature in French. Many contemporary writers represent African people who live in a changing society and a changing world, though they still find it difficult to interact with the reader in Africa through their texts.

In this scenario, the number of children's books published in Africa has been slowly increasing, opening a path that would enable these authors to directly address local children. The writers and editors who have been dedicating themselves to this effort communally hope that children in Africa will see themselves, their society and their culture reflected in books. It could be said, therefore, that they have assumed the point of view of the black Negritude writers.

Jeanne de Cavally, for example, was a modern writer and pioneer of children's literature in Ivory Coast, beginning her career in the 1970s when she was a teacher recommending texts to her pupils and finding that they could only source books about Europe or France. Thus, she thought that 'if a child knows well the history of his country, he will be attracted by its values' and decided to 'write Africa for African children' (Dabo 1982).

However, until Tadjo published children's literature in Ivory Coast, only a few literary works existed for African children in French-speaking West African countries. Children who wanted to read could only find books depicting the life and society of Westerners. Tadjo explained, 'There must be literature in which a child can find his environment, develop emotionally and be stimulated intellectually. Without literature derived from the child's own country and reality, it would be unbalanced'. According to her, African children can be conscious of who they are and their environment in which they live only when they have access to literature in which they find themselves (interview on 20 November 2017).

Lalinon Gbado described such a reading experience more concretely:

> Books can help a child in many ways. They help him understand the world, life, and relationships between people. … He can know people could be angry, satisfied, talk to each other or not. Books can help the child understand himself a little. He can know what he likes, what he doesn't like, what he wants or what he doesn't want. … Therefore, books help a child develop and construct his personality (interview on 23 July 2014).

According to her, when a child finds the environment he/she knows in literature, assimilates himself/herself into the main character, and travels the story world, it helps the child better understand himself/herself and his/her environment. Lalinon Gbado and other African writers have tried to produce such literary works, which had long been lacking in the region.

3-3. Being Yourself

Lalinon Gbado has a clear concept about what kind of self-consciousness she wants African children to have and reflects it in the books she publishes. In an interview she cautioned that, even if she wants children to learn about their own society and own culture through reading books, she does not recommend them either being 'locked in' to one culture or simply 'gazing at their navels'. She said, 'It is necessary to be yourself (*être soi*) before you connect with others' (Beau 2013).

What is then to 'be yourself'? We posed this question to her, to which she responded, 'It's that the child can demonstrate his potential. That means he can demonstrate his abilities, like helpfulness, kindness, intelligence and vitality'; in other words, it means 'to be aware that you have something' (interview on 20 October 2018). 'Being yourself', to Lalinon Gbado, means that a child knows about themselves, believes that they can demonstrate their abilities and really is in a state where they can do so.

She also noted that a child must be aware of what they have and needs 'to be ready to share this 'something' to participate in a give-and-take relationship' (interview on 20 October 2018), highlighting how 'being oneself' is important for a child to live with others.

Explaining the meaning further, Lalinon Gbado said,

> That is to be yourself, to demonstrate yourself, to become what you are, and to interact with others, to create yourself and to keep you alive without losing your own thoughts, without erasing your aspiration, without missing your dreams. However, you must be open to others and listen to others' words (interview on 20 October 2018).

We interpret these answers as a wish to bestow African children with books in which they can read their life, learn about their abilities, feel that they have the power to demonstrate them and self-confidently build relationships with others.

After considering Lalinon Gbado's view, we must recall some works of contemporary African literature. In her novel *Le Ventre de l'Atlantique* [*The Belly of the Atlantic*] (2003) Senegalese writer Fatou Diome described poor Senegalese youth with great longing for European life and culture living on a small island. Emmanuel Dongala, a writer from Republic of the Congo, in his aforementioned novel *Johnny chien méchant* depicted a teenager named Johnny becoming a cruel child soldier, who is very docile to his senior officer, after accepting a suspicious explanation about the ethnic conflict that had broken out in his country.

Though these are literary works, the writers attempt to represent part of the reality of African youth, in which the characters are strongly influenced by others' ways of thinking and values and do not know what they can or should do in their own country. Diome and Dongala seem to ask African readers, what can be done for their youth, and how they can give them hope in Africa. Lalinon Gbado likely aims to publish books that respond to these questions, hoping that African children will trust their abilities, find ways to live as they keep their hope alive, and coexist with others without being unilaterally influenced by their view or values even when facing problems.

4. Beninese Children's Literature

4-1. Texts Treating Social Issues

In the final section, we critically read some children's literary works published by *Editions Ruisseaux d'Afrique* in line with Lalinon Gbado's views examined in the previous section.

An artist might undertake creative work led by his/her desire to create or by his/her inspiration. When a Beninese artist creates, his/her imagination world is not free from the environment around him/her: his/her experience and the values of his/her society may be embedded in his/her work.

Among the books of *Editions Ruisseaux d'Afrique* are some texts that deal with the social issues affecting children. Mayaba, for instance, published 15 children's literary works in Ivory Coast and Benin from the beginning of the 2000s, among which are *La robe de Ninie* [*Ninie's Dress*] (2002) and *Le syllabaire de Gadjo* [*Gadjo's Primer*] (2003).

The story of *La robe de Ninie* features Ninie, the story's main character, who is a clever schoolgirl and has worked hard and is top of her class, for which she will receive a citation at the end of term. However, she is unhappy because she does not have a 'Sunday best'.

Although her parents are poor, her mother, who is aware of Ninie's worries, secretly sews her a dress in one night. Though the dress is too big for Ninie, she is delighted with it and goes to the ceremony. Despite her school friends laughing at her loose dress, she is happy because she has been rewarded with a beautiful dress and some *pagne* [cloth] for another.

The main character of *Le syllabaire de Gadjo* is a schoolboy, Gadjo, who has recently begun learning how to read and write at school. One day, as Gadjo is enjoying a book, his father asks him, 'Does your book speak to me too?', but Gadjo knows well that it does not because his father has never studied at school. The father then decides to learn to read and write, though Gadjo's school has no literacy classes for adults. Witnessing the father's disappointment, Gadjo's teacher encourages his pupil: 'You can teach your father, Gadjo'. Helped by his son, the father makes a great effort and succeeds in learning to read. Those around him then claim that he is 'a person who has courage', and Gadjo feels proud of him.

Though both stories describe the serious themes of poverty, schooling difficulties and the promotion of literacy, Mayaba applies some techniques that draw readers into her story. At the beginning of *La robe de Ninie*, the narrator says to the reader, in French,

> Hello, my name is Hortense. I live in the village of Birni. I have lots of friends here. One of my favourite friends is Ninie. Do you know the story of her dress, the famous history of the dress of Ninie?

Here the last phrase in French is: '*Connais-tu l'histoire de sa robe, la famouse histoire de la robe de Ninie?*' and the author uses the second-person pronoun *tu* here, which is used with a person with whom one is on friendly terms; thus, the reader perceives this as if they were listening to a friend. In this way, the narrator invites the reader into the world of the story.

Illustrations also play an important role in these books. The story of *La robe de Ninie* is set in a real village in the north of Benin, named Birni. Roger Yaratchaou Boni, a painter from the region, said he painted landscape and houses that he really knew (interview on 21 October 2018). Children from Benin, as well as other surrounding countries, may probably find landscapes somewhere in their country similar to those represented in the book, even if some differences exist when examining them in detail. What will then be the reaction of children upon witnessing things they are familiar with in a book? From our modest experience as nursery-school teachers in Japan, they will be more interested in the story. However, as Senegalese children's literature writer Coumba Touré observed, 'We have hardly been represented in books' (interview on 23 November 2017), and it is rare for African children to see children similar to themselves or landscapes they know in literature. Hence, those who read *La robe de Ninie* will most likely be drawn into the story and read it more intensively than, for example, Japanese children.

Mayaba herself illustrated *Le syllabaire de Gadjo*. The bright colours contrast the book's serious theme, and the fact that the characters are not drawn in detail seems to help readers concentrate on the story. Mayaba revealed that child readers often tell her that they can draw like her (interview on 10 October 2018) and believes that they talk to her in this way because they feel close to her illustrations: their style lightens the seriousness of the humiliating situation of a father who learns to read and write from his little son, and helps the readers follow the story.

In our interview with Mayaba, she recounted her attempts at providing mental assistance to the children she met particularly girls who had difficulties continuing their studies at school due to poverty or family problems. Her literary works seem to be born from these experiences because the main character in each is courageous and never gives up hope. She told us, 'Poverty is not destiny. I wanted to say to my readers of *La robe de Ninie* that you should not be at a loss or worried, you can find a way out of your troubles somehow' (interview on 10 October 2018). Though Mayaba's work depicts serious social problems, she encourages children to overcome them.

4-2. Challenging Tradition

Some female Beninese writers of children's literature have taken a critical stance on traditional values and practices. One of them is Emeline Assogba, who rewrote an oral tale with *Il était une fois une petite girafe* [*Once Upon a Time There was a Little Giraffe*] (2007). The main character, Nanga, is loved by her husband; however, as the couple cannot have children, the husband decides to find a second wife. Soon, the second wife gives birth and begins to look down on Nanga. One day in the forest, Nanga meets a beautiful giraffe which claims to have been sent by God and metamorphoses into a girl, coming to live with Nanga. Having her own child, Nanga becomes happy; however, when the second wife discovers Nanga's secret, the girl disappears.

Assogba claimed that this story represents the reality of African women: 'In Africa, when a married woman doesn't have a baby, all members of her husband's family will interfere with the couple, and consequently, the husband is forced to get a second wife. In this story, the same thing happens, and the second wife insults the first one' (interview on 20 October 2018).

The second wife, who has plagued Nanga, dies from magical powers and Nanga is happy again because she can live with the giraffe, her husband and the children left by the second wife. The story of a sterile woman who achieves happiness can be read as an objection to social sanctions traditionally imposed on women with no children. Assogba, a young working mother, rewrote an oral tale that her grandmother had narrated to her in her childhood from her point of view as a contemporary woman, by which traditional values must change, and a couple without children can be happy if they love each other.

4-3. Writing Village Life

Serge Adjaka writes young adult novels while working as a high school mathematics teacher. His works depict the traditional values, behaviour, and relationships of Fon farmers.

In his first young adult novel, *Le génie des termitières* [*The Spirit of Termites' Nest*] (Adjaka 2015), a farmer named Kindo goes to meet Aziza, the spirit of the termites' nest, following a fortune-teller's advice to save the life of his daughter, who is suddenly suffering from a serious illness. Those who want to meet Aziza must bear three terrible experiences, and it is said that if you escape from fear, you lose reason. After withstanding those challenges Kindo meets Aziza and asks him a favour. Aziza then holds out a magic water jar, inside of which a burning fire can be seen, and orders Kindo to break it into pieces. After following Aziza's order Kindo's daughter recovers, and, oddly enough, those who have been vengeful towards him because of litigations on his palm farm then lose their lives.

In Adjaka's second novel, *La case des ancêtres* [*The Shrine of Ancestors*] (2017), the protagonist Saka has lost his father and has been raised by his uncle. Saka is now an adult and wants to save money to get married and help his mother; therefore, he asks his uncle to return half of his father's palm farm, which the uncle has been managing since Saka's father's death. The uncle, who does not want to relinquish even half of the property, stipulates a contract with the serpent spirit Dan and ask him to kill Saka. Dan then appears to Saka in the forest at night and commands him to step inside his magic basket on the ground from which one can never get out. Saka resists Dan and is saved by his father's spirit just as he is on the verge of being thrown into the basket. In the end, it is the uncle whose life is taken by Dan, ordered by the spirit of Saka's father.

What is common to Adjaka's works is that the two stories take place in Gbolli-Kpodji, a village located in central Benin where Adjaka's father was born. Readers also find in them the villagers' view of the world in which the palm farm is the most important property bequeathed from one generation to the next, where the behavioural pattern of choosing a spell is the last resort to resolve a quarrel and where spirits and ancestors can intervene in human life. Adjaka said to have observed this thinking at Gbolli-Kpodji, when his father became *daah* [king] of the village in a confused situation (interview on 11 October 2018), and explained that Aziza and Dan are spirits that appeared in the stories told to him by his father during childhood.

Adjaka does not seem to depict past events in his novels because the descriptions of the village and the villagers' daily life are concrete and detailed, giving a realistic impression; moreover, the text shows a modern expression of time with 'at 16:00' (Adjaka 2015: 13). These stories can then be read as if they were about contemporary people who are still alive. In this regard, Adjaka explained that 'the stories talk about the past, but even today the same things happen in the village' (interview on 11 October 2018).

How do we interpret these stories, which are far from the Western worldview? Tadjo called such a faith in spirits and curse 'invisible' (Tadjo 2013: 1), indicating 'the belief in vital forces animating all earthly creations, alive or dead' (Tadjo 2013: 1). She also emphasised that as 'it is so grounded in the active imagination for many Africans – whether from rural or urban setting', 'doing away with it for ideological or religious reasons would impoverish the complexity of spiritual life on the continent' (Tadjo 2013: 6).

Adjaka claims that he is interested in 'the good, weak and nasty aspect of human beings' (interview on 11 October 2018), though what he actually tries to write about are Beninese people living today with the 'invisible', rather than human beings in general. When an African child reads Adjaka's books, they will find the surrounding environment reflected in them especially the mental world of African people and they will be conscious of themselves living in such a world.

5. Conclusion

In this chapter, we have considered a co-edition system as an example of African Potentials among French-speaking Western African countries by specially focusing on Benin. At the beginning of the 2000s, Beninese writer and editor Lalinon Gbado, along with other African publishers, developed co-edition publishing and increased the number of children's books in the region. She devised this scheme by harmoniously combining the skills of editing and publishing developed in Europe, her relationship with publishers with the same purpose and the will and talents of Beninese artists. Small publishing companies thus managed to overcome the challenges of lack of funding and experience and were able to publish books and distribute them in the region, where the leading publishing companies of developed countries had monopolised the market of books by writers originally from these countries even after their independence. For a long time, many African literature works written in French in which the writers detailed their society, culture, values and themselves had been published in France and read by Western, rather than African readers. However, many children's literary works are nowadays published in African countries and directly address young African readers.

In those works of children's literature, young African readers can integrate themselves into the main character of the story and learn about themselves and the world around them. Such production of children's literature seems to be deeply connected to the Negritude movement led by black intellectuals, which is the origin of African literature in French: they wrote about being subordinated in the world and expressed who they were through their literary works.

However, that is not to say that children's literature in Africa encourages children to be 'locked into' their own culture. The examination of Lalinon Gbado's expression, 'being yourself', demonstrates her efforts to publish works that help children to know themselves and be able to maintain their own hopes and dreams before building give-and-take relationships with others.

Based on this concept, Lalinon Gbado's *Editions Ruisseaux d'Afrique* has co-edited children's books that enable the reader to become aware of social problems and of the traditional values particularly affecting women and that encourage the child reader to live with hope. It has also published works that depict how Beninese villagers coexist with invisible creatures and traditional faith and inspire the child reader to think about life in such a society.

Although the financial difficulties experienced by local publishing companies in French-speaking West African countries remain serious, adults who believe that books play an important role for children continue to create and publish children's literature. These are books full of desire for children to believe in their own potential and explore ways to live better without relying excessively on Western cultures and information.

This chapter provided a more concrete perspective on the factors that have hindered the development of publishing in the region. It also examined opinions about children's literature of contemporary African writers and, especially, of Lalinon Gbado to determine the effects of the current publishing situation on the formation of African children's personalities and the importance of the co-edition of works by African writers and illustrators in the region. In addition, by criticising some locally published works, we showed the themes and expressions through which local publications address African child readers.

Endnotes

[1] In this chapter, the term 'Africa' is used to indicate the geographical location of 'sub-Saharan Africa'.

[2] 'Children's literature' here refers to books written for children from infants up to those in their mid-teens. They are picture books consisting of, for example, modern stories, rewrites of oral literature and young adult novels. 'Children's books' refers to those written entirely for children: they are, in addition to children's literature, short historical novels, books offering practical knowledge, encyclopaedias, and so on.

[3] These countries are Benin, Burkina Faso, Ivory Coast, Guinea, Mali, Niger and Senegal (the former French colonies), and Togo which is a former French trust territory, where French is mainly used in education, administration and other public areas of society. Most of the books published in these countries are written in French. In this chapter the expression 'French-speaking West African countries' can be interchangeable with 'West African countries that use French as an official language'.

[4] In this chapter, we have omitted titles from the names of the persons whom we interviewed and cited. We would like to thank all who answered our questions.

[5] When we cite, for the first time, a publisher's name, an institution's name, or a book title in French, a literal translation will follow in square brackets.

[6] According to *Publication Yearbook 2018*, UNESCO suspended its annual world's publication statistics in 1996, and no more statistics were ever released by any institutions (Publishing News 2018: 357). It has been impossible, in recent years, to know what percentage African countries' publications are present among the world's publications.

Acknowledgements

This work was supported by JSPS KAKENHI Grant Numbers

JP17K18480, JP17H02328 and JP16H08318, and ILCAA Joint Research Project 'Présence Africaine: Text, Thought and Movement'.

References

Adjaka, S. (2015) *Le génie des termitières [The Spirit of Termites' Nest]*, Cotonou: Editions Ruisseaux d'Afrique.

────── (2017) *La case des ancêtres [The Shrine of Ancestors]*, Cotonou: Editions Ruisseaux d'Afrique.

Association des amis de la Joie par les livres (1989) 'No. 1–Les livres africains pour la jeunesse: Catalogue des éditions en français [The African Books for Children: Catalogue of Publications in French]', *Takam Tikou*, June 1989 (http://cnlj.bnf.fr/fr/detail_revue/Les_livres_africains_pour_la_jeunesse_catalogue_des_editions_en_francais/1) (accessed: 8 May 2020).

Assogba, E. P. (2007) *Il était une fois une petite girafe [Once Upon a Time There was a Little Giraffe]*, Cotonou: Eiditions Ruisseaux d'Afrique.

Atchadé, B. and Djogbénou, L. (2016) 'À la découverte de la vie: Entretien avec Béatrice Lalinon Gbado [Discovering the Life: Interview with Béatrice Lalinon Gbado]', *Takam Tikou*, 16 March 2016 (https://takamtikou.bnf.fr/dossiers/dossier-2016-la-belle-histoire-de-la-litt-rature-africaine-pour-la-jeunesse-2000-2015/la-d-) (accessed: 8 May 2020) .

Beau, N. (2013) 'De Ruisseaux d'Afrique à Ruisseaux du monde, rencontre avec Béatrice Lalinon Gbado [From African Stream to World's Stream, Meeting Béatrice Lalinon Gbado]', *Takam Tikou*, 20 March 2013 (https://takamtikou.bnf.fr/dossiers/dossier-2013-patrimoine-et-transmission/de-ruisseaux-d-afrique-ruisseaux-du-monde) (accessed: 8 May 2020).

Dabo, A. (1982) 'Jeanne de Cavally, écrivain [Jeanne de Cavally, writer]', *Amina*, No. 114, p. 21 (https://aflit.arts.uwa.edu.au/AMINAcavally82.html) (accessed: 8 May 2020).

Diome, F. (2003) *Le ventre de l'Atlantique [The Belly of the Atlantic]*, Paris: Editions Anne Carrière.

Dongala, E. (2002) *Johnny chien méchant [Johnny Mad Dog]*, Paris: Le Serpent à plumes.

Ducournau, C. (2017) *La fabrique des classiques africains: Ecrivains d'Afrique subsaharienne francophone [The factory of African classics: Writers from Sub-Saharan French-Speaking Africa]*, Paris: CNRS Editions.

Foucault, J., Manson, M. and Pinhas, L. (eds) (2010) *Edition de jeunesse francophone face à la mondialisation [Publication of Children's Books in French-Speaking Countries Facing the Globalisation]*, Paris: L'Harmattan.

Hugues, L. (2008) 'Les coéditions panafricaines: Quel enjeux pour la littérature de jeunesse en Afrique francophone subsaharienne ? [The Pan-African Co-editions: Which Stakes for the Sub-Saharan French-Speaking Africa's Children's Literature?]', in L. Pinhas (ed.) *Situations de l'édition francophone d'enfance et de jeunesse [Situations of Publication for Children and Youth in French-Speaking Countries]*, Paris: L'Harmattan, pp. 243–255.

Keïta, F. (2008) 'L'édition pour la jeunesse en Côte d'Ivoire : Histoire et état des lieux [The Publication for Children in Ivory Coast: History and Inventory]', in L. Pinhas (ed.) *Situations de l'édition francophone d'enfance et de jeunesse [Situations of Publication for Children and Youth in French-Speaking Countries]*, Paris: L'Harmattan, pp. 205–223.

Kesteloot, L. (1963) *Les écrivains noirs de langue française: Naissance d'une littérature [The Black Writers of French Language: Birth of a Literature]*, Brussels: Université libre de Bruxelles.

Kloeckner, H. (2003) 'A quand une édition scolaire africaine? [When will an African Publication of School Textbooks comme?]', *Africultures*, No. 57, pp. 71–85.

Mayaba, H. (2003) *Le syllabaire de Gadjo [Gadjo's Primer]*, Cotonou: Editions Ruisseaux d'Afrique.

Mayaba, H. and Boni, R. Y. (2002) *La robe de Ninie [Ninie's Dress]*, Cotonou: Editions Ruisseaux d'Afrique.

Nakamura, T. (2013) *Carib–World Theory: Plural Places Fighting against Colonialism and Their History*, Kyoto: Jinbunsyoin (in Japanese).

Ohta, I. (2016) 'Introduction to the five-volume collection of papers on "African Potentials": Steps towards conflict resolution and attainment of coexistence', in M. Matsuda and M. Hirano-

Nomoto (eds) *Cultural Creativity for Conflict Resolution and Coexistence: African Potentials as Practice of Incompleteness and Bricolage*, Kyoto: Kyoto University Press, pp. i–xxii (in Japanese).

Pinhas, L. (2005) *Editer dans l'espace francophone [Publishing in French-Speaking Arena]*, Paris: Alliance Internationale des Editeurs Indépendants.

Pinhas, L. (ed.) (2008) *Situations de l'édition francophone d'enfance et de jeunesse [Situations of Publication for Children and Youth in French-Speaking Countries]*, Paris: L'Harmattan.

Publishing News (2018) *Publication Yearbook 2018*, Tokyo: Shuppan News (in Japanese).

Sunano, Y. (2004) 'On Aimé Césaire', in A. Césaire, *Notebook of a Return to the Native Land / Discourse on Colonialism* (translated into Japanese by Y. Sunano), Tokyo: Heibonsya, pp. 219–311 (in Japanese).

Tadjo, V. (2003)'Littérature africaine et mondialisation [African Literature and Globalisation]', *Présence Africaine, New Series*, No. 167–168, pp. 113–116.

———— (2013) 'Lifting the cloak of (in)visibility: A writer's perspective', *Research in African Literatures*, Vol. 44, No. 2, pp. 1–7.

Tervonen, T. (2003) 'Sur le chemin de l'indépendance: Entretien avec Béatrice Lalinon Gbado, directrice des Editions Ruisseaux d'Afrique (Bénin) [On the Way to Independence: Interview with Béatrice Lalinon Gbado, Manager of Editions Ruisseaux d'Afirique (Benin)]', *Africultures*, No. 57, pp. 101–103.

Chapter 10

Writing from the In-between: Binyavanga Wainaina's Literary Practices

Maiko Kanda

1. Introduction: African Potentials in a Time of Terror

Mass migrations and refugee movements across borders have become global phenomena over the years. It is difficult to ignore that the Arab Spring's joyous spirit of democratisation was unmistakably and shortly followed by opposite consequences in Syria. Civilian movements for democracy were suppressed by the authoritarian government, and civil wars were initiated by anti-governmental forces, armed ethnic or religious militia and multinational armies. A new spate of refugee migration to Europe thus began in 2014 (Talhami 2014). At first, the European countries welcomed these migrants on humanitarian grounds. However, their numbers were so large and the speed of their displacement was so fast that the residents of the European host countries became anxious about the ultimate outcomes: would the refugees leave after a brief duration or would they settle down somewhere in Europe where they had remained stranded? Conflicts also began to occur between incoming populations and the residents of the European nations that sheltered them.

These European host societies have been caught in a forced process of rapid diversification. The current circumstances are doubtlessly different from the globalisation of the 1990s and 2000s. People belonging to the developed nations could celebrate globalisation, which was considered a predominantly economic matter. They believed that the global expansion of their capital and the global labour influx to their shores would eventually contribute to their prosperity. It was taken for granted that the immigrant labour forces would accept the new norms and assimilate into their host societies over time.

A few terrorist incidents occurred in several European cities approximately two decades later. The host societies then became aware for the first time that most of the attackers were home-grown in Europe. The new influx of refugees began when the host nations were engaged in retrospection of their immigration policies of the near past. Hamid Dabashi, an Iranian intellectual, chose the expression *Time of Terror* as the title of his 2009 book, which indicates the period after 9/11. Twenty years have passed since that time, but communities still seem to be stuck within those moments when the framework of societal emotions metamorphosed from humanitarianism to exclusionism.

Unfortunately, exclusionary movements have become a worldwide trend. A feeling of hierarchical superiority can be observed across the world whether or not the Others are newcomer immigrants. Numerous examples may be cited such as the insistence to construct a border wall between the US and Mexico[1] or hate speech in Japan against Korean residents.[2] Such discriminatory sentiments may be traced to colonialism. However, we should not attribute the current global situation solely to colonialism. The current multicultural circumstances should make global societies more horizontal than hierarchical. Thus, populations cannot be inclined anymore toward segregation merely through a sense of superiority. Instead, a sense of threat of deprivation from personal benefits may drive the present forms of exclusion. In other words, the Others are now perceived as competitors in the daily life of resident populations. Therefore, the present difficult times require a new framework of consideration.

The conceptual term 'African Potentials' describes the inherent cognitive processes, institutions and capabilities that have developed organically from the multicultural daily living realities of African citizens and that can be compiled and utilised to resolve real-world problems. Africa's multicultural circumstances could thus offer a prior model through which nations can tackle the recent phenomenon of exclusion. Many African societies have maintained horizontal multiculturalism in conditions of vast ethnic diversity.

This balance is not always stable: it is somewhat volatile. However, equilibrium tends to be maintained by the general citizenry through daily practices and not via the top-down policies established by government institutions.

2. Postcolonial Literary Criticism and African Potentials

The purpose of this chapter is to illuminate the writing practices of Binyavanga Wainaina as an exemplar of African Potentials. However, the focus of postcolonial literary criticism must be elucidated at the beginning of the discussion because this theoretical framework first allowed for the discovery of characteristic literary texts from colonised nations across the world.

Literature can express subtle nuances such as voices, cadences, feelings and experiences that are not otherwise apparent in statistical figures or historical grand narratives. Just one title from African literature is enough to prove this statement. In *Things Fall Apart*, Chinua Achebe depicted the delicate moods and shades of people who had not earned a place in historical accounts. Painting vivid and specific images of the cultural practice of Igbo, the book describes how a successful person and marginalised characters in the same traditional community sought to establish individual paths without apprehending the consequences of their subjective choices.

This novel challenged the prevailing binary oppositions posited between Africa and the West in English literature: Africa was savage; the West was civilised. *Things Fall Apart* emphatically asserted that every society possesses a worldview, language and culture. Each culture has its own value system, beliefs and wisdom that may be logically apprehended even by cultural outsiders. These representations of Africa initiated the new domain of postcolonial literature and even more fruitfully, they encouraged younger generations of Africans to author texts from their perspectives.

Multicultural conditions must have seemed so ordinary and transparent to first-generation African novelists, like Achebe, that they weren't really interested in writing about the ways in which they functioned in their daily contexts. Their personal experiences of colonialism and post-independence neo-colonialism initially focused their interests on the hierarchical structures that existed between colonial rulers and their subjects.

The suppressed resists the suppressor using local or ethnic elements rooted in traditional culture: such alternative narratives were compatible with postcolonial literary criticism, which grew in popularity over time. Postcolonialist scholars lauded Achebe's challenge against the one-way representations of Africa in Western works of literature as the best practice of postcolonial literature. In this critical context, depicting the ethnic viewpoint constituted a worthy counterattack against the Western standpoint, but nothing more. Postcolonial academics underestimated the original means to coexist or negotiate with other communities and societies that every ethnic culture had evolved through longstanding historical experiences. Thus, postcolonial critics could never envision the notion or power of African Potentials.

Hamid Dabashi argued in *Post-Orientalism: Knowledge and Power in Time of Terror* that postcolonial criticism has only highlighted hierarchical relationships. He censured the prominent postcolonial critics Edward W. Said and Gayatri C. Spivak for considering the Euro-American white male as their fictive principal interlocutor. Dabashi referred to Said's taking the time and expending undue force in his works to convince the West and questioned whether any of the prevailing circumstances were altered by Said's sincerity. According to Dabashi, the postcolonial postulation of Western scholarship as the singular interlocutor also signified its continued acceptance of the agency of the West to express everything and thus perpetuated Euro-centrism (Dabashi 2017: 272–273).

Dabashi suggested that the West's approval was no longer required. Instead, he sought global horizontal solidarity that was not merely based in rhetoric but yielded practical results. Thus, Dabashi proposed that the interlocutor should be altered from the fictive white male to the marginalised or suppressed people of the real world. In so doing, the hierarchical scope could be transformed into a horizontal frame of reference that incorporated multiple agencies. Such a perspective would be identical to African Potentials as described above.

Dabashi also listed some revolutionary figures as models of this practice. According to him, the extraordinary legacies of revolutionary thinkers and activists such as Che Guevara, Franz Fanon, Malcolm X and Ali Shari'ati evidenced their success in crossing a number of confounding borders to achieve a global conception of emancipation. The principle of revolution for emancipation should be global. Therefore, their transborder activism is significant. All those great figures were not bound by their own physical trappings such as a geographical 'home', but pursued an ideal of revolution. It could be geopolitically 'inauthentic', as Dabashi termed it, but paradoxically, it has, at the same time, a truly revolutionary authentic character as a creative agency in the specific context of revolutions (Dabashi 2017: 279–280).

The present chapter intends to add a new name, Binyavanga Wainaina, to Dabashi's list of revolutionary thinkers. Wainaina was a Kenyan writer. He was born in 1971 and died in 2019. His legacy of international publications in the course of his short life includes only a single book, *One Day I Will Write About This Place*, which appeared in print in 2011 (Wainaina 2011b). The internet acted as his primary battlefield, and he engaged vigorously with online writing. His writings spanned representations of Africa, ethnicity issues, LGBTQI+ activism and more. They encouraged marginalised peoples to join together in solidarity and created a space where their voices and stories could be heard in present-day African societies.

This chapter intends to posit the body of Binyavanga Wainaina's writing as an exemplar of African Potentials. The conceptual construct of 'in-between' is crucial to this discussion. When objects are classified into particular groups, people tend to believe in essential differences that drive divisions between 'this' and 'that'. However, such clear demarcations do not always apply to human life. What about race, ethnicity and culture? In-between is, literally, a space between multiple realms. For example, the distinctions drawn between neighbouring ethnic cultures may essentially be based on a single larger difference. There would thus exist an ambivalent zone of gradational transition and hybridisation. How, then, can a hard line be drawn to divide this and that? In another context, some people could be prevented from receiving or accepting their cultural inheritances because of a social void created by certain limiting factors. Such individuals could 'qualify' to be counted as members of their traditional societies according to customs, but their actual assimilation could be questionable. In-between is therefore a conceptual space from which questions are continually asked about the reasonableness of essentialist attitudes.

Social norms could also become boundaries between right and wrong, superior and inferior. Being valid only in like populations, their criteria may not be universal as collectively subjective. However, societal norms work powerfully within particular communities and the regions they dominate and the majority population always occupies the spaces marked 'right' in the criteria. As a result, the Other becomes marginalised and invisible: for example, the colonised in a hierarchical structure, and sexual minorities or people with disabilities in a horizontal structure. In such instances, an in-between space may emerge through the actions of some minority individuals who decide to transcend boundaries to revise the present circumstances.

Wainaina lived consciously in the in-between and wrote mindfully from the in-between. His writing sought horizontal balance or solidarity. This chapter attends primarily to two of Wainaina's texts, *How to Write About Africa* (Wainaina 2011a) and 'Discovering Home' (Wainaina 2009). Initially, the chapter grounds itself in Dabashi's concept of the interlocutor to explore the originality and impact of *How to Write About Africa*. Second, the chapter contemplates the possibility of an identity free from ethnic affiliation. The post-election violence that occurred in Kenya in 2007–2008 evidenced that the issue of ethnicity was again attaining importance. The present chapter does not intend to offer an infallible resolution to the current situation. However, an awareness of Wainaina's achievements could contribute to this end by steering the ethnocentric tone taken by societies in this 'time of terror' toward a more just and equitable attitude.

3. The Issue of How to Write About Africa: From Achebe to Wainaina

The African literary environment has become reinvigorated since the 2000s. Economies are developing rapidly and online literary communities are flourishing thanks to information and communication technology driven advancements. The institution of several literary prizes is also one among the varied reasons for this boom in the continent's literary output. Founded in 1999, the Caine Prize for African Writing[3] is the most prestigious of these literary awards. It has become a stepping stone to fame for promising young African writers. Binyavanga Wainaina won this prize in 2002 for his short story, 'Discovering Home'.

Despite his award-winning career, Wainaina only became internationally renowned in 2005. *How to Write About Africa* starts with the advisory sentence, 'Always use the word "Africa" or "Darkness" or "Safari" in your title' (Wainaina 2011a: 5). This article[4] is filled with useful advice for the creation of 'best-selling' content about Africa. Of course, this advice is also an exercise in sarcasm and irony against common contemporary media representations of Africa. It became the most-forwarded article in the history of the online magazine that published it (Wainaina 2010) and undoubtedly became Wainaina's best-known work.

How to Write About Africa should be read for another reason that does not involve its sarcasm and humour. The text is also crucial for postcolonial literature in its direct and explicit focus on the issue of how Africa is represented to the world at large. In *Orientalism*, Edward Said collected substantial similar representations about the Orient to depict the West's desire to obtain conceptual and intellectual control of the Orient. Since Said's work, the methodology of examining and evaluating representations of Others in works produced by the West became established in literary criticism.

In the context of African literature, Chinua Achebe accused Joseph Conrad's *Heart of Darkness* of racism toward Africans at a university lecture in 1975, three years before the publication of Said's *Orientalism*. For Achebe, *Heart of Darkness*, 'better than any other work that I know displays that Western desire and need' (Achebe 2010: 2–3). He quoted many parts from Conrad's novel and explicated the unreasonableness of each description of Africa. For example, Achebe remarked on the polar differences between Kurtz's African mistress and his European fiancé.

The difference in the attitude of the novelist to these two women is conveyed in too many direct and subtle ways to need elaboration. But perhaps the most significant difference is the one implied in the author's bestowal of human expression to the one and the withholding of it from the other. It is clearly not part of Conrad's purpose to confer language on the 'rudimentary souls' of Africa. In place of speech they made 'a violent babble of uncouth sounds.' They 'exchanged short grunting phrases' even among themselves. But most of the time they were too busy with their frenzy (Achebe 2010: 9).

Achebe mentioned repeatedly that African characters were unfairly depicted in *Heart of Darkness* as ugly to be posited as foils to the West. Above all, Achebe attended significantly to the issue of the possession of language. The novel did not accord its African characters the honour of owning any systematic languages, an act synonymous to depriving the African people of their right to tell their own story. Thus, Achebe called it dehumanisation. Unlike Said, Achebe did not academically scrutinise Western practices, but he did elucidate that Western desires promoted a specific type of representation of Africa. Achebe's concerns were more practical: could people living in the actual world be forever haunted by the stereotypes presented in the novel?

The real question is the dehumanization of Africa and Africans which this agelong attitude has fostered and continues to foster in the world. And the question is whether a novel which celebrates this dehumanization, which depersonalizes a portion of the human race, can be called a great work of art. My answer is: No, it cannot (Achebe 2010: 13).

The intense tone taken by Achebe's denial of *Heart of Darkness* created a controversy, garnering much critical consideration. It is nevertheless true that his tone accords a piercing sense of urgency to the topic. The lecture in question was delivered at the University of Massachusetts in 1975. Hence, the reason for Achebe's urgency is easy to understand if one envisions the manner in which American society at that time viewed the African people. Achebe's audience would most likely be aware of several fairly recent incidents in Africa, such as struggles for independence and the Biafra War. At the same time, they would have been immersed in the 'savage' images of Africa that were prevalent. Thus, he avoided the typical and 'pedagogic' style of closing the lecture, shifting instead to his opinions about the negative representations of Africa:

> But as I thought more about the stereotype image, about its grip and pervasiveness, about the wilful tenacity with which the West holds it to its heart; when I thought of the West's television and cinema and newspapers, about books read in its schools and out of school, of churches preaching to empty pews about the need to send help to the heathen in Africa, I realized that no easy optimism was possible. And there was, in any case, something totally wrong in offering bribes to the West in return for its good opinion of Africa (Achebe 2010: 20).

The final sentence of this quoted speech suggests Achebe's determination to declare a direct resistance to the Western imagery. No doubt, the hierarchical relationship based on colonialism was his primary thought. Achebe also seemed to appoint the Western white male as his interlocutor in his attempts to recover the humanity of Africans. However, it is questionable whether it is necessary to seek the West's help in reclaiming the dignity of Africans. Achebe's strong declaration, in fact, betrayed his intentions and contributed to the persistence of the authority of the West as the sole agent of representation.

Around three decades later, the world has realised that Achebe's foresight was correct: 'no easy optimism was possible'. The more advanced media technology becomes, the worse the representation of the Other becomes. Wainaina's definitive article appeared when the high expectations for the age of the internet had turned into disappointment.

How to Write About Africa was originally published in 2005 in *Granta*, a renowned online literary magazine. Its basic sentence pattern is imperative, using words such as 'must' or 'need to' with excessive enthusiasm in a tone and cadence reminiscent of the voice of a shady business consultant whose nationality, sex and racial or ethnic origin are unknown. This consultant/narrator advises readers about expressive techniques and encourages prospective writers who are hesitant to take a stance: 'Do not feel queasy about this: you are trying to help them to get aid from the West' (Wainaina 2011a: 10). One of the consultant's recommendations is the following:

> After celebrity activists and aid workers, conservationists are Africa's most important people. Do not offend them. You need them to invite you to their 30,000-acre game ranch or 'conservation area,' and this is the only way you will get to interview the celebrity activist. Often a book cover with a heroic-looking conservationist on it works magic for sales. Anybody white, tanned and wearing khaki who once had a pet antelope or a farm is a conservationist, one who is preserving Africa's rich heritage. When interviewing him or her, do not ask how much funding they have; do not ask how much money they make off their game. Never ask how much they pay their employees (Wainaina 2011a: 11).

Celebrity activists are a relatively new stereotype about Africa. In essence, however, the usual combination is sustained: white heroes and Mother Nature. This prototype dates to the imperialist era and postulates Western societies simultaneously as conquerors and guardians of Africa. The Africans are invisible in this storyline and slide quietly into the backdrop.

This exhortation is also as much a representation of the West. The list of 'don'ts' discloses consumption issues related to media images as well as the global economy. It constitutes a sharp criticism of the act of representation by the West as much as the phenomenon itself. Wainaina revealed that he received a call of complaint from a conservationist with the accusation that he had written about *him*.

> I had not mentioned anyone by name, but he was personally affronted. Yes, he's a conservationist, and yes, he has hosted a celebrity or two – but he didn't trade in game animals, and he paid his workers well. Sure, I said. It's beyond the pale, he said. I have never really understood what that means, where that is, the pale, and why such a mild-seeming phrase promises interpersonal Armageddon (Wainaina 2010).

Objections, anger and accusations: such reactions to representations of Africa have been oft-repeated for more than half a century. Wainaina reversed this trend, writing about white conservationists in general. The tactic worked so well that a specific individual felt personally attacked. Finally, *How to Write About Africa* accomplished a 'writing back' against Western sensibility.

The style of Wainaina's writing in this article is particularly noteworthy: it is not pleading or prohibitionary; rather, it issues a strong recommendation. Africans and also discerning readers across the globe immediately recognise that *How to Write About Africa* is ironically intended. However, it reads like a how-to manual, and thus another interpretive possibility cannot at all be denied: it could just reflect simple encouragement in the traditional, easy-to-digest style of writing about Africa. The consummate consultant suggests the technique described in the quoted section below to all writers who need tips about writing about Africa:

> Among your characters you must always include The Starving African, who wanders the refugee camp nearly naked, and waits for the benevolence of the West. Her children have flies on their eyelids and pot bellies, and her breasts are flat and empty. She must look utterly helpless. She can have no past, no history; such diversions ruin the dramatic moment. Moans are good. She must never say anything about herself in the dialogue except to speak of her (unspeakable) suffering (Wainaina 2011a: 8–9).

Video footage of the news programmes on TV, cover photos on photojournalism magazines, news photographers' exhibitions, images from the Biafra War, the Famine in Ethiopia, the Dadaab Refugee Camp: countless images of the type Wainaina describes are imprinted on the minds of the citizens of the world. Everyone will be reminded of at least one encounter with a capitalised stereotype similar to this description.

Like the African mistress in *Heart of Darkness*, 'The Starving African' woman is not allowed to possess language. However, Wainaina's description does not end with her appearance. He adds text that could be termed 'stage directions' of the sort not generally uttered aloud behind the visualisations. The woman cannot speak, as always. No one reasonably represents her. However, Wainaina's stage directions play a contradictory role, explaining the utility of suppressing her and at the same time, confessing the transgression of the very act of dehumanisation. What Wainaina describes is arrogance: the global media's unshakeable belief in a sole agency to see and write about peculiarly African phenomena.

Accusations of Western arrogance are not new to African writing. However, *How to Write About Africa* does not intend, at all, to make the West understand the 'Real Africa', neither does it offer the opposing assertions of the 'real experiences' of genuine Africans. Instead, it deals with the issue of representation only within the Euro-American context. It takes advantage of the how-to format to encourage repeat stereotypes. It may look like it accepts Western superiority and seem like a servile offering of a twisted 'bribe', in Achebe's terms. However, it acts like a Trojan horse. It infiltrates the territory of the dominant discourse that, when grasped, discloses the hidden egoism of outdated arrogance and exposes it as ridiculous. Africa is never exploited in Wainaina's representation.

As for representation, images are now dispersed worldwide via the internet in the space of a few minutes. As they are transferred from one person to another, images become sequentially linked to many people across many regions. In the present context, there can never be one particular agent who owns full responsibility for the representation of an image. Thus, literary agency is no longer necessarily vested in white Western hands. Africans can also purposefully utilise conventional Western ways of representation for their benefit. The issue of representation has now transcended geographical boundaries. Although benevolent white individuals may still subscribe to the hierarchical structures of writing practices, the West is no longer a single interlocutor. *How to Write About Africa* developed and utilised the strategy of turning a series of stereotypes into a platform of punch lines that the Other could use to assert disagreement with the colonialist context. Now, multiple versions of such platforms proliferate on the internet.

4. Writing from the In-between: Comparing Wainaina's Approach with Ngũgĩ's Literary Philosophy

'Discovering Home' is Binyavanga Wainaina's Caine Prize-winning short story. A revised version of this story was divided into several chapters and included in his 2011 memoir, *One Day I Will Write About This Place*. The final part of the original story equates to the narrative in Chapter 22 of this book. It is also the highlight of his memoir, as the title sentence is inscribed at the end of this chapter. The original 'Discovering Home' describes the homeplaces of both his parents. The present chapter's discussion of the issue of ethnicity focuses primarily on the story of his mother's side in Chapter 22 because the tracing of the concept of 'home' from this side helps to illustrate Wainaina's exceptional standpoint vis-à-vis ethnicity.

Before such a discussion can be undertaken, however, it is necessary to review the work of Ngũgĩ wa Thiong'o. Wainaina's and Ngũgĩ's paternal ethnic affiliations were identical. Thus, Ngũgĩ's famed literary legacy could have been a burden for Wainaina as a writer.

Binyavanga Wainaina was born of a Gikuyu father and a Bafumbira (originally from Uganda)[5] mother in Nakuru, a city that hosted a large Gikuyu population. However, Wainaina could not acquire Gikuyu as his first language. In his words, 'My third language, Gikuyu, is nearly nonexistent; I can't speak it. It is a phantom limb, kimay – and this only increases my desire to observe and belong to this intelligence and its patterns' (Wainaina 2011b: 125).

Wainaina's family name loudly announces his authenticity as a member of the Gikuyu. However, his first name, Binyavanga, is seemingly unclear in Kenya. He is the second son of the Wainainas; thus, he was named after his maternal Bafumbira grandfather according to the Gikuyu custom. His first name is thus ironically devoid of meaning because of the faithful application of traditional processes. It also caused some trouble in his life. For example, a member of the ground crew at an airport checked his Kenyan passport and asked him about the origins of his name. A person who met him on the street asked him what type of half-breed he was (Wainaina 2011b: 208–209). Such incidents would greatly annoy

Wainaina.

Generally, in Africa, one's ethnic identity forms the firm foundation of the individual. Despite his family name, Wainaina's phantom limb sensation prevented him from declaring his ethnic authenticity. Besides, he did not inherit (or learn) his mother's language and culture and thus he had a cultural void on the maternal side, also. He lived 'being both but having neither'. As the quotation above shows, he felt a strong desire for a kind of 'Gikuyu-ness'. A major part of this feeling could have emanated from his daily life experiences. Yet, it cannot be overlooked that Wainaina was a writer and as such, he could not necessarily be free from his great predecessor in African literature and Gikuyu novelist, Ngũgĩ wa Thiong'o.

Ngũgĩ wa Thiong'o started his career in 1964 when his first novel *Weep Not, Child* was published in the name of James Ngugi. He reverted to his Gikuyu name Ngũgĩ wa Thiong'o in 1967 after two more publications. His work focused on ordinary people exploited by being at the mercy of the authorities of the moment, and he finally arrived at 'A Statement' in his notable book *Decolonising the Mind* in 1986: 'This book, *Decolonising the Mind*, is my farewell to English as a vehicle for any of my writings. From now on it is Gĩkũyũ and Kiswahili all the way' (Ngũgĩ 1997: xiv).

For Ngũgĩ, *his* people were the primary readers of his writings. He dealt with their daily problems resulting from colonialism and its aftermath. However, they could not access Ngũgĩ's works as long as he used English as his means of expression. He thus shifted to the Gikuyu language. This act seemed to be quite natural to ensure comprehensibility between the author and his readers, but it was also an epoch-making development for postcolonial literature.

Most of celebrated postcolonial literature has been written by authors who have used the languages of their former-colonisers.[6] They have, of course, incorporated some local/ethnic expressions into their works, aiming for alienation effects. They have intended to insert 'incomprehensibility' in the modern literary context into European languages. This writing style has certainly succeeded. At the same time, however, this type of postcolonial literature also assumes a Euro-American sensibility as its imaginary reader – or the interlocutor. Perhaps, this condition is also an unavoidable result of colonialism: it has been implanted into most postcolonial writers through their education that only the European languages were appropriate means of modern literature. In normal conditions, artists have the creative freedom to select their means of expression. However, the postcolonial condition is full of contradictions. They have a strong urge to convince the West, but have to rely on languages of the past colonial regime to achieve their ends. Therefore, Ngũgĩ's ultimate statement represented his own complete solution to the problem in postcolonial literature. It combined his determined objection against the cultural-economic domination of the West and his quest to preserve the integrity of ordinary citizens of Africa.

For Ngũgĩ, a language was much more than a mere communication tool. His linguistic-cultural standpoint is aptly reflected by the quotation that follows:

> Culture embodies those moral, ethical and aesthetic values, the set of spiritual eyeglasses, through which they come to view themselves and their place in the universe. Values are the basis of a people's identity, their sense of particularity as members of the human race. All this is carried by language. Language as culture is the collective memory bank of a people's experience in history (Ngũgĩ 1997: 14–15).

Ngũgĩ's suggestion that language is a collective memory bank would be accepted by many postcolonial writers because most take the utilisation of their local/ethnic heritages for granted. An invisible premise then appears: every individual possesses a sense of ethnic affiliation, which becomes a firm foundation of the individual identity. Does the loss or absence of an ethnic language then signify a critical deficiency in a postcolonial artistic creation?

Despite his Gikuyu family name, Binyavanga Wainaina could not share the ethnic heritage stored in the collective memory bank because he did not possess its key, the language. Therefore, he may seem inauthentic as an African intellectual. However, his ethnic vacuum did not result from the humiliation of the use of local languages experienced by Ngũgĩ in his school days during the colonial era (Ngũgĩ 1997: 11). It could be argued that Wainaina slipped into an ethnic vacuum because of colonialism. However, his parents could come together because of English, a communication tool shared by them. It would thus be productive to regard his ethnic vacuity, not as a dreadful lack of belonging or 'should-be', but as a new facet of the region's history.

As mentioned above, Wainaina was positioned in two ethnicities, 'being both but having neither'. The 'being both' part should be stressed in this context. It must not be very rare on the African context for people to be born into double ethnic affiliations. However, people are easily inclined toward a single affiliation myth. The traditional customs of each paternal or maternal society should exist behind the scenes of one's personality. Recently, the results of the census have begun to make people aware of each of their ethnic affiliations.[7] Wainaina's vacuum raises a question concerning this premise constructed by traditional customs and current social research results.

> Being Binyavanga is to me also exotic – an imaginary Ugandan of some kind resides in me, one who lets me withhold myself from claiming, or being admitted into, without hesitation, an unquestioning Gikuyu belonging (Wainaina 2011b: 161).

Wainaina lived in the in-between space of two ethnicities. In his space, a sense of belonging was always fluid. An individual's story concerning his/her roots tends to be directed toward the core of his/her ethnicity. However, one can tell a story about home and family even when one's ethnicity cannot easily be categorised. Such a space may be untethered by affiliations, but it can still speak of the story as the harmony of individuals. Wainaina discovered a home in Uganda that emerged as a synchronic experience.

Wainaina's mother, Rosemary, was born in Bufumbira, where her ancestors settled from contemporary Rwanda in the late 1800s. She identified herself as a Mufumbira who spoke Kinyarwanda. She had eleven siblings and some of them, including her, left their hometown for education or other reasons. Continuing political crises since the 1970s and the genocide in Rwanda kept the family apart for over 30 years. Just before Christmas in 1995, the Wainainas decided to travel across Uganda to meet Rosemary's parents for their wedding anniversary and celebrate Christmas together. That was Rosemary's first opportunity to reunite with her family.

Although Wainaina sensed a cultural void on his maternal side, it was not an empty space; it was full of images of the *kabaka*, old kingdoms, banana trees, Tutsi women, Hutu servants and Idi Amin. For him, Uganda was an imaginary presence crafted by fragmented conversations. Travelling across Uganda, a young Wainaina would find himself turning his imaginary creation into firm reality. He stated that driving around the Bufumbira range, 'a sense of where we are starts to seep into me. We are no longer in the history of Buganda, of Idi Amin, of the *kabakas*, or civil war, Museveni' (Wainaina 2011b: 157). He could now achieve a solid sense of the place. Even so, Wainaina could not fill his void with a sense of belonging to Bufumbira. Instead, he reaffirmed the void in himself when he noted that his mother fit the surroundings.

> Mum looks almost foreign now. Her Kinyarwanda accent is more pronounced, and her face is not as reserved as usual. Her beauty, so exotic and head-turning in Kenya, seems at home here. She does not stand out anymore; she belongs. The rest of us seem like tourists (Wainaina 2011b: 157).

Wainaina was in one of his places of origin. Yet, he remained a stranger in that place. He pestered his grandfather to find out about their family history. It could have been an aspect of exploring his roots, but his grandfather was confused by Wainaina's questioning. Ultimately, his void was not filled; he remained unsatisfied. However, the condition was not as desperate as it sounds because he was not the only person who lacked a firm sense of belonging. Most people who had gathered there were the same to a certain extent. However, they could still create a Utopia-like atmosphere decades after their separation.

> I am filled with magic and I succumb to the masses. In two days, we feel like a family. In French, Swahili, English, Gikuyu, Kinyarwanda, Kiganda, and Ndebele, we sing one song, a multitude of passports in

our luggage (Wainaina 2011b: 163).

These words describe the ideal repatriation experience of diasporas. Yet, there was no recognisable element connecting all of them except for the original family members in Bufumbira. Certainly, they were more or less united by blood ties, but those bonds had become invisible. Cousins did not share the memories of childhoods spent with each other. In such circumstances, diasporas such as the Jewish communities across the world could rely on visible signifiers indicating their national/ethnic affiliations. They could share aspects of identity such as the language or religion. In the African context, ethnicity would be the primary shared element. However, Wainaina's extended family members did not share ethnic markers. Even the elderly couple did not seem to care about ethnic traditions. If they had a reason to meet at that time, it would be the familiar Christian custom of entire family members gathering for family anniversaries and Christmas festivities. At the beginning of Chapter 22, the narrator Wainaina likens the reunion to the cliché of a Christmas movie (Wainaina 2011b: 161). There was nothing special. What, then, happened among them to make them feel like a family?

His 'family' emerged in their encounter as a collective experience with synchronicity. The literary form of the memoir allowed Wainaina to sustain a monologue as the first-person narrator. Even from the limited view of the first-person narrator, he was able to evince that a generation or more of each extended family unit in each destination had led a life that required coping with hardship. At the reunion in Bufumbira they seemed to speak of different geopolitical (hi)stories, not mentioned by the narrator. Each exodus to Bufumbira did not move toward a single centre, something essential. Instead, Bufumbira became the converging point of the multiple voices of the extended family; all the voices told their (hi)stories in different languages and resonated with the polyphony of the family. That momentary sense of family was not attributable to ethnic identity. It was the cathartic effect of the removal of external factors that had, for many decades, prevented them from reuniting.

What are the potential implications of this Bufumbira polyphony in the face of the spread of the climate of ethnocentrism in recent years? It has been a long time since the nation was conceptualised as an imagined community. Now that the national grand narratives have been criticised, to advocate national unity beyond ethnocentrism has become outdated. Wainaina's chapter on Bufumbira makes the contention that ethnicity is not absolute. It is overly reductive to base entire identities on ethnicity. Of course, some people value their ethnic language and culture as the foundation of their individual identity. However, individuals can find their places, even if they do not cling to entire sets of elements that comprise ethnicity such as languages, cultures, lands and so on. The place that young Wainaina swore that one day he would write about is such a space, free from affiliations but full of solidarity.

5. Conclusion: From Another In-between

Binyavanga Wainaina's writing ethos and real-life activism motivate us to make the next move. By criticising a blind belief in essentialism, he transgressed borders drawn between binary oppositions of colonialism, and between different ethnicities. Postcolonial critic Homi K. Bhabha described this type of gesture in the following terms:

> Being in the 'beyond,' then, is to inhabit an intervening space, as any dictionary will tell you. But to dwell 'in the beyond' is also, as I have shown, to be part of a revisionary time, a return to the present to redescribe our cultural contemporaneity; to reinscribe our human, historic commonality; *to touch the future on its hither side*. In that sense, then, the intervening space 'beyond,' becomes a space of intervention in the here and now (Bhabha 2008: 10).

Bhabha is primarily alluding to the hierarchical colonial relationship. However 'in the beyond' could also be equivalent to the in-between space. *How to Write About Africa* would then be an example of an intervention as envisaged by Bhabha.

Not long after its publication, *How to Write About Africa* became a platform showcasing 'our human, historic commonality' among our contemporaries, especially in the postcolonial world. Because this article was first published on the internet, it was repeatedly forwarded and it subsequently generated a series of such 'How to Write About' endeavours: 'How to Write About India', 'How to Write About Haiti', 'How Not to Write About Iran' and so on. The statuses, aims and results of the contributors of such articles differ widely. Yet, the emergence of the synchronic phenomenon proves that multiple subjects have emerged to intervene in the current global situation. *How to Write About Africa* has made each of them visible on the same ground, and for more effective intervention, it has promoted solidarity among them.

In terms of horizontal multiculturalism, Wainaina projected himself as an individual who lived in between two ethnicities. He did not deny ethnic culture itself as a whole, but he questioned the strict divisions between ethnic categories as they related to real people living in contemporary societies. He described his 'home' as a conceptual place of his own, which did not depend on ethnic affiliation and a fixed land in reality. Such a space may appear to be a temporal Utopia in the face of a global expansion of exclusion. However, the conception of such a space could also offer a moment of hope. Wainaina's writing depicted such African Potentials.

Binyavanga Wainaina died on 22 May 2019. He focused in his last years on the suppression of the LGBTQI+ people by governments of African countries. As his first move toward this activism, he published a short story in 2014 and termed it the 'lost chapter' of his memoir *One Day I Will Write About This Place*. This lost chapter was titled, 'I am a Homosexual, Mum'[8] and it tackled the topic of his coming-out as gay at the moment of his mother's death. In this short story, Wainaina described his coming-out as the ideal farewell scene that could not be achieved in reality.

He published this short story as a reaction to the anti-homosexuality legislation enforced in both Uganda and Nigeria. He continued his intervention after the coming-out story, revealing that he was HIV positive on World Aids Day in 2016. In 2018, he announced that he was planning to get married to his longstanding partner in South Africa the next year.[9] Unfortunately, however, his marriage could not be actualised because of his illness. His interview with Kevin Mwachiro reveals his reasons for coming-out:

More importantly for me, I felt I had to come out to be useful. In the closet I could not be useful. I could not think of myself as a writer in the closet while harbouring queer concerns. I see the person who I like. I like the adventurer and I try placing myself in vulnerable situations exposing myself to hard questions, which is hard, very hard. That is the hardest part. Being gay in Africa for me involves being behind a wall, or involved me behind a wall and I'm not behind the wall, which makes one uncertain about certain things. That is harder, but all in all I feel good (Mwachiro 2015: 99).

Many societies in Africa are still so intolerant toward LGBTQI+ people that few who do not identify as heterosexual can openly assert their gender or sexuality. There is a clear divide between the visible majority and the invisible minority. Appearing out from behind the wall implies making the invisible minority visible as a specific individual named Binyavanga Wainaina was able to achieve. It is a gesture that turns a demonised group into human beings of equal status.

By coming out, Wainaina opened up another in-between space. This space was, at first, only wide enough for one person. However, it became ever-broader as people in the same situation felt empowered to join in. Those identifying as LGBTQI+ could now hold firm in their own agency as human beings. It will, of course, take a long time to make the existence of the sexual minorities more visible and accepted across African societies. Nevertheless, lamenting Wainaina's demise, the present study is optimistic in the possibilities that can be actualised by African Potentials. In the end, it is the general public that can voluntarily negotiate this multicultural situation to achieve a balance in their society, rather than uncritically capitulate to the top-down control by governments.

Endnotes

[1] Donald Trump, the 45th president of the United States, pledged throughout his presidential campaign that he would build a US-Mexico border wall. The construction of the wall is not complete, but he has not

given up on the idea. Trump is seeking a second term in 2020.

2 Korean residents in Japan have been discriminated against for a long time. Around the mid-2000s, hate speech against Korean residents became radical, primarily on internet-based platforms. In 2009, an anti-Korean activist group delivered a hate speech using a megaphone pointed toward an elementary school designated for the Korean residents of Kyoto. Faced with the increase of hate speech, Osaka city, which has a large population of Korean residents, passed an ordinance against hate speech in 2016.

3 The Caine Prize for African Writing changed its name as The AKO Caine Prize for African Writing in January 2020.

4 In general, *How to Write About Africa* is frequently labelled as an *essay*. The word essay implies the straight-forward expression of ideas by an author. However, the point of the humour of this piece of writing rests in a fictive narrator who volleys 'useful' advice to aspiring writers. Thus, the creativity of this text should be appreciated as a form of fiction. Wainaina himself called it an 'article' in the sequel of 2010. Hence, this chapter also adopts the term.

5 Bafumbira is the name of the ethnic group whose area of residence is called Bufumbira, which is now located in the Kisoro District of Uganda. This area was annexed to Uganda from Rwanda at the Europe Convention of Brussels in 1910.

6 Of course, numerous writers across the world use local/ethnic languages for their artistic creations. However, it is quite rare for them to be spotlighted in terms of market value in the global economy. The category of postcolonial literature is no exception; Euro-American centrism is still dominant. Unfortunately, this nomenclature appears inclusive at first sight, but may be exclusive in reality.

7 Generally, the ethnic classification under the heading 'Distribution of Population by Ethnicity/Nationality' in the census does not allow for a classification of multiple ethnicities/nationalities. The media tend to focus on which group has the largest numbers, as if the ethnic identities were entered in a competition.

8 'I am a Homosexual, Mum' was published on the internet on the day after the author's 43rd birthday on 18 January 2014.

9 These announcements were posted on his Twitter account.

Acknowledgements

This work was supported by JSPS KAKENHI Grant Number JP16H06318.

References

Achebe, C. (2010) 'An image of Africa: Racism in Conrad's Heart of Darkness' in *An Image of Africa*, London: Penguin Books, pp. 1-21.

Bhabha, H. K. (2008, first published in 1994) *The Location of Culture*, New York: Routledge.

Dabashi, H. (2017, first published in 2009) *Post-Orientalism: Knowledge & Power in a Time of Terror*, New York: Routledge.

Mwachiro, K. (2015) 'A lost chapter found: Interview with Binyavanga Wainaina' in T. Sandfort, F. Simenel, K. Mwachiro and V. Reddy (eds) *Boldly Queer: African Perspectives on Same-Sex Sexuality and Gender Diversity*, The Hague: Hivos, pp. 97–101.

Ngũgĩ wa Thiong'o (1997, first published in 1986) *Decolonising the Mind: The Politics of Language in African Literature*, Oxford: James Currey.

—— (2012, first published in 1964) *Weep Not, Child*, New York: Penguin Classics.

Said, E. W, (2003, first published in 1978) *Orientalism*, London: Penguin Classics.

Talhami, G. (2014) 'The Syrian refugee crisis in 2014', *Encyclopedia Britannica*, 23 October 2014 (https://www.britannica.com/topic/Syrian-Refugee-Crisis-in-2014-The-1997834) (accessed: 18 January 2020).

Wainaina, B. (2005) 'How to write about Africa', *Granta 92* (https://granta.com/how-to-write-about-africa/) (accessed: 4 February 2021).

—— (2009, first published in 2001) 'Discovering home', in C. Brazier (eds) *Ten Years of the Caine Prize for African Writing*, Oxford: New Internationalist, pp. 79-98.

—— (2010) 'How to write about Africa II: The revenge', *Bidoun*,

Issue 21 (Bazaar II, summer 2010) (https://bidoun.org/articles/how-to-write-about-africa-ii) (accessed: 11 January 2021).

—— (2011a) *How to Write About Africa (Kwanini? Series)*, Nairobi: Kwani Trust.

—— (2011b) *One Day I Will Write About This Place: A Memoir*, Minneapolis: Graywolf Press.

Chapter 11

The Social Orientation of Kiswahili Poetry

Fuko Onoda

1. Introduction

Achebe and Senghor repudiated the effectiveness of 'art-for-art's sake', or the idea that art should be separated from didactic or utilitarian functions, in the African context (Senghor 1966; Achebe 1975). Recently, Nyamnjoh has also contended that individual achievements only become valuable in African societies when they serve collective interests (Nyamnjoh 2017).

Kiswahili literature also seems to be incompatible with the principle of art-for-art's-sake, filled as it is with lessons, warnings and political messages. Kiswahili writers are expected to speak to concerns shared by local communities rather than baring personal feelings or details about their individual lives. In the world of Kiswahili literature, art appears oriented to society, not art itself.

For the purposes of the present chapter, this characteristic reversal of 'art-for-art's-sake' is labelled 'social orientation'. The chapter intends to elucidate the social orientation of Kiswahili poetry by describing its development vis-à-vis its historical context. In so doing, the chapter uncovers the characteristics of art forms that proliferate in Kiswahili and other African languages, revealing evaluation criteria that differ fundamentally from Western assessments of art. These criteria could postulate an entirely non-Western conception of art forms.

This chapter attempts to probe the social orientation of Kiswahili poetry through the methodology of mapping poetic developments and changes against the historic contexts of the region.

Kiswahili poetry originated in the islands of present-day Kenya and has, over time, expanded its range of influence. Its forms have been altered to become accessible to more diverse populations across wider spaces. The changes effected to Kiswahili poetics coincide with significant historical events in the region. This fact seems to suggest that Kiswahili poetry is characteristically closely associated with its society. In other words, Kiswahili poetry wields the power to directly affect its linguistic community.

In geographical terms, this chapter will focus on pre-colonial East African coastal history and poetry before boundaries were established by the West as well as the colonial and postcolonial poetic culture of Tanzania. This country is specifically selected for the colonial and postcolonial review because Kiswahili poetry contributed significantly to the institution of an original socialist policy called the *Ujamaa* Policy which was implemented in Tanzania after its independence.

Three important historical events occurred in the focal region. The changes observed in Kiswahili poetry can also correspondingly be classified into three stages. The first major historical event of the region involved Oman's invasion and colonisation of the East African coast in the early 19th century. Before this time, almost all Kiswahili poems were religious epics claiming Islam's superiority but at that juncture, the poetry shifted from religious to more secular and familiar themes. Before Oman's intervention into the region, Kiswahili poetry had remained closed within the boundaries prescribed by the culture of Muslim scholars. Afterwards, it became popular. Muyaka bin Haji, a poet from Mombasa, led this change.

The second historical event occurred in the 20th century with the colonisation of East Africa by Germany and the United Kingdom. At this time, the script of Kiswahili poems changed from Arabic to Latin. As a result, Kiswahili poetry, which had been the culture unique to the coastal region, became accessible to the people of inland ethnic groups. The poets engaged in this process of transformation included Shaaban Robert, Amri Abedi and Saadani Kandoro.

The third significant historical event was Tanzania's attaining independence in the mid-1960s. People from various ethnicities in this newborn country began to compose poems in the national language, Kiswahili. Thus, the attribute of Kiswahili poets expanded from being limited to *Waswahili* (Swahili people) of the East African coast to encompassing all Tanzanian citizens. The character of Kiswahili poetry transformed from a regional art form to the national literature of Tanzania. Notable poets of this stage of the evolution of Kiswahili poetry include M. Mnyampala and E. Kezilahabi.

The above overview clarifies that Kiswahili poetry underwent repeated evolutionary changes that expanded its reach at each important historical milestone to include larger numbers of people within its ambit. Of course, criticism is unavoidable because such necessary summarisations are also likely to be reductive in describing complicated realities. However, the presentation of the development history of Kiswahili poetry in three stages will enable the visualisation of the connections between social realities and poetry and will illuminate the social orientation of Kiswahili poetry.

2. The First Stage: Change of Content

It is pertinent to overview the history of the East African coastal region before attempting to discuss the first of the three important historical events. This part of the world had prospered as an important hub for Pacific Indian Ocean trade for more than a millennium. Arabs began to migrate to the coast around the 7th century. A group of people who identified themselves as *Waswahili* emerged by the middle of the 13th century. *Waswahili* is not an accurate ethnic name; rather, it is a self-appointed identity representing Kiswahili-speaking Muslims born or living in the coastal regions of East Africa.

Kiswahili became popular as a trading language both in the coastal regions and inland. Nearly forty Swahili sultanates flourished by the end of the 15th century in the coastal regions of East Africa. The Portuguese arrived at the beginning of the 16th century and conquered coastal towns to control the trade routes of the Indian Ocean.

The events that triggered the first stage of change in Kiswahili poetry began to occur around this time. Oman drove out the Portuguese forces in Muscat in the mid-17th century and subsequently seized the Portuguese-controlled areas of East Africa. The ruler of Bu Said Oman, Sayid Said (Said bin Sultan), relocated the Sultanate's capital to Zanzibar at the beginning of the 19th century. Eventually, Oman dominated the coastal regions of East Africa from southern Somalia to southern Tanzania (Stapleton 2013).

To describe the first stage of change in Kiswahili poetry, the current chapter focuses on Muyaka bin Haji, a poet who lived in Mombasa. He was active as a renowned poet when Oman was trying to stretch its tentacles to Mombasa. However, the state of Kiswahili poetry before Muyaka must be discussed before clarifying the changes he brought about.

Muslim scholars established the Kiswahili writing system in Arabic around the 17th century. Afterwards, Quran schools (*madarasa*) were established along the East African coast as well as in inland trading bases to teach people how to read and write Kiswahili. Almost all extant Arabic manuscripts from this area represent religious and didactic epic poems about historical wars or the Prophet's life. All such epics were written in the poetic form called *utenzi*, which was created and enjoyed by Muslim scholars or elite lay people familiar with Arabic literary traditions. This poetic form required a compilation of at least 100 stanzas to be accomplished to be counted as a piece of work (Harries 1962; Knappert 1979). Therefore, it could convey enough information for intellectuals to adequately elaborate on Islamic teachings or translate Arabic histories. In this period, Kiswahili poetry remained completely bound by the prescribed culture of Muslim scholars.

Muyaka bin Haji al-Ghassany (1776–1840?), a Muslim scholar and a poet born into a family of water transporters in Mombasa, transformed this condition of Kiswahili poetry. He is believed to have composed more than 150 poems between 1810 and 1840 (Abdulaziz 1979). His oral poetry was passed down through word of mouth for forty years before being collected and transliterated into the Arabic and Latin scripts.

Many of Muyaka's political poems represent calls to the people of Mombasa to unite and prepare to fight Oman. The poem quoted below was composed in the tense circumstances when Oman had already occupied Zanzibar and was approaching Mombasa (Knappert 1979). In this poem, Muyaka praises the greatness and terrifying power of Mombasa to inspire people with pride and to raise public morale.

T'umwi ukifika Zinji, Zinji la Mwana Aziza
Wambile waje kwa unji, unji tutawapunguza
Hawatatupiga msinji, jengo wakalitimiza!
Wakija wakitekeza, maneno ni ufuoni.

Wakija wakitekeza, katika nyamba na fungu
Wataona miujiza, vituko vya ulimwengu
Wambaje, watayaweza, kuvumilia matungu?
Wemapo simba wa bangu, maneno ni ufuoni.

Wemapo simba wa bangu, wenye utambo na vimo
Watalia 'Ole wangu', Wangie ndani mwa shimo
Watak'atika manungu, mtemo hata mtemo
P'anga zao na mafumo, hazifai ufuoni. (Abdulaziz 1979: 130)

Messenger! When you reach Zanzibar, the home of Mwana Aziza,
Tell them to come in large numbers, so that we may reduce them.
They shall not lay their base here to complete the colonisation!
If they come on shore, the result will be written on beaches.

If they come on shore, here on cliffs and sand banks,
They will meet with a miracle, the shock of the world!
What do you think, will they bear the agony?
When the lions of war rise, the result will be written on beaches.

When the lions of war rise, with their strong feet
The enemy will cry, 'Woe to us!' before they fall into graves
They will be cut into pieces, stroke by stroke
Their swords and lances will be of no avail on the beaches.[1]

Muyaka's contribution is simply articulated by his local reputation as 'the poet who brought Kiswahili poetry from "the mosque to the market"'. He preferred the poetic form called *shairi* to the *utenzi*, which had already become known as the form suited to the writing of relatively long poems. Unlike the *utenzi*, which requires at least 100 stanzas, *shairi* can be as short as a single stanza. Therefore, this form could express trivial events that the *utenzi* could not handle. Using this form, Muyaka eloquently described secular themes pertaining to diurnal living and politics instead of Islamic sermons and war histories of previous poetic expression. Kiswahili poetry, which had long been an art to be enjoyed by intellectuals such as Muslim scholars, became popular with the masses at this time. *Shairi* is still the most popular form of Kiswahili poetry (Abdulaziz 1979).

This change occurred in Mombasa, not in the islands of Pate or Lamu, where the *utenzi* originated (Knappert 1979). Perhaps the location of poetic change is linked to Mombasa's violent opposition of Omani rule even as its surrounding territories tried to establish friendly relations or accepted invasion fairly quickly. The need to inject a sense of crisis and urgency to inspire people into a martial mood may have prompted this major transformation and popularisation of poetry.

Nevertheless, it is important to note that Kiswahili poetry changed its form to appeal to a larger group of people during a social crisis than it could previously reach. Thus, the transformation evidences the social orientation of Kiswahili poetry and is testimony to its power to affect social outcomes.

3. The Second Stage: The Script Change

The European countries entered the region after Oman and this second wave of invasions also caused the second stage of the changes observed in Kiswahili poetry. Mainland Tanganyika became a German protectorate in 1885, after the Scramble for Africa in the 1880s. The British, who had already extended their hegemony throughout the Indian Ocean since the 19th century, made Zanzibar a protectorate after a short war in 1890. African resistance movements occurred in various places in mainland Tanganyika against German rule. These uprisings included the Abushiri revolt, the Maji maji resistance as well as insurgencies by the Ngoni and Hehe peoples. However, the insurrections were divided and were ultimately suppressed because the ethnic groups were unable to overcome their differences. German East Africa was dismantled when World War I ended with the defeat of Germany, and most of the German-occupied lands came under the purview of a British mandate named Tanganyika Territory (Lliffe 1979).

Britain and Germany both attended to Kiswahili as the dominant language actively promoted it to disseminate their messaging during their colonial rules. In the 1880s, Christian missionaries translated the Bible into Kiswahili, which had already diffused through trading hubs into the mainland. The missionaries used the Latin script for their Kiswahili Bible. Britain, the eventual ruler of four East African regions, adopted Kiswahili as its lingua franca in British East Africa, a territory that encompassed Uganda, Kenya, Tanganyika and Zanzibar (Mdee 1999).

Kiswahili was, until this time, a dialect continuum: there was no standard version of the language. In 1930, the Inter-Territorial Language Committee was established to linguistically unite British East Africa. A Zanzibar dialect (*Kiunguja*) was chosen to be the standard Kiswahili, whose orthography was also established in the Latin alphabet. This language committee did not include a native Kiswahili speaker and thus native speakers strongly questioned the validity of the new standard Swahili (Mdee 1999).

The standard Swahili and the Latin orthography established at this time were taught to locals at colonial schools. A large amount of English literature, including texts by Swift, Banyan, Shakespeare and Lewis Carroll among others, was translated and published. The Latin writing system became quickly rooted among Christianised Africans. The Arabic script also rapidly became marginalised (Mazrui 2007), presumably for three reasons: first, the simplicity of the Latin alphabet; second, the natural affinity between Kiswahili and the Latin alphabet; and third, the Latin alphabet was not obviously connected to a specific religion, whereas the Arabic script was strongly associated with Islam and was not easily accepted by non-Muslims.

The establishment and dissemination of standard Swahili and its Latin orthography could have led to discontinuities between the *Waswahili* and others. However, the second major change in Kiswahili poetry enabled the opposite result.

Shaaban bin Robert (1909–1962), a *Mswahili* (a singular form of *Waswahili*) born in Tanga, German East Africa, was the first poet to initiate this stage of the transformation of Kiswahili poetry. He was the first to write poems and novels of high artistic value using standard Swahili with Latin orthography. The artistry of his works was appreciated by the *Waswahili* and because they were composed in standard Swahili using the Latin alphabet, they were legible for the non-*Waswahili*. In sum, his poetry acted as a bridge between the *Waswahili* and others: they encouraged people to accept poems composed using these new tools as an aspect of the indigenous culture (Mazrui 2007).

One of his poems expresses his love for Kiswahili, comparing the language to breast milk. The third, seventh and ninth stanzas of this poem are quoted below (Biersteker 1996: 41–42).

III
Lugha yangu ya utoto, hata sasa nimekua,
Tangu ulimi mzito, sasa kusema najua,
Ni sawa na manukato, moyoni mwangu na pua,
Pori bahari na mto, napita nikitumia,
Titile mama litamu, jingine halishi hamu.

VII
Lugha kama Kiarabu, Kirumi na Kiingereza
Kwa wingi zimeratibu, mambo ya kupendeza
Na mimi nimejaribu, kila hali kujifunza
Lakini sawa na bubu, nikizisema nabezwa
Titi la mama litamu, jingine halishi hamu.

IX
Natoa na kubakisha, kwa lugha ya Kiswahili
Naweza kujibisha, swali bila ya shikeli
Kwa lugha nyingine yesha, rai niweze hili
Lakini nakopesha, kulipwa sina dalili
Titi la mama litamu, jingine halishi hamu.

III
My language of childhood, even now as an adult,
Once a difficult language, now I know how to speak it,

It is like a fragrance, in my heart and nose,
The savannah, the coast, the river, where ever I pass I use it,
The mother's breast is sweetest, no other satisfies desire.

VII
Language like Arabic, Latin, and English,
Have been significant, concerning much that is pleasing,
And I have tried, in every way to study them,
But like a mute, if I speak them, I am despised,
The mother's breast is sweetest, no other satisfies desire.

IX
I give and take, in Kiswahili
I can and do argue, a question without difficulty
In another language, 'Yes, sir,' in your opinion can I do this,
But I lend, to be paid back there is no sign.
The mother's breast is sweetest, no other satisfies desire.[2]

This love-poem for Kiswahili became a slogan for the union of multiple ethnic groups during the Tanganyika independence movement. The transition of the script from Arabic to Latin transformed Kiswahili poetry from a *Waswahili* monopoly to an art form that could be enjoyed by a much larger population. Thus, there emerged for the first time the possibility of uniting diverse groups into one united by language. Kiswahili-speaking citizens could now overcome the differences between their ethnic groups. National awareness was awoken within the tribal consciousness.

The rules of Kiswahili poetry also passed on to those who had newly acquired the language. A book entitled *Sheria za Kutunga Mashairi na Diwani ya Amri* (Rules of Poetry Writing and Amri's Anthology) was published in 1954 to explain the rules of Kiswahili poetry. It was authored by Amri Abedi (1924–1964), a Kiswahili poet from Ujiji in Tanganyika. Inland cities, such as Ujiji and Dodoma, were trading hubs from the time before the advent of Western colonists. The people of these cities were followers of Islam and were familiar with the trade language, Kiswahili. They also identified as *Waswahili*. Many of Abedi's poems express his adherence to the

Islamic faith.

Abedi's explanation of the rules of Kiswahili poetry may be summarised as follows. According to him, four rules must be remembered: first, all stanzas must have the same number of lines (*beti*); second, all lines must have the identical number of syllables (*mizani*); third, the rhymes (*vina*) at the middle and the end of each line must align; and fourth, each stanza must offer a completed thought (Abedi 1954: 16–20). Abedi's poem quoted below is an exemplar of these rules. This poem expresses anger at colonialism and is unusual for Abedi, whose poems were primarily written on religious themes.

V

Vya bure vyao vitabu, wao haviwatakasi
Wamevipangia babu, kuupumbaza unasi
Na usawa umeghibu, hata ndani ya kanisi
Uhuru jambo halisi, kuukosa ni taabu

VI

Na ufanye la harubu, u mweusi, u mweusi!
Kamwe hulipwi thawabu, sawa na aso mweusi
Wewe zako ni sulubu, kuwakhudumu wakwasi
Uhuru jambo halisi, kuukosa ni taabu.

VII

Dharau zinatusibu, kudharawiwa Weusi
Maponjoro hutujibu, kwa maneno ya matusi
Asili ya hii taabu, ni kwamba tu mahabusi
Uhuru jambo halisi, kuukosa ni taabu. (Abedi 1954: 98)

V

Their meaningless books cannot purify souls
The old men fooled people with the book
And equality is lost even inside the church
Freedom is essential, it is painful to lack it.

VI
They insult you, 'Black, black!', even if you endure the hard work
And you will never get the same reward as a non-black person
All of our hard work is to further enrich the wealthy people.
Freedom is essential, it is painful to lack it.

VII
We have been suffering from contempt only because of our blackness
We will not reply to derogatory remarks
This captivity is the cause of all sufferings
Freedom is essential, it is painful to lack it.[3]

The publication of Abedi's Latin script book on the rules of Kiswahili poetry enabled non-*Waswahili* poets to attempt compositions in Kiswahili. Kiswahili poetry gradually became a popular means of encouraging the freedom movement as the struggle for independence intensified.

A poem by Saadani Kandoro (1926–) is quoted next. Kandoro was born in Dodoma and became a member of the Tanganyika African National Union (TANU), the political party that led Tanganyika's independence movement (Kandoro 1972: 141). Amri Abedi also was a TANU member who became the first African mayor of Tanganyika's largest city, Dar es Salaam. Kandoro's poem is simpler and more appealing to the masses in comparison to Abedi's poem quoted above.

I
Raia tumekutana, mbele ya wakubwa wetu
Raia tumeungana, kuunda taifa letu
Na sisi tuwe mabwana, tutawale nchi yetu
Ondoka nchini mwetu, mwishoni mwa mwaka huu.

III
Nchi tunayoinena, hii Tanganyika yetu
Nchi yote kuungana, Afrika ni ya kwetu
Afrika yakazana, tokeni, tokeni mwetu

Ondoka nchini mwetu, mwishoni mwa mwaka huu. (Kandoro 1972: 141)

I
Citizens have gathered under our leaders
Citizens have united to create our country
Become gentlemen and govern our country
Leave our country by the end of this year.

III
The 'country' we refer to is this Tanganyika
All countries should be united because Africa is ours
Unite Africa, get out, get out from our land
Leave our country by the end of this year.[4]

A standard Swahili written in the Latin alphabet was a system imposed by the Western colonial government. However, this inflicted system made unity between diverse ethnic groups possible and eventually made a united population successfully overturn a colonial government. Prominent Kiswahili poets such as Shaaban bin Robert and Amri Abedi played an especially important role. Instead of adhering to traditions shaped in the Arabic alphabet, they quickly accepted the foisted change which carried their messages to a larger population of readers. The changes they made to Kiswahili poetry resulted from their prompt reaction to societal demand. Their society needed clarion calls to resist Western colonisation; therefore, Kiswahili poetry answered the need. The social orientation of Kiswahili poetry became evident once more.

4. The Third Stage: Change of the Attribute of Poets

Tanganyika attained independence from the British Empire in 1961 and became a republic with Julius Nyerere as its president. In 1963, Britain shut down the protectorate. Zanzibar became a constitutional monarchy under the Sultan from Oman. However, the Zanzibar Revolution occurred only a month later. Around 10,000 Arabs were slaughtered and thousands fled to the Arabian Peninsula (Clayton 1981). In 1964, The People's Republic of Zanzibar and

Pemba was born from the Zanzibar Revolution. This republic then merged with mainland Tanganyika to form the Republic of Tanzania. The new republic established Kiswahili as its national language and English as its official language. Kiswahili became a symbol of national unity as a common language used by more than 120 ethnic groups in the joint republic.

The first president of Tanzania, Julius Nyerere, advocated 'African socialism' alongside Senegal's Léopold Sédar Senghor and Guinea's Sékou Touré. He speculated that equal and peaceful societies existed in pre-colonial Africa on the basis of three principles: mutual respect, sharing of property and duty of labour. He called such social norms *ujamaa*, the Swahili term for 'community'. According to Nyerere, restoring the African-specific spirit of *ujamaa*, which was lost through colonialisation, would enable the actualisation of an African style of socialism that was different from Marx's notion of socialism resulting from the development of capitalism (Hyden 1980: 98).

Nyerere adopted the spirit of *ujamaa* as his basis for nation building. In the city of Arusha, in February 1967, three years after Tanzania was born, he formally declared the imposition of socialism and nationalised the major companies of the country under the *Ujamaa* policy which aimed to combine scattered settlements into one artificial village called the *Ujamaa* village where farmers would migrate. He expected collaborative labour undertaken in a large farming operation to create egalitarianism. The state's economic independence was expected to improve through the implementation of new agricultural infrastructure along with increased productivity through mechanisation and the introduction of chemical fertilisers.[5]

A few months after the declaration, Nyerere requested prominent Kiswahili poets to use their talents to promote better awareness in people of their citizenship responsibilities following the implementation of the declaration (Blommaert 2014: 92). The poets met Nyerere's expectations by forming a literary-political association, the Society for Kiswahili Composition and Poetry in Tanzania (UKUTA: *Chama cha Usanifu wa Kiswahili na Ushairi Tanzania*). UKUTA purposed to develop Kiswahili literature to educate the populace about the spirit of *ujamaa*. Blommaert (2014: 93) generically labelled the many poems, novels and plays that were composed during this period to celebrate the *Ujamaa* policy as '*ujamaa* literature'.

Poets were central to UKUTA, and *ujamaa* literature often took the form of poetry. Poems praising the *Ujamaa* policy were written using traditional forms such as *utenzi* and *shairi* and were published in newspapers (Blommaert 2014: 95). UKUTA also organised poetry contests for citizens on occasions such as the anniversary of the founding of TANU, the only political party in Tanzania at that time. UKUTA tried to instil patriotism in citizens and to popularise the custom of expressing praise of the *Ujamaa* policy by using traditional forms of poetry.

UKUTA's greatest contribution to the government was the creation of a new genre of poetry enabling messages to reach even the illiterate masses. M. Mnyampala (1917–1969), one of the prominent poets of the time, a founder of UKUTA and a member of TANU, established a poetry genre called *ngonjera*. *Ngonjera* is a form of dramatic poetry in which characters discuss political themes mostly following the rules of *shairi*. Many *ngonjera* poems follow a set pattern: a wise supporter discusses the *Ujamaa* policy with an ignorant challenger who opposes him, and ultimately the supporter persuades and converts the challenger. The primary aim of the *ngonjera* was to educate people about the spirit of *ujamaa* (Nyoni 2007). This form of poetry was introduced as an adult literacy programme for the dissemination of political ideas (Kerr 1995).

A poem entitled *Sielewi Azimio* (I don't understand the declaration) by Mnyampala is reproduced below as an example of a *ngonjera*. In this poem, a child asks his father the meaning of the Arusha Declaration, and the father tells the child its significance. The complete poem has fourteen stanzas; only the first, spoken by the child's and the fourth, uttered by the father, are presented here.

Mwana:
Baba tafadhali sana, nakuomba kwa hisani,
Mimi ningali kijana, mengi sijayabaini,
Sijaelewa maana, ni mgeni duniani,
Azimio la Arusha, nambie nilielewe.

Baba:
Asante ewe mwana, maneno yako matamu,
Utakayo yana maana, una akili timamu,
Lau ungali kijana, takwambia ufahamu,
Azimio la Arusha, laneemesha taifa. (Mnyampala 1969: 5)

Child:
Father, please listen, I have a favour.
I am just a boy and there are many things I don't know.
I am a newcomer to this world so I haven't understood the meaning.
Teach me about the Arusha Declaration, so that I can understand it.

Father:
Thank you, my son, for your sweet words,
You are wise and what you wish is something important,
Although you are still young, let me tell you clearly,
The Arusha Declaration is to enrich the nation.[6]

Ngonjera were widely introduced in education. It became compulsory for high-school students to write *ngonjera* as part of their graduation-year exam requirements (Blommaert 2014). According to Askew (2014), who surveyed post-independence Kiswahili newspapers in Tanzania, all eleven papers of the time incorporated poetry columns and printed many poems by readers on the themes of patriotism, socialist ideals and praise for Nyerere. The fact that the people became the composers of patriotic poetry, as well as its recipients, indicates the success of the government's and UKUTA's literary activities.

A poem titled *Azimio la Arusha* (The Arusha Declaration) was published in a column called *Maoni ya Washairi Wetu* (Opinions of our Poets) in the Tanzanian newspaper *UHURU* on 10 April 1969. The 11-stanza poem was written by Ally Zedi Rajabu, a reader from Musoma, a town on the east coast of Lake Victoria. The first three stanzas of the poem are quoted below.

1.
Allahuma natamka, shairi kuliandika.
Mola ndiye mtajika, aso khiyana hakika.
Msingi utajengeka, kumalizika haraka.
   Azimio la Arusha, mwanga kwetu Tanzania.

2.
Usukani kushikika, wetu baba msifika.
Nyerere kakamilika, uwezowe msifika.
Ndiye Rais hakika, neema ndo kumvika.
   Azimio la Arusha, mwanga kwetu Tanzania.

3.
Napongeza natamka, Baba Taifa sifika,
Mwenge muhimu kaweka, kumulika vibaraka.
Wachafuzi kuchapika, Tanzania kutunzika.
   Azimio la Arusha, mwanga kwetu Tanzania. (Rajabu 1969)

1.
Oh lord, let me speak, let me write a poem.
God is the one who is celebrated, who certainly has no evil.
The foundation will be solidified, to complete quickly.
The Arusha Declaration, a light for our Tanzania.

2.
The leadership is firm, let us praise our father.
Nyerere is a perfect man, let us praise his ability.
He certainly is the president, grace is with him.
The Arusha Declaration, a light for our Tanzania.

3.
I congratulate and praise the father of the nation.
The precious torch is set to shine puppets.
The subversives are beaten, and Tanzania is protected.
The Arusha Declaration, a light for our Tanzania.[7]

Almost all poems classified as *ujamaa* literature followed the traditional rules of poetry and required rhyming lines and syllabic correspondence. Such rules emanated from the *Waswahili* culture of the residents of the East African coast and seemed incongruent with the values and rules of the new socialist state peopled with discrete ethnic groups. From the end of the 1960s and into the 1970s, some elites from the inland regions of Tanzania pointed out this inconsistency and established a new genre of Kiswahili free verse to express real life in plain language. They included scholars such as E. Kezilahabi, M. Mulokozi and K. Kahigi.

The Kiswahili free verse updated both the forms and themes of Kiswahili poetry. Poets would usually express community values in the traditional fixed verse, making their poems seem didactic and moral (Topan 1971). Kiswahili fixed verse was conventionally geared toward the well-formed expression of shared values and teachings. On the other hand, Kiswahili free verse could delve into personal sentiments and private lives of modern individuals. Poets became more individualists and began to deviate from the public. Such a definition of poets and poetry was a completely new experience for the traditional communities of Tanzania (Topan 1971; Abdulaziz 1979).

This new style of Kiswahili poetry aroused antipathy in the *Waswahili*. The *Waswahili* had allowed other communities to create Kiswahili poetry as long as they followed the traditional rules. Once the newcomers turned their backs on the rules and started to experiment, however, the *Waswahili* began to censure their work as not being true to the Kiswahili poetic ethos.

The debate between traditionalists and reformists about the proper forms and contents of Kiswahili poetry lasted more than ten years. The traditionalists comprised primarily the *Waswahili*, who emphasised the importance of the rules of poetry; the reformists consisted of young elites who opposed the imposition of traditional rules. The traditionalists argued that free verse was a culture influenced by the West and that the African-origin fixed verse should be adopted. The reformists refuted this argument, citing that fixed verse originated in Arabic poetry and that the traditionalists were trapped within the bounds of Arabic cultural colonialism. The reformists also contended that Kiswahili was no longer a *Waswahili* tongue; it was the common language of East Africa and the traditional rules of Kiswahili poetry were not suitable for the expression of issues that concerned a complex and diverse modern population.

A poem by E. Kezilahabi (1944–2020), entitled *Kisu Mkononi* (Knife in My Hand), clearly evinces the individualist character of free verse. In particular, the second stanza of the poem alludes to a suicidal feeling (Topan 1971; Senkoro 1988; Ranne 2006) which was said to shock contemporary readers (Wamitila 2008). The poem is quoted below:

Wakati miaka inaibwa mmoja mmoja,
Kurudi nyuma, kusimama, kupunguza mwendo
Siwezi, kama gurudumu nitajiviringisha.
Mteremko mkali huu.
Lini na wapi mwisho sijui:

Mbele chui mweusi, nyuma mwanga
Nionako kwa huzuni vifurushi maelfu vya dhambi.
Kisu, maisha kafiri haya
Kama kutazama nyuma au mbele
Ni kufa moyo mzima!

Sasa kama Simba-Mtu shauri nimekata.
Ya nyuma sana nisijali, ya mbele sana niyakabili.
Kwa ujasiri na uangalifu nitazunguka
Nikifuata kamba kama ng'ombe aliyefungwa,
Kila mpigo wa moyo wangu
Huu mpigo muziki wa maisha. (Kezilahabi 1974: 13)

When years are stolen, one by one,
To go back, to stand still, to slow the pace
I cannot, like a wheel I shall go round.
This steep fall,
When, and where the end is, I don't know.

In front is the leopard of darkness, behind the light

In which with great sorrow, I glimpse thousands of parcels of sins.
Knife, a pagan life this is
To look back, to look forward
Is to prove fatal!

Now like Lion-Man I have made the decision.
Not to mind what has gone past, and to face what is coming.
With great courage and caution, I shall go around
Following the rope like a tied bull,
Considering every heartbeat of mine,
Every beating, as the music of my life.[8]

The birth of Tanzania, a nation that adopted Kiswahili as its national language, changed Kiswahili poetry. Kiswahili poetry transformed into a form of national literature from its modest roots in a local and closed culture. Thus, all citizens, not just conservative intellectual *Waswahili*, could now become composers of Kiswahili literature. The third paradigm shift in Kiswahili poetry occurred with the attribute of poets. Meanwhile, Tanzanian society was driven by a strong need to make the *Ujamaa* policy, the symbol of newborn Tanzania, a success. Numerous patriotic and propaganda poems were contributed to newspapers by the general public as well as prominent poets, evidencing that Kiswahili poetry responded immediately to the social need of the hour.

The birth of Kiswahili free verse was also associated with this third change. As mentioned above, people with diverse backgrounds could now enter the world of Kiswahili poetry as composers. Being aware of various kinds of world literature, these elite poets forged realistic forms and wrote poems on themes familiar to their lives.

After the third change, and after becoming a part of the national literature, Kiswahili poetry diversified and became a multi-layered tool for every Tanzanian's everyday self-expression.

5. Conclusion

This chapter followed the major transfigurations of Kiswahili poetry with reference to its historical context. This methodology enabled the elucidation that Kiswahili poetry changed repeatedly to extend its reach to increasingly diverse groups of people at every significant historical event that occurred along the East African coast and in Tanzania. In addition, Kiswahili poems were written to appeal to contemporary social needs each time these regional societies faced significant events. The present chapter labels this characteristic the 'social orientation' of Kiswahili poetry.

Free verse, a form that was introduced along with the expansion of the attribute of Kiswahili poets, is the only exemplar of a form of the genre that was more individual than social in its orientation. However, the culture of writing about personal emotions in free verse never really prospered in Kiswahili poetry, underlining its social orientation in the regions under discussion. The culture of individual self-expression remained limited to elite poets and is still unknown to the ordinary masses.

On the other hand, people still like to convey social and political messages through their writing and recitation of fixed-styled poetry. As the threat of COVID-19 has spread through the world since the beginning of 2020, people in Tanzania are writing poems that raise morale and caution against the spread of the infection. Several famous musicians of Swahili hip-hop form of *Bongo Flava* have released songs carrying similar messages.[9] The intimacy of Kiswahili language arts with societal needs is also reaffirmed by this current example.

It would be interesting to probe whether the characteristics of Kiswahili poetry revealed in this chapter are observable in the art forms of other African languages.

Endnotes

[1] Translated by the author based on an English translation by Abdulaziz (1979: 130–131).

[2] Translated by Biersteker (1996: 41–42).

[3] Translated by the author.

[4] Translated by the author.

[5] A closer scrutiny of the *Ujamaa* policy reveals that its achievements

included improvement in infrastructure and education. The literacy rate of Tanzania soared from 40 per cent to 90 per cent during this period. However, negative effects such as hunger also accrued due to poor harvests on village lands unsuitable for agriculture. In addition, conflicts arose between different ethnic groups occupying a single area. Trouble was also caused by the forced repatriation of both unemployed urban residents and hooligans to *Ujamaa* villages. Repeated cultivation of the same tracts of land led to the depletion of nutrients in the soil. As a result, wealthier farmers used bribery to escape the confiscation of their lands, while the motivation of those who were less fortunate diminished. These factors contributed to reduced productivity. The yield of almost all crops decreased between 1974 and 1977 (Mboya 1971; Coulson 1982). The depression, the oil crisis and the war against Uganda contributed to Tanzania's economic crisis. Finally, the *Ujamaa* policy was abandoned after the acceptance of the Structural Adjustment Policy in 1982. Nyerere resigned in 1985, blamed for the policy's failure. The ideal of a socialist state based on Africa's unique philosophy was thus frustrated. Tanzania introduced a multiparty system in 1992. After winning the first general election in 1995, Chama cha Mapinduzi (CCM), which succeeded Tanganyika Africa Union (TANU), continues as the ruling party.

[6] Translated by the author.

[7] Translated by the author.

[8] Translated by the author.

[9] Here are examples of some COVID-19-related songs and artists of Bongo Flava found on YouTube, 'Corona' by Diamond Platnumz, 'Corona' and 'Rais Magufuli' by Paulo Siria, 'Corona' by Beka Flavour, 'Corona' by Asala, 'Magufuli-Corona' by Rayvanny, 'Corona Virus' by Daudi Mwanisenga, 'Coronavirus' by Danny P Mboka, 'Corona' by Lava Lava.

Acknowledgements

This work was supported by JSPS KAKENHI Grant Number JP16H06318.

References

Abdulaziz, M. H. (1979) *Muyaka: 19th Century Swahili Popular Poetry*, Nairobi: Kenya Literature Bureau.

Abedi, K. A. (1954) *Sheria za Kutunga Mashairi na Diwani ya Amri*, Nairobi: Kenya Literature Bureau.

Achebe, C. (1975) *Morning Yet on Creation Day*, London: Heinemann Educational Publishers.

Askew, K. (2014) 'Tanzanian newspaper poetry: Political commentary in verse', *Journal of Eastern African Studies*, Vol. 8, Issue 3, pp. 515–537.

Biersteker, A. (1996) *Kujibizana: Questions of Language and Power in Nineteenth- and Twentieth-Century Poetry in Kiswahili*, East Lansing: Michigan State University Press.

Blommaert, J. (2014) *State Ideology and Language in Tanzania, Second and Revised Edition*, Edinburgh: Edinburgh University Press.

Clayton, A. (1981) *The Zanzibar Revolution and Its Aftermath*, London: C. Hurst & Company.

Coulson, A. (1982) *Tanzania: A Political Economy*, Gloucestershire: Clarendon Press.

Harries, L. (1962) *Swahili Poetry*, Oxford: Clarendon Press.

Hyden, G. (1980) *Beyond Ujamaa in Tanzania*, London: Heinemann Educational Books.

Kandoro, S. (1972) *Mashairi ya Saadani*, Dar es Salaam: Mwananchi Publishing.

Kerr, D. (1995) *African Popular Theatre: From Pre-Colonial Times to the Present Day*, Oxford: James Currey.

Kezilahabi, E. (1974) *Kichomi*, Nairobi: Heinemann Educational Books Ltd.

Knappert, J. (1979) *Four Centuries of Swahili Verse: A Literary History and Anthology*, London: Heinemann Educational Books.

Lliffe, J. (1979) *A Modern History of Tanganyika*, Cambridge: Cambridge University Press.

Mazrui, A. (2007) *Swahili Beyond the Boundaries: Literature, Language, and Identity*, Athens: Ohio University Press.

Mboya, G. R. (1971) 'The feasibility of ujamaa villages in Kilimanjaro', in J. H. Proctor (ed.) *Building Ujamaa Villages in*

Tanzania, Dar es Salaam: Tanzania Publishing House, pp. 64–68.

Mdee, J. S. (1999) 'Dictionaries and the standardization of spelling in Swahili', *Lexikos*, Vol. 9, pp. 119–134.

Mnyampala, M. (1969) 'Sielewi Azimio', *Swahili*, Vol. 39, No. 1-2, pp. 5–6.

Nyamnjoh, F. B. (2017) 'Incompleteness: Frontier Africa and the currency of conviviality', *Journal of Asian and African Studies*, Vol. 52, Issue 3, pp. 253–270.

Nyoni, F. P. (2007) 'Music and politics in Tanzania: A case study of Nyota wa Cigogo', in K. Njogu and H. Maupeu (eds) *Songs and Politics in Eastern Africa*, Dar es Salaam: Mkuki wa Nyota Publishers, pp. 241–272.

Rajabu, A. Z. (1969) 'Azimio la Arusha', *UHURU*, 10 April 1969.

Ranne, K. (2006) 'Drops that open Worlds – Image of water in the poetry of Euphrase Kezilahabi', M.A. Thesis, Institute for Asian and African Studies, Faculty of Arts, University of Helsinki.

Senghor, L. (1966) 'The hidden force of Black African Art', *Vogue*, Vol. 148, No. 10, pp. 236–239, 276–277.

Senkoro, F. E. M. K. (1988) *Ushairi: Nadharia na Tahakiki*, Dar es Salaam: Dar es Salaam University Press.

Stapleton, T. J. (2013) *A Military History of Africa Volume 1: The Precolonial Period: From Ancient Egypt to the Zulu Kingdom (Earliest Times to ca. 1870)*, Santa Barbara: Praeger.

Topan, F. M. (1971) 'Swahili literature plays major social role', *Africa Report*, Vol. 16, Issue 2, pp. 28–30.

Wamitila, K. W. (2008) 'Utangulizi,' in E. Kezilahabi, *Dhifa*, Nairobi: Vide-Muwa Publishers.

Chapter 12

Amos Tutuola as a Quest Hero for Endogenous Africa: Actively Anglicising the Yoruba Language and Yorubanising the English Language[1]

Francis B. Nyamnjoh

1. Introduction

Everything moves – people, things and ideas – in predictable and unpredictable ways. The circulation of things, ideas and people is not the monopoly of any particular group, community or society. Mobility and circulation lead to encounters of various forms, encounters that are (re)defining in myriad ways. If people, their things and their ideas circulate, it follows that their identities, personal or collective, move as well. And through encounters with others, mobile people are constantly having to navigate, negotiate, accommodate or reject difference (in things, ideas, practices and relations) in an open-ended manner that makes of them a permanent work in progress. No mobility or interaction with others leaves anyone, anything or any idea indifferent, even if such interactions are not always equal and do not always result in immediate, palpable or tangible change. No encounter in mobility results in uncontested domination or total passivity. Even as some may wilt completely in the face of domination, some resist it fervently, and others are able to navigate and negotiate the tensions and contradictions brought about by the reality of domination in complex, creative and innovative ways. Sometimes this holds potential for new and more convivial forms of identity.

This is the framework I bring to my reflections on indigenous languages in Africa, their encounters, navigation and negotiation with colonial languages. I draw on *Drinking from the Cosmic Gourd: How Amos Tutuola Can Change Our Minds* (Nyamnjoh 2017), a book in which I discuss the writings of the late Amos Tutuola, a Nigerian writer who was mocked and dismissed by his fellow Nigerian writers for, among other things, his non-standard use of English.

In accepting a binary and exclusionary logic of civilisation, however, the writers dismissive of Tutuola missed the very point of his works. In his writings, Tutuola actively sought to yorubanise English and anglicise Yoruba, reflecting how Africans have never been passive in their embrace, internalisation, consumption and reproduction of European languages. His understanding of English is incomplete, but this does not diminish his ability as a Yoruba story teller with ambitions of reaching out and cultivating readership over and above his immediate Yoruba cultural context.

His deliberate effort to bring Yoruba and English into conversation exemplifies the conviviality of his life as a composite being always in the process of becoming – through encounters with fellow humans, and with nature and super-nature. In Tutuola's writings, Yoruba influences English and vice versa. One language and worldview mobilises another to make his storytelling intricate.

Tutuola repeatedly acknowledged that his English is borrowed, not to be mistaken for his message or used as a measure of his intelligence. Language to him is nothing more than a container, an envelope or a messenger, even if an active, lively and enlivening one. He cautions against dwelling on language at the risk of losing out on the contents or the message.

Long before encounters with Europe, Africans cultivated conviviality in and from encounters among indigenous languages; hence the more appropriate term of 'endogenous' languages. Endogenous is used here as an extension to the notion of indigenous, to evoke the dynamism, negotiability, adaptability and capacity for autonomy and interdependence, creativity and innovation in African societies, cultures and languages. It counters the widespread and stubborn misrepresentation of African cultures and languages as static, bounded, vernacular and dialect. It counters the idea that African societies need the benevolence and enlightenment of colonial languages to aspire, compete and self-sustain as part of a civilised modern world. The term endogenous, more so than indigenous, reflects how for centuries Africans have Africanised European languages. They do not relent, even when colonising and postcolonial forces are bent on deleting, reformatting and installing a whole new linguistic software in the African mind and social imaginary.

2. Tutuola's Quest for Conviviality

This address explores how Tutuola successfully employed his creative imagination, in conversation with Yoruba folktales, to use and appropriate the English language. His stories activate himself and others to cope with the tensions and contradictions of colonial encounters.

Tutuola navigates between languages and worldviews, sharing African modes of thought in a colonial language. In a dynamic world of myriad encounters and agentive forces, he promotes conviviality between different traditions and generations of being and becoming African. He gives incompleteness a chance rather than embracing the extravagant illusion of completeness fuelled by spurious affirmations of superiority and autonomy. He speaks more to the logic of inclusion and less to that of exclusion and the violence of zero-sum games of conquest and conversion.

Tutuola felt the coloniser's language needed to be 'altered sufficiently to bear the weight of an African creative aesthetic, infused with elements of the African literary tradition' (Achebe 2012: 55). He saw language and art as communication tools across social categories and worlds of unequal encounters. Tutuola stressed the need for conviviality between change and continuity, individual freedom and collective interest, tradition and modernity, Africa and the rest. Conviviality between the world of physical appearances and that which does not easily lend itself to sensory perception in a straightforward manner. His writing poses a challenge to conventional assumptions about indigeneity and authenticity versus imports and hybridity, and forces us to rethink what really counts as 'indigenously African' in a dynamic manner.

Tutuola's intention was to ensure survival for his Yoruba culture and language by telling his stories in English. However, he was doggedly determined to think and write in English the way he would think, speak and write in Yoruba (Lindfors 1970, 1999a; Larson 2001:

1–25). This was a successful way of denying the English language and its universe of origin the victory it craved by seeking to transform its African enthusiasts (Skulls *à la* The Complete Gentleman in *The Palm-Wine Drinkard*) into complete gentlemen and complete ladies, English style. To Steven Tobias, 'Tutuola's use and manipulation of both language and the fantastic play pivotal and complementary roles in his formulation of a discourse of resistance' against the, often, deplorable dehumanisation to which he and his fellow Nigerians were subjected under British colonialism (Tobias 1999: 69). In this way, argues Tobias, Tutuola 'turns the colonial power structure on its ear in an attempt to reclaim the centre for himself and his culture' (Tobias 1999: 71).

3. A Spanner in the Pursuit of Colonial Modernity

Tutuola published his first two and most influential novels – *The Palm-Wine Drinkard* (1952) and *My Life in the Bush of Ghosts* (1954) – in the 1950s with one of the most prestigious literary publishers in London: Faber and Faber. The publisher did not overly interfere, editorially, with Tutuola's use of the English language, despite the fact of his modest formal schooling and his clearly imperfect mastery of the language and grammar in the eyes of purists. Many non-African readers (English and Americans in the main) were ambivalent but fascinated by Tutuola's young English and 'unhinged imagination' but Nigerians who had drunk profoundly from the wells of colonial education were angered, especially by the publication of his first book, *The Palm-Wine Drinkard*. 'They had learned that dexterity in handling language was a necessity for a literary career, and they found Tutuola's critical reception befuddling' (Owomoyela 1997: 868).

These elites considered Tutuola a spanner in the pursuit of colonial modernity. Like his barely human Skull that had ambitions of becoming The Complete Gentleman by borrowing body parts in *The Palm-Wine Drinkard*, Tutuola, barely schooled in colonial education and its instances of legitimation, resorts to borrowing the English language of his colonisers to tell his tall Yoruba tales. Tutuola was considered as beneath human because of the perceived savageness of his mind and its primitive imagination by an African elite aspiring for full humanity by means of whitening up in the eyes of their European colonisers.

Such Africans, keen to bleach themselves culturally till they were virtually white, felt that Tutuola was pulling them down and back to the status of bare or incomplete humanity of the dark caves of their dark continent that they were determined to escape.

To the colonially educated Nigerians, for Tutuola's publisher and European readers to display such open fascination with his exotic subject matter and his atrocious English grammar was nothing short of suspect (Lindfors 1975: xiii). The crystallising modern Nigerian elite were perplexed. They could not understand how imperial Britain could expect to be taken seriously when, on the one hand, it presented itself as the model of perfection in civilisational pursuits, to be copied, mimicked and reproduced without question by its colonial subjects, while on the other hand, it continued to promote and display such fascination with the very same primitivism and savage superstitions, incompetence and underachievement that were supposedly a justification for Britain's initial colonial incursions with civilising pretensions.

4. The Beauty and Reality of Incompleteness

As a winner takes all project, colonialism and colonial education encouraged the adoption of the *colonial language* in its purest authentication. In the case of Yorubaland and the rest of colonial Nigeria, this was English – which was generally perceived to be superior to the local languages, which were often referred to condescendingly as vernaculars and dialects of the colonised. The anthropologist and writer Okot p'Bitek introduces in his epic poem *Song of Lawino* (p'Bitek 1989 [1966]), the colonially illiterate narrator Lawino. She, Lawino, has much in common with the barely colonially literate Tutuola and is treated in the same condescending manner by the 'fully' or marginally better schooled Africans. The tendency was for schools to punish grammatically incorrect English such as Tutuola's. In certain cases, some overly enthusiastic converts adopted the colonial language in their families to the exclusion and detriment of their own mother tongues.

These preferences for colonial languages persist. Adaobi Tricia Nwauban, a 21st century Nigerian novelist, admitted in a BBC interview as recently as November 2016 how she grew up in a context where the English language was privileged to the detriment of her mother tongue, the Igbo language – so eloquently celebrated by Chinua Achebe in his sumptuous menus of proverbs. The Igbo language was banned at home and treated as a punishable offence if spoken at school. This fixation with colonial Eurocentrism is not confined to language as a vehicle. In the social sciences and humanities, just as in journalism and related worlds of storytelling, representations of Africa as a necessarily negative trope in the language of Eurocentric modernity perfected in the era of imperial imagination and conquest continue to be re-actualised in a manner that defies the very logic and science by which they are purportedly inspired.

The vast majority of African people continue to be sidestepped by a colonial and colonising education that pretends to be complete. Unlike the Skull in Tutuola's *The Palm-Wine Drinkard*, who recognises the importance of interdependence through debt and indebtedness and insists on the need to acknowledge and pay one's debts, colonial education and the imposition of the superiority of European languages portray themselves as being beyond debt and indebtedness. This attitude can only result in borrowing without acknowledging and, therefore, pretending to be purer than these languages actually are. Such imperialist languages and cultures can only claim superiority by stubbornly and deafly insisting that their contacts with other languages and cultures are zero-sum exercises of one-dimensional conquests and conversions, with little or no conversation, let alone creative borrowings for self-enhancement. Of course, the history of language dynamism belies any such pretensions.

The under-privileging of local African languages in favour of colonial languages has had the added detrimental effect of taking attention away from the cultures, worldviews, cosmologies and traditions of knowing and knowledge production that were developed and sustained in conversation with these languages for centuries prior to European colonisation. If Tutuola's stories are any indication, the universes represented by sidestepped endogenous languages are structured around the reality of incompleteness as a normal way of being and becoming. Such a reality is one that privileges interconnections and interdependencies, as well as an idea of power that is disabused of the illusion of permanence.

5. (Re-)appreciating African Realities and Forms of Knowledge

An African literature shy of and embarrassed by its endogenous languages, and its mythical and folkloric past, even if this past was indeed barbaric and primitive, impoverishes itself. An uncritical and elitist embrace of the one-dimensionalism of colonial education in colonial languages and its palatability regimes serves to render invisible or peripheral dynamic popular modes of self-expression and meaning making that predated European colonialism.

African literature has much catching up to do with African musicians and filmmakers who have embraced endogenous languages and popular articulations of reality in all their complexities. The popularity of their songs and films suggests that, indeed, there is no longer shame in telling stories, no matter how 'backward' they may seem, and bringing into creative conversation African and colonial languages. Some filmmakers are comfortable going to their home villages to produce videos that disgruntle their African compatriots dazzled by the lure and allure of imperial modernity. If anything, Tutuola confidently teaches by example that Nigerians and Africans by extension 'must not be ashamed of their old way of life, if they are to produce a literature worthy of their own aspirations' (Harold R. Collins, reprinted in Lindfors 1975 [1961]: 66–68).

In his quest to recognise and provide for interconnections and interdependencies in lieu of zero-sum games of winner takes all, Tutuola opts to bring Yoruba and English into a conversation that is fruitful and enriching to him and the tasks he has at hand. He tells his stories in the ways he sees fit, drawing unapologetically on his rich cultural repertoire as a man of many worlds, local and distant, Nigerian and foreign, African and intercontinental.

Through his creative appropriation of Yoruba and English languages and cultural influences in his writings, Tutuola draws the attention of his reader to incompleteness, and to the need to recognise, cherish and draw on it as a strength. In this regard, dichotomisation between tradition and modernity, and between orality and the written word is highly problematic and misrepresentative of the full value of Tutuola's contribution as a frontier writer. He brought tradition and modernity, nature and culture, the natural and the supernatural, orality and the written, Africa and Europe into conversation in a manner that challenges the rigid thinking of evolutionary pretensions about human encounters and progress (Soyinka 1963; Barber 1995; Tobias 1999; Newell 2006: 71–72).

Tutuola was driven by his determination to keep the past alive and protect his culture. He resisted being forced, in the name of completeness, to choose between the ways of others and the ways of his own people. 'I don't want the past to die. I don't want our culture to vanish' (Tutuola interviewed by Mike Awoyinfa, quoted in Lindfors 1999b: 143). Tutuola did not allow his lack of higher formal education and sophistication in European literary styles and canons – his incompleteness, in other words – to stand in the way of his mission. 'So far as I don't want our culture to fade away I don't mind about English grammar' (Tutuola interviewed by Mike Awoyinfa, quoted in Lindfors 1999b: 143).

Who validates and authenticates the level of one's education in order for one to tell one's own personal story or write about one's own society and cultural conventions? Should a writer's skills be judged by the ability to communicate in a second language or in the language of their birth and upbringing? The idea of an exogenously dictated level of education somewhat denies the likes of Tutuola the ambition of telling their stories, because they are bound to fall short of the level of completeness, competency or achievement expected for one to qualify as storyteller. It also denies a particular representation of their worlds and encounters with others that only they, with their background and experience, can make possible, however modest their level of formal education and whatever their mastery or lack thereof of the styles and canons dictated by the gendarmes of literary validation. For a sense of the type of scrutiny Tutuola's writings have had to go through in this regard, see Lindfors (1970, 1999a) and Larson (2001: 1–25).

Compared to Chief Daniel Olorunfemi Fagunwa, who wrote exclusively in Yoruba, and whose influence on Tutuola is undeniable (Lindfors 1970: 325–329; Cooper 1998: 42–44), by opting to share the same Yoruba stories with a wider readership by writing in English, even if not an English sanctioned by England nor its Nigerian acolytes (Lindfors 1970: 331), Tutuola has probably brought more recognition and representation for Yoruba culture and folktales at the global marketplace of cultural production. In this connection, Abiola Irele, who considers Tutuola's novels as 'an extension of Fagunwa's work in Yoruba' and as representing, albeit problematic, 'a continuous progression from the indigenous to the European,' has argued that 'insofar as his language is the spontaneous recreation in English of the structures of the Yoruba language, which provides the linguistic and cultural framework of his imagination,' Tutuola could be seen as an 'unconscious artist' (Irele 2001: 17). Reluctance to see him as literary has led others to dismiss his work as 'an "aberrant" literary strain which represents a "cul-de-sac in African literature"' (Neumarkt 1975 [1971]: 188–189; Newell 2006: 186).

According to Yinka, Tutuola's son, these Nigerian critics of his father:

> ... took it upon themselves to defend the English language more than the English and the Americans combined, and refused to see anything good in the efforts of a semi-illiterate writer (by Western standards) but an undeniable professional raconteur (by Yoruba standards). To them anything, everything, must be judged, evaluated, and recommended only if they passed Western tests and standards. And that was a time when they were fighting Western colonialism, imperialism, culture, influence, you name it, through the writings of their novels, poems, etc.

Yinka adds that his father stood his ground, because he knew what he was doing.

6. Tutuola's Writings as an Archive on the Future of Endogenous Languages

A closer look at the universe depicted by Tutuola suggests it has far more to offer Africa and the rest of the world than the one-dimensional logic of conquest and completeness championed by European imperialism and colonialism. Tutuola's universe is one in which economies of intimacy go hand in hand with a market economy, and where pleasure and work are expected to be carefully balanced, just as balance is expected between affluence and poverty, nature, culture and supernature. Tutuola draws on popular philosophies of life, personhood and agency in Africa, where the principle of inclusive humanity is celebrated as a matter of course, and the supremacy of reason and logic are not to be taken at face value. Collective success is emphasised, and individuals may not begin to consider themselves to have succeeded unless they can demonstrate the extent to which they have actively included intimate and even distant others. These include family members and friends, fellow villagers and even fellow nationals and perfect strangers, depending on one's stature and networks.

Despite his unconventional English domesticated by his Yoruba syntax, modest and less than intellectual education in elite African terms, Tutuola has contributed significantly to the resilience of ways of life and worldviews that could easily have disappeared under the weight of extractive colonialism, globalisation and the market economy. His are stories of an accommodating resilience against a tendency towards metanarratives of superiority and conquest championed by the aggressive zero-sum games of the powerful. Tutuola's stories emphasise conviviality and interdependence, including between market and gift economies.

Tutuola's writing also serves as an *archive for endangered ways of life and of what is possible* in spite of colonialism and its zero-sum games of exclusive and exclusionary victories. Driven by his determination to keep the past alive and protect Yoruba culture, to resist being forced to choose between the ways of others and the ways of his own people, Tutuola did not allow his lack of higher formal education –

his incompleteness – to stand in the way of his mission to preserve an African way of being human.

His desire to write was informed and justified by a deep unease with the blazing lights of colonial civilisation – lights as dazzling and blinding as the flood of light from one of his characters in *My Life in the Bush of Ghosts* (Tutuola 1954), the Flash-Eyed Mother. Aware of the corrosive and infectious nature of colonial education, Tutuola felt he might have become a worse writer or not written at all had he embraced colonial education uncritically, or had he the opportunity to be duped completely and blunted by its pretensions. His imperfections in this connection were a blessing.

Tutuola had no pretensions to sophistication in the mother of all civilisations which colonial education was supposed to bring about. Because of the freedom this afforded him, Tutuola was able to write his books in a way that today offers Africans a rare window of opportunity to see how current asphyxiating and impoverishing epistemologies championed by reductionist Cartesian rationalism raised to an ideology could be enriched by complementary traditions of knowledge production, traditions initially disqualified and inferiorised under colonialism and its metanarratives of conquest.

Tutuola suggests ways for vulnerable Africans to challenge victimhood and assert their personalities. In his stories, very ordinary Africans are quite simply extraordinary in their capacity to challenge brutal and brutish games of power and conquest. Rich and poor are co-implicated and mutually entangled in Tutuola's universe of the elusiveness of completeness. His stories challenge the illusion of the autonomous, omnipotent, omniscient and omnipresent individual, culture or civilisation, by inviting the reader to embrace and celebrate incompleteness as the normal order of being and of things. The stories suggest an epistemology of conviviality in which interdependencies are privileged and delusions of grandeur and completeness discouraged.

Tutuola and his writings celebrate compositeness, the humility of incompleteness and the potency of a language and its disposition for conviviality.

Endnotes

¹ This Chapter was first written as a Keynote Address at the 2019 SAALT and SAALS Conference on Indigenous Languages in Contemporary African Societies, 30 June–4 July 2019, University of Pretoria; first published in *Acta Academica*, 2020, Vol. 52, Issue 1, pp. 89–98.

Acknowledgements

This work was supported by JSPS KAKENHI Grant Number JP16H06318.

References

Achebe, C. (2012) *There Was a Country: A Personal History of Biafra*, London: Allen Lane.
Barber, K. (1995) 'African-Language literature and postcolonial criticism', *Research in African Literatures*, Vol. 26, No. 4, pp. 3–30.
Collins, H. R. (1975 [1961]) 'Founding a new national literature: The ghost novels of Amos Tutuola', in B. Lindfors (ed.) *Critical Perspectives on Amos Tutuola*, Boulder: Three Continents Press, pp. 59–70.
Cooper, B. (1998) *Magical Realism in West African Fiction: Seeing with a Third Eye*, London: Routledge.
Irele, F. A. (2001) *The African Imagination: Literature in Africa and the Black Diaspora*, Oxford: Oxford University Press.
Larson, C. R. (2001) *The Ordeal of the African Writer*, London: Zed Books.
Lindfors, B. (1970) 'Amos Tutuola: Debts and assets', *Cahiers d'Études Africaines*, Vol. 10, No. 38, pp. 306–334.
─────── (ed.) (1975) *Critical Perspectives on Amos Tutuola*, Boulder: Three Continents Press.
─────── (1999a) 'Amos Tutuola's search for a publisher', in B. Lindfors (sole author) *The Blind Men and the Elephant and Other*

Essays in Biographical Criticism, Trenton: Africa World Press, pp. 109–133.

——— (1999b) 'A "proper farewell" to Amos Tutuola', in B. Lindfors (sole author) *The Blind Men and the Elephant and Other Essays in Biographical Criticism*, Trenton: Africa World Press, pp. 135–146.

Neumarkt, P. (1975 [1971]) 'Amos Tutuola: Emerging African literature', in B. Lindfors (ed.) *Critical Perspectives on Amos Tutuola*, Boulder: Three Continents Press, pp. 183–192.

Newell, S. (2006) *West African Literatures: Ways of Reading*, Oxford: Oxford University Press.

Nyamnjoh, F. B. (2017) *Drinking from the Cosmic Gourd: How Amos Tutuola Can Change Our Minds*, Bamenda: Langaa RPCIG.

Owomoyela, O. (1997) 'Amos Tutuola', in C. B. Cox (ed.) *African Writers, Volume II*, New York: Charles Scribner's Sons, pp. 865–878.

p'Bitek, O. (1989 [1966]) *Song of Lawino*, Nairobi: East African Educational Publishers.

Soyinka, W. (1963) 'From a common back cloth: A reassessment of the African literary image', *The American Scholar*, Vol. 32, No. 3, pp. 387–396.

Tobias, S. M. (1999) 'Amos Tutuola and the colonial carnival', *Research in African Literatures*, Vol. 30, No. 2, pp. 66–74.

Tutuola, A. (1952) *The Palm-Wine Drinkard*, London: Faber and Faber.

——— (1954) *My Life in the Bush of Ghosts*, London: Faber and Faber.

Index

A

Achebe 10–11, 173, 237–238, 242–243, 246, 259, 288
   to Wainaina 240–246
Afar 4–5, 72
   justice and conflict resolution system 74–77
Africa
   and convivial linguistic practices 89–92
   endogenous 283–294
   how to write about 240–246
   multilingualism in 89–92
African ethos 19–40
African languages 21, 26, 28, 94, 122–128, 149–162, 170, 191, 259, 278
   and literature 1–14
   dynamism in 1–14
African literature 173, 211, 220, 222, 228–229, 237, 241, 248, 289, 291
   languages and 1–14
   written in French 212–214
African multilingual norm 124–129
African multilingualism 5, 19, 22, 30, 36, 136–138
   flexibility and the potential of 121–141
African Potential/s 1–14, 19, 22–23, 36, 91, 110, 137, 210, 218, 228, 254–255
   towards conceptualisation of 1–14
   postcolonial literacy criticism and 237–240
African realities
   and forms of knowledge 289–291
Angola 3–4, 57–63, 157
   as a multilingual society 48–50
   Portuguese colonial policy and 50–57
antilanguage 103
   to national identity marker 104–106
Arab 25–28, 30, 38–39, 72, 82, 152, 187, 200, 235
arts 94, 159, 195–196, 278
assimilation 3, 25–26, 30, 32, 37, 54

patterns of cultural 191–194

B

Bantu 4, 13, 34, 48–52, 56–65, 98–99, 101, 130, 149, 159
    noun classification 94–95
Benin 2, 197–198, 209–210, 213, 223–224, 227–228
Beninese children's literature 223–228
Binyavanga Wainaina *see* Wainaina
brass band 200–202

C

categorial view of language 91, 93–95, 101, 110
children's books 9, 162
    creation and publication of 209–230
children's literature 9, 211–212, 219–223
    Beninese 223–228
class
    (as social stratification) 57, 107, 186, 201, 204
    (as a component of grammatical system) 94, 98, 105
    (as a school unit) 7, 169, 171-173, 183, 223-224

classification 49, 109, 202, 256
    Bantu noun 94–95
colloquial Swahili 5, 28, 30, 36, 89–113
colonial modernity
    a spanner in pursuit of 286–287
colonial policy and Angola 50–57
conceptualisation 3, 36
    of African Potentials 1–14
    of language hybridisation 32–36
    of language/s 25–30, 92–97
conflict reconciliation speech 4, 69–84
conflict resolution 4, 70–71
    the Afar justice and 74–77
content 63, 106, 180, 192, 195, 201, 241
    change of 261–264
convivial linguistic practices 89–92
conviviality 2–3, 12, 22, 27, 30, 91–93, 109–110, 137, 284, 292–293
    Tutuola's quest for 285–286
courtly arts 195–196
cultural transformation 2
    patterns of 195–196

Yoruba traditional music and its 189–196

customary justice system 74–76

D

dance band 200–202

de-contextualisation 106–110

de-standardisation 5, 89–113

documentation 4, 69–84, 125

dùndún 191–194, 196, 200, 204–205

dynamism 284, 288

    and conviviality 109–110

    linguistic 89–113

    in African languages and literature 1–14

        in linguistic structures 97–102

        socio-linguistic 47–66

E

East African 2, 6, 110, 149–162, 260–262, 265, 275, 278

    non-Arab Arabophone societies 19–40

economy 6, 107, 151, 156, 244, 292

Editions Ruisseaux d'Afrique 210–211, 216–219, 223, 229

elite 56–57, 182, 202, 204, 262, 275, 277–278, 286–287, 292

    emergence of 185, 198–200, 216, 254

endogenous Africa 11, 283–294

endogenous languages 12, 284, 289, 292–293

English language 11–12, 19

    Yorubanising the 283–294

ethnic identity 8, 94, 248, 252

    the 'Yoruba' as an 188–189

ethos 2–3, 19–40, 253, 275

F

flexibility 5, 10, 136–138

    and the potential of 'African multilingualism' 121–141

fluidity 21, 92, 95, 97–98, 108, 110, 126, 138

    syntactic hybridity and 98–102

frame of reflection 3, 47–66

French 212–214, 219–220

H

history 2, 11, 13, 20, 89, 186, 214, 241, 260–261, 288

    of African literature in French 219–220

    of *dùndún* 191–194

    of Lagos and its inhabitants 197–198
    of Yorubaland 186–188
hybridisation 30–36, 239

I

identity
    marker 104–105
    the future of Angolan 57–59
    the 'Yoruba' as an ethnic 188–189
ideology 92–97, 110, 125–126, 134, 199, 293
    standard language 93
in-between 10
    writing from the 247–256
incompleteness 3, 12, 22, 91, 96, 138, 285, 290, 293
    in language ideology 92–97
    the beauty and reality of 287–289
instruments 198, 204–205
    traditional religions and musical 189–191

J

justice system 73
    the Afar 74–77

K

Kenya 3, 22, 30, 36, 108-109, 149, 151–152, 154, 157, 240, 247, 251, 259, 265
Kenyan colloquial Swahili 89–113
Kiswahili 6–7, 11, 105, 248
    development of education 154–156
    in trade and economy 152–154
    poetry 259–279
    potentiality for African development 151–160
    the social orientation in 259–279
knowledge 9, 62, 80, 83, 94, 138, 154–156, 161, 210, 218, 288, 293
    forms of 289–291

L

Lagos 8, 185, 187, 194, 196–199, 204
    brief history of 197–198
    popular music in 199–204
Lalinon Gbado 210–211, 216–219, 221–223, 228–229
language attitudes 133–134
language hybridisation 30–36
language ideology 92–97

language policy 48, 66, 90, 127, 129, 136, 138, 161, 170
    trends in Angolan 59–63
language practice 2, 5–6, 25, 69, 71, 123, 134–136
    in Tanzania 121–141
language use 3–4, 70, 121, 130–131, 136
    recognition on 132–133
language/s
    dynamism of African 1–14
    endogenous 292–293
    socio-linguistic dynamism among 47–66
    the conceptualisation of 25–30, 92–97
    two types of 25–30
lingua franca 6, 24, 26–27, 89, 149, 158–159, 265
    development of an incomplete 95–97
linguistic dynamism 3, 5, 47–66, 89–113
linguistic margins of the Arab world 22–25
linguistic structures 20, 36
    dynamism in 97–102
literary philosophy 247–253
literary practice 10, 173
    Binyavanga Wainaina's 235–256
literature
    African children 220–221
    an opportunity to experience 171–174
    dynamism in African languages and 1–14

M

mi-ino teke 76–77
modernity 12, 21, 25, 91, 285, 288–290
    a spanner in pursuit of colonial 286–287
Mohamed, Said Ahmed 8, 174–175
multilingual norm 6, 123, 137
    language and the African 125–126
    translanguaging and the African 124–129
multilingual society 22, 170
    Angola as a 48–50
multilingualism 2–5, 89–94, 110, 136–138
    as a modern African ethos 19–40

flexibility and the potential of African 121–141

music 2, 277

    commercial recording of Nigerian 196–197

        in Lagos 200–204

        Yoruba popular 8–9, 185–206

musical instrument 189–191, 195

N

national identity 4, 58–60

    marker 103–105

national language 4, 6–7, 19–23, 48, 60–65, 89–90, 121, 127, 149–155, 161, 172, 182, 260, 271

Ngũgĩ/'s 10

    comparing Wainaina's approach with 247–253

    literary philosophy 247–253

Nigeria 8, 185, 196–197, 201, 204, 212, 254, 287

Nigerian music

    commercial recording of 196–197

non-Arab 3

    Arabophone societies 2, 19–40

norm 5–6, 21, 30, 95–96, 109, 121–123, 137, 172, 201, 240, 271

language and the African multilingual 125–129

O

opportunity 30, 57, 129, 154, 162, 203, 251, 293

    to experience literature 171–174

orientation 11, 137

    of Kiswahili poetry 11, 259–279

P

palmwine 200, 202–205

pattern 8, 19, 22, 98, 101, 227, 243, 247, 272

    of cultural assimilation 191–194

    of cultural transformation 195–196

peace-making step 76–77

philosophy 27, 37, 55

    Ngũgĩ's literary 247–253

poetry 2, 11, 172–173, 194

    Kiswahili 259–279

poet 214, 219, 260–263, 265, 267, 269–270, 278

politics 6, 23, 70, 77, 97, 151, 264

popular music 8–9

Yoruba 8, 185–206
Portuguese 4, 22, 48–49, 57–58, 60–61, 64–66, 127, 150, 153, 155, 158, 261
   colonial policy and Angola 50–57
postcolonial literary criticism 10
   and African Potentials 237–240
practice 1–2, 4, 6, 20–22, 25, 30, 35–36, 69, 71, 94–96, 110, 159, 173, 192, 225, 283
   a case of language 5, 121–141
   actual language 134–136
   Binyavanga Wainaina's literary 10, 235–256
   multilinguism in Africa and convivial language 89–92
publication 2, 53, 127, 150, 212–219, 229, 239, 241, 248, 253, 269, 286
publishers 9, 62, 149, 154, 209–210, 212, 214–217, 228

R

recognition 7, 64, 91–92, 101, 130–131, 137, 158, 170, 213–214, 219, 291
   dynamism and 103–109
   on language use 132–133
reconciliation 4, 64
   speech 4, 69–84
recording 8, 70, 136, 203, 205
   of Nigerian music 196–197
relative marker 100–101
re-vernacularisation 5
   of Sheng 106–108

S

sákárà 200, 202
script 260
   change 264–270
Sheng 5, 36
   as Kenyan Colloquial Swahili 5, 89–113
social issues 175
   texts treating 223–225
social orientation 11
   of Kiswahili poetry 11, 259–278
social structure 47, 71–73
socio-linguistic dynamism 3, 47–66
spoken language 7, 53, 154, 157
   Swahili in Tanzania 169–171
standard language 91, 95–96, 110, 113
Swahili 5, 7, 89–113

in Tanzania 169–171
syntactic hybridity and fluidity 98–102

T

Tanzania 6–8, 21, 29, 149, 151–157, 160, 182–183, 260–262, 271–278

language practice in 5, 121–141, 171–174

Swahili in 169–171

texts 53, 172, 211–214, 220–221, 237, 240, 265

treating social issues 223–225

tradition 9, 12, 21, 37, 70, 74, 121, 133, 173–174, 285, 290

challenging 225–226

traditional music 8–9, 186, 195–196, 198, 200, 204

Yoruba 189–194

traditional religion 198

and musical instruments 189–191

transformation 2, 13, 51, 122, 153, 157, 260, 264, 266

cultural 8, 185–206

translanguaging 6, 36, 95, 122–125, 132, 134, 136–138

conceptual framework 124–129

Tutuola, Amos 12

as a quest hero for endogenous Africa 11, 283–294

quest for conviviality 285–286

U

urbanisation 9, 185, 196–204

V

vernacularisation 95–97

W

Wainaina 10, 104, 107

from Achebe to 240–253

literary practices 10, 235–256

West African countries 9

literature for children 9, 209–230

publishers in French-speaking 214–216

writing/s 10, 12, 63, 65, 175, 214, 262–265, 267, 278, 284–291

from the in-between 10, 235–256

Tutuola's 292–293

village life 226–228

written language 7

304

    in Tanzania 171–174

Y
Yoruba 2, 8–9, 12
    as an ethnic entity 188–189
    language 11, 51, 154, 283–294
    popular music 8, 185–206
Yorubanising the English language 11, 283–294

www.ingramcontent.com/pod-product-compliance
Lightning Source LLC
Chambersburg PA
CBHW070808300426
44111CB00014B/2458